Better Homes and Gardens®

MEAT
COOKBOOK

BETTER HOMES AND GARDENS BOOKS
Editor: Gerald Knox
Art DIrector:
  Ernest Shelton
Assistant Art Director:
  Randall Yontz
Production and
Copy Editor:
  David Kirchner
Meat Cook Book Editors:
  Elizabeth Woolever,
    Senior Food Editor
  Diane Nelson,
    Associate Food Editor
Food Editor:
  Doris Eby
Senior Associate Food Editor:
  Sharyl Heiken
Senior Food Editor:
  Sandra Granseth
Associate Food Editors:
  Flora Szatkowski
  Patricia Teberg
Meat Cook Book Designer:
  Sheryl Veenschoten
Graphic Designers:
  Faith Berven
  Richard Lewis
  Harijs Priekulis

ACKNOWLEDGEMENT: Our sincere
thanks go to Robert E. Rust,
Extension Meat Specialist, Iowa
State University, for his help in
the production of this book.

Our seal assures you
that every recipe in the
Meat Cook Book is
endorsed by the Better
Homes and Gardens Test
Kitchen. Each recipe
is tested for family appeal,
practicality, and
deliciousness.

Contents

Beef and Veal 5

Pork, Ham, 41
and Bacon

Lamb 75

Ground Meat 91

Sausage 121

Variety Meats 135

Wild Meats 145

Leftovers 151

Meat Guide 164

Index 172

Whether you're an expert at cooking meat
or a beginner who's still intimidated
by the thought of even buying it, you'll find
useful information in the following pages.
Explanations of the hows and whys plus other
pertinent tips appear throughout the recipe pages.
For help in identifying the cuts you see
at the store and in determining how to cook them,
study the opening pages of the first three
chapters. Here you'll find many of the most
common cuts of beef, pork, and lamb—all
illustrated and described.
Similar information also opens the chapters on
sausages, variety meats, and wild meats.
General guidelines for buying, storing, cooking,
and carving meat appear in the last chapter.

Roasts from the Rib

The rib bone, shaped somewhat like a curved "T", determines the name and appearance of rib cuts. Since the meat is derived from supporting muscles along the backbone, it is among the most tender and desirable.

Beef Rib Roast Select bone-in (2 to 4 rib bones) or boneless roast. A solid round of meat —the rib eye muscle— identifies the cut. Commonly called standing rib or prime rib. *Roast.*

Veal Rib Roast is cut from the rib or rack and resembles a beef rib roast, except it is smaller. A **Rib Crown Roast** is 2 rib sections sewn together in a circle with the rib bones on the outside. Either roast may be frenched. *Roast.*

Steaks and Chops from the Rib

Steaks and chops include a rib bone unless they've been boned or cut from between the ribs.

Beef Rib Eye Steak
Boneless cut from the rib eye muscle. *Broil, panbroil, or panfry.*

Veal Rib Chop Resembles a beef rib steak. *Braise or panfry.*

Beef Rib Steak Consists of the tender rib eye muscle and usually the less tender rib cap muscle on top of the eye. Cut about 1 inch thick. *Broil, panbroil, or panfry.*

Since beef is too large to be handled in one piece, the carcass is cut into sides, quartered, then divided into wholesale cuts as shown. Veal cuts are smaller and lighter in color. For specific meat cuts, check the following identification and cooking information.

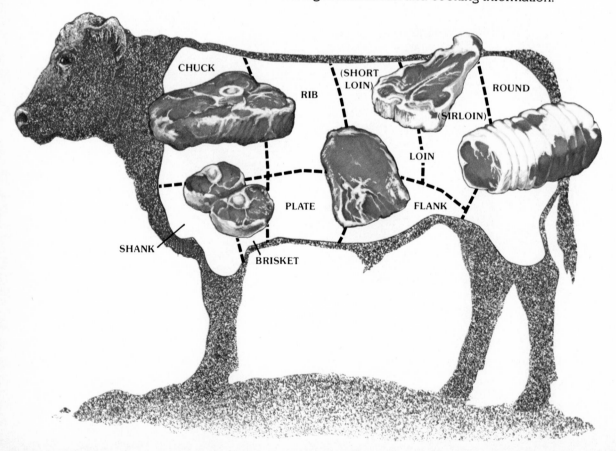

CHUCK

RIB

(SHORT LOIN)

(SIRLOIN)

ROUND

LOIN

PLATE

FLANK

SHANK

BRISKET

Ribs

Rib bones are covered by alternating layers of lean meat and fat.

Beef Short Ribs

Can be cut from the plate or chuck, or the ribs immediately below the rib steak section. Short ribs from the chuck usually have more lean meat than the others. *Braise or cook in liquid.*

Beef Plate Spareribs

Come from the same section as plate short ribs, but the rib bones are cut longer and are generally less meaty. Usually sold in long strips that can be laced accordion-style onto a barbecue spit for rotisserie grilling. Spareribs also come from the chuck, but are called Flat Ribs. *Braise or cook in liquid.*

Beef Rib Back Ribs

Actually the rib bones removed from rib steaks or roasts. Generally well-trimmed of fat and meat and separated into individual bones. Often labeled Finger Ribs. *Braise or cook in liquid.*

Veal Breast Riblets

Cut from ribs in the breast section. Fairly lean. *Braise or cook in liquid.*

Roasts from the Chuck

The blade bone or arm bone identify cuts from the chuck (known as the shoulder in veal). The activity required of the shoulder muscle makes the meat less tender.

Beef Chuck Arm Pot Roast

Oval-shaped cut about 2 inches thick having a cross section of the round arm bone. *Braise.*

Beef Chuck Blade Pot Roast

Contains a cross section of blade bone (the bone resembles a reverse "7" near the neck, and a flat blade next to the rib). *Braise (roast high quality).*

Veal Shoulder Blade Roast

Resembles a beef blade pot roast. *Braise or roast.*

Veal Shoulder Arm Roast

Similar to a beef arm pot roast. *Braise or roast.*

Boneless Beef Chuck Eye Roast

A cut obtained by boning the meat adjacent to the blade bone. *Braise or roast.*

Beef Chuck Cross Rib Pot Roast

Rectangular piece containing 3 chuck ribs plus the meat that lies across them, hence "cross rib." Really little more than 3 large meaty short ribs hooked together. Commonly called Boston roast or bread and butter roast. *Braise.*

Steaks and Chops from the Chuck

Chuck steaks and chops are identical to chuck pot roasts, except thinner.

Beef Chuck Blade Steak

Many muscles interspersed with fat and connective tissue. Cross section of blade bone. *Braise.*

Boneless Beef Chuck Shoulder Steak

Cut obtained by boning the meat near the round arm bone. Often labeled boneless shoulder cutlet. *Braise or panfry.*

Veal Shoulder Blade Steak

Similar to a beef blade steak. Sometimes called a shoulder chop. *Braise or panfry.*

Beef Chuck Arm Steak

Includes a cross section of the round arm bone. May be labeled Swiss steak or round bone steak. *Braise.*

Veal Shoulder Arm Steak

Resembles a beef arm steak. Sometimes called round bone chop. *Braise or panfry.*

Meat from the Brisket

Comparatively thin, less tender muscles and fat in alternate layers. Includes plate in veal; called breast.

Beef Brisket

Long flat piece having thick layers of lean meat with little fat. Can be processed for corned beef brisket. *Braise or cook in liquid.* (Some brands of corned brisket can be baked.)

Veal Breast

Frequently marketed as a roast for stuffing. *Braise or roast.*

Steaks and Chops from the Loin

A cross section of backbone or hip bone identifies loin cuts. The loin is the most naturally tender portion of the animal.

Beef Tenderloin Steak Boneless steak, 1 to 2 inches thick, cut from tenderloin muscle. Often called filet mignon. *Broil, panbroil, or panfry.*

Beef T-Bone Steak Contains a section of backbone commonly called a T-bone because it resembles the letter "T." Muscles include the large top loin or loin eye muscle and the smaller tenderloin muscle. Cut from the short loin between top loin and porterhouse steaks. *Broil, panbroil, or panfry.*

Beef Top Loin Steak Small steak cut from the short loin section nearest the rib. Consists of the top loin or loin eye muscle. Also known as club steak, New York strip, and Kansas City steak. *Broil, panbroil, or panfry.*

Veal Top Loin Chop Similar to a beef top loin steak. *Braise or panfry.*

Beef Porterhouse Steak Resembles a T-bone steak in muscle and bone structure except the tenderloin muscle is larger. Comes from short loin section nearest the sirloin. *Broil, panbroil, or panfry.*

Veal Loin Chop Slice from the full loin, usually about 1 inch thick. Similar to a beef steak from the short loin. *Braise or panfry.*

Beef Sirloin Steak Bone and muscle structure varies throughout the sirloin section. Slices nearest the short loin (pin bone steaks) contain the tip of the hip bone. Flat bone sirloin steaks contain the widest section of hip bone. Just behind these are 1 or 2 steaks with a round or oval-shaped bone. Slices nearest the round contain a wedge-shaped cross section of hip bone. For all practical purposes, however, it is necessary to remember only the name "sirloin." Muscles include the top sirloin muscle and the tenderloin muscle. *Broil, panbroil, or panfry.*

Boneless Beef Top Sirloin Steak Slice of the top sirloin muscle with bone removed. *Broil, panbroil, or panfry.*

Roasts from the Loin

Meat from the loin is generally considered to be the most tender available. Usually sold as steaks rather than roasts, except for the tenderloin.

Beef Tenderloin

Long tapering muscle that extends the full length of the loin (the thick end of the tenderloin is in the sirloin). Usually comes with outside cartilage still around the muscle. *Roast or broil.*

Veal Loin Roast Consists of the entire loin section. *Roast.*

Ground Meat

Usually made from lean trimmings and the less tender and less popular cuts of meat. Grinding the meat makes it more tender.

Ground Beef Meat from the flank, shank, plate, and chuck is commonly used for grinding into ground beef. *Bake, broil, panbroil, or panfry.* For more information, see pages 107 and 166.

Ground Veal Made from any cut of veal. Sometimes sold as a combination package of ground veal, pork, and lamb. Presently no attempt is made to define or limit the fat-to-lean ratio. *Bake, broil, panbroil, or panfry.*

Meat from the Plate

The plate area, which includes the ends of the rib bones, contains a high percentage of bone in proportion to meat. Although short ribs and skirt steaks may be cut from the plate, most of the meat is boned and ground or cut into stew meat.

Boneless Beef Plate Skirt Steak Actually the diaphragm muscle. Often sold trimmed, flattened slightly, rolled, and skewered. *Braise, broil, panbroil, or panfry.*

Steaks from the Round

Contain cross sections of leg bone. Fat and connective tissue separate four distinct muscles.

Veal Cutlet Cut from leg; often tenderized mechanically. *Braise or panfry.*

Veal Leg Round Steak Resembles a beef round steak. Tip muscle is included. *Braise or panfry.*

Beef Round Steak Large oval cut with a cross section of the round leg bone. Leaner and less tender than loin steaks. The 4 muscles are the top (largest), bottom, eye, and tip (which may or may not be present). *Braise or panfry.*
Beef Top Round Steak Most tender cut of round. *Broil, panbroil or panfry.*
Beef Bottom Round Steak Sometimes includes both the bottom and eye muscles. *Braise or panfry.*
Beef Eye Round Steak Small oval muscle. Often sold as breakfast steak. *Braise, panbroil, or panfry.*
Beef Round Tip Steak Sliced from large end nearest the sirloin. *Broil, panbroil, or panfry.*

Beef Cubed Steak Mechanically tenderized meat from round or chuck. *Braise or panfry.*

Roasts from the Round

The characteristic shape of the top, bottom, eye, and tip muscles identifies cuts from the round (the same area in veal includes the sirloin and is known as the leg).

Beef Top Round Roast Consists of the single large top round muscle (most tender part of the round). *Roast.*

Beef Bottom Round Roast Consists of the single bottom round muscle. *Braise (roast high quality).*

Beef Round Tip Roast Triangular-shaped cut from the area where the round meets the sirloin. *Braise (roast high quality).*

Beef Eye Round Roast Consists of the small cylindrical eye round muscle. *Braise (roast high quality).*

Veal Leg Round Roast From the tip and center portion of the leg; contains a section of leg bone. Often called leg of veal. *Braise or roast.*

Veal Leg Sirloin Roast The full sirloin portion of the leg. (Section is also cut into steaks.) *Roast.*

Beef Round Rump Roast Includes the top, bottom, and eye round muscles. A boned, rolled, and tied roast is often labeled rolled rump. May come with bone; called a standing rump. *Braise (roast high quality).*

Beef Heel of Round Boneless wedge- or triangular-shaped roast from the lower portion of the round. Contains considerable connective tissue. *Braise or cook in liquid.*

Meat from the Flank

The flank area contains fairly coarse muscles. Most flank meat other than flank steak is sold as ground beef.

Beef Flank Steak Thin, oval-shaped boneless cut with many long muscle fibers and little fat. Often scored to shorten fibers.

Also called London broil. *Broil or braise.*

Meats for Soups, Stews, and Kabobs

Beef Round Cubes for Kabobs Boneless lean cubes of meat cut from the tip portion and heel portion of the round. *Braise or broil.*

Veal Cubes for Kabobs Boneless lean cubes from the leg. Cubes may be threaded on wooden skewers and sold as city chicken. *Braise.*

Beef Shank Cross Cuts Cross-sectional pieces cut from the shank bone, usually 1 to 2 inches thick. During simmering, the tough connective tissue softens and becomes more tender. *Braise or cook in liquid.*

Veal for Stew Cubed shoulder meat. *Braise or cook in liquid.*

Beef for Stew Lean meat cubes cut from the less tender areas, such as the chuck, round, and plate. *Braise or cook in liquid.*

Beef Soup Bone Section of arm bone, fore shank, or neck bone containing little or no meat. Sometimes called marrow bone or knuckle bone. *Cook in liquid for soup.*

Standing Rib Roast with Yorkshire Pudding

1 4-pound beef rib roast	2 cups all-purpose flour
4 eggs	1 teaspoon salt
2 cups milk	

Place meat, fat side up, in 15½x10½x2-inch roasting pan. Sprinkle with a little salt and pepper. Insert meat thermometer. Roast in 325° oven about 2¼ hours for rare or till thermometer registers 140°; about 3 hours for medium (160°); or about 3¼ hours for well-done (170°). Remove meat from pan. Cover with foil; keep warm. Reserve ¼ cup drippings in pan. Increase oven to 400°. Beat eggs at low speed of electric mixer for ½ minute. Add milk; beat 15 seconds. Add flour and salt; beat 2 minutes or till smooth. Pour over drippings in pan. Bake in 400° oven about 40 minutes. Cut in squares; serve at once with roast. Serves 8.

Horseradish- and Barley-Stuffed Rib Roast

⅓ cup quick-cooking barley	2 cloves garlic, minced
¼ cup sliced green onion	1 5- to 6-pound boneless
¼ cup prepared horseradish	beef rib roast

Cook barley according to package directions. Fold in green onion, horseradish, garlic, and ¼ teaspoon *salt*. Unroll roast; spread evenly with barley mixture. Reroll and tie securely. Place roast, fat side up, on rack in shallow roasting pan; sprinkle with a little salt and pepper. Insert meat thermometer. Roast in 325° oven for 2¾ to 3 hours for medium-rare or till thermometer registers 145°. Let roast stand about 15 minutes. Remove strings and carve. Makes 10 to 12 servings.

Chateaubriand with Béarnaise Sauce

An exceptionally thick steak cut from the beef tenderloin is often referred to by the French name, chateaubriand. It is usually broiled or grilled. This recipe, however, uses the roast-size center portion of the tenderloin. It is roasted at 425° to give a browned exterior while keeping the rare interior.

Béarnaise sauce is the classic accompaniment. If desired, substitute 1 teaspoon fresh snipped tarragon for ¼ teaspoon of the dried.

1 1½- to 2-pound center-cut beef tenderloin	¼ teaspoon dried tarragon, crushed
2 tablespoons butter, softened	¼ teaspoon dried chervil, crushed
3 tablespoons tarragon vinegar	½ cup butter, softened
1 teaspoon finely chopped green onion *or* shallot	4 egg yolks
4 whole black peppercorns, crushed	¼ teaspoon dried tarragon, crushed

Place meat on rack in shallow roasting pan. Spread with 2 tablespoons butter. Insert meat thermometer. Roast *in 425° oven* for 40 to 45 minutes or till thermometer registers 140° (outside will be browned; the inside, rare). Remove to serving platter; keep warm.

In small heavy saucepan blend next 5 ingredients. Simmer about 5 minutes or till liquid is reduced by half. Strain; stir in 1 tablespoon cold *water*.

Divide the ½ cup butter into three portions. Add one portion to vinegar mixture; stir in egg yolks. Cook and stir over *low* heat till butter melts. Add another portion of the butter and continue stirring. As mixture thickens and butter melts, add remaining butter; stir constantly. When butter is melted, remove from heat. Stir in ¼ teaspoon tarragon. Season with salt to taste. Serve sauce with meat. Makes 5 or 6 servings.

A barley filling accented with horseradish and garlic makes Horseradish- and Barley-Stuffed Rib Roast *a sophisticated choice for entertaining.*

Sauerbraten-Style Roast

Marinating adds a spicy flavor to this roast. Serve it hot with gravy or prepare ahead, then chill and glaze for an easy buffet entrée.

1 3- to 4-pound boneless beef heel of round roast
2 medium onions, sliced
1 cup dry red wine
¾ cup cranberry juice cocktail
⅓ cup vinegar
1 tablespoon sugar
1 tablespoon salt
1 tablespoon lemon juice
½ teaspoon ground cloves
¼ teaspoon ground ginger
¼ teaspoon pepper
2 tablespoons cooking oil

Place meat in a plastic bag; set in shallow pan. For marinade combine onions, wine, cranberry juice cocktail, vinegar, sugar, salt, lemon juice, cloves, ginger, and pepper. Pour marinade over meat; close bag. Marinate for 2 to 3 days in the refrigerator, turning meat occasionally. Remove meat, reserving marinade. Pat excess moisture from meat with paper toweling. In Dutch oven brown meat slowly on all sides in hot oil. Add reserved marinade. Cover; roast in 325° oven for 2 to 2¾ hours or till tender. Remove meat from pan juices. Serve hot or cold. Serves 9 to 12.

To serve meat hot: Skim fat from pan juices. Measure 1½ cups juices; return to Dutch oven. Blend ½ cup cold *water* into ¼ cup all-purpose *flour;* stir into pan juices. Cook and stir till thickened and bubbly. Add a little kitchen bouquet, if desired. Pass gravy with the hot sliced meat.

To serve meat cold: Chill meat; discard pan juices. In a 1-cup glass measure soften 1 envelope *unflavored gelatin* in ⅔ cup cold *water*. Set in small saucepan of hot water; heat and stir over low heat till gelatin is dissolved. Combine ⅔ cup *mayonnaise or salad dressing* and ¼ cup dijon-style *mustard;* stir in dissolved gelatin. Chill till partially set. Spread mustard mixture evenly over chilled meat. Garnish with ¼ cup sliced pimiento-stuffed *olives*. Chill till mustard mixture is set. Slice meat thinly.

Beef Wellington

Notice that the beef tenderloin is roasted at 425° instead of the usual 325°.

1 4-pound beef tenderloin
2 cups all-purpose flour
½ teaspoon salt
⅔ cup shortening
2 2¾-ounce cans liver pâté
1 beaten egg
2 teaspoons instant beef bouillon granules
¼ cup all-purpose flour
⅓ cup burgundy
½ teaspoon dried basil, crushed

Place meat on rack in shallow roasting pan. Insert meat thermometer. Roast *in 425° oven* for 35 to 45 minutes or till thermometer registers 130°. Remove meat from pan; let cool. Reserve pan drippings.

For pastry combine the 2 cups flour and salt; cut in shortening till size of small peas. Add ⅓ to ½ cup cold *water, 1 tablespoon* at a time, tossing with a fork till all is moistened. Form into ball. On floured surface roll to 14x12-inch rectangle; spread pâté to within ½ inch of edges.

Center the meat atop pastry. Bring up long sides of pastry and overlap atop meat. Brush on some of the egg; seal. Trim excess pastry from ends; fold up. Brush on egg; seal. Place, seam side down, on greased baking sheet. Reroll pastry trimmings. Make decorative cutouts; place atop meat. Brush remaining egg over pastry. Bake in 425° oven about 35 minutes (meat will be rare). Place on warm serving platter.

Heat and stir reserved pan drippings with bouillon granules and 1½ cups *water* till granules dissolve. Blend ½ cup cold *water* into the ¼ cup flour; stir into hot mixture. Add burgundy and basil. Cook and stir till thickened and bubbly; season to taste. Pass with sliced meat. Makes 12 servings.

Roasting Beef and Veal

Individual cuts of meat vary in size, shape, and tenderness. Because of these differences, use the roasting times only as a guide.

Cut	Approx. Weight (Pounds)	Internal Temperature on Removal from Oven	Approx. Cooking Time (Total Time)
Roast meat at constant oven temperature of 325° unless otherwise indicated.			
BEEF			
Rib Roast	4 to 6	140° (rare) 160° (medium) 170° (well-done)	2 to 2½ hours. 2½ to 3¼ hrs. 2¾ to 4 hrs.
Rib Roast	6 to 8	140° (rare) 160° (medium) 170° (well-done)	2½ to 3 hrs. 3 to 3½ hrs. 3½ to 4¼ hrs.
Boneless Rib Roast	5 to 7	140° (rare) 160° (medium) 170° (well-done)	2¾ to 3¾ hrs. 3¼ to 4¼ hrs. 4 to 5½ hrs.
Boneless Round Rump Roast	4 to 6	150° to 170°	2 to 2½ hrs.
Round Tip Roast	3½ to 4	140° to 170°	2¼ to 2½ hrs.
Rib Eye Roast (Roast at 350°)	4 to 6	140° (rare) 160° (medium) 170° (well-done)	1¼ to 1¾ hrs. 1½ to 2 hrs. 1¾ to 2¼ hrs.
Tenderloin Roast (Roast at 425°)	4 to 6	140° (rare)	¾ to 1 hr.
VEAL			
Leg Round Roast	5 to 8	170° (well-done)	2¾ to 3¼ hrs.
Loin Roast	4 to 6	170° (well-done)	2¼ to 3 hrs.
Boneless Shoulder Roast	4 to 6	170° (well-done)	3 to 4 hrs.

Roasting directions: Season the roast by sprinkling with a little salt and pepper. Insert a meat thermometer into the center of the roast so that the bulb reaches the thickest part of the lean meat. Make sure the bulb does not rest in fat or touch bone. Place roast, fat side up, on a rack in a shallow roasting pan. *Do not* cover, add water, or baste. Except as noted above, roast meat in 325° oven till the meat thermometer registers the desired internal temperature. To check doneness, push the thermometer into meat a little farther. If the temperature drops, continue cooking the meat to the desired temperature. Let meat stand about 15 minutes for easier carving. Remove string from rolled and tied roasts, and carve meat across the grain (see pages 168 and 170 for carving and gravy-making tips).

Veal a la Royale

2 tablespoons chopped onion
2 tablespoons butter *or* margarine
2 cups small dry bread cubes
½ pound bulk pork sausage, cooked and drained
¼ cup chopped pitted ripe olives
¼ teaspoon poultry seasoning
¼ teaspoon ground sage
⅛ teaspoon salt
⅛ teaspoon pepper
2 tablespoons water *or* beef broth
1 4-pound boneless veal leg round roast
3 hard-cooked eggs, chilled
3 tablespoons cooking oil
3 tablespoons butter

Cook onion in the 2 tablespoons butter or margarine till tender. Combine with bread cubes, sausage, olives, poultry seasoning, sage, salt, and pepper. Toss with water or beef broth to moisten. Butterfly meat so when spread out it forms about a 12x8-inch rectangle (see page 164). Trim any excess fat. Spread ⅔ of the bread mixture to within 1 inch of edges of meat. Align eggs, end to end, across center of meat. Pile remaining bread mixture around and over eggs. Fold sides and ends of meat over eggs to reshape into a roast. Secure with metal skewers as needed, then tie securely crosswise and lengthwise; remove skewers.

In 5-quart Dutch oven brown meat on all sides in mixture of hot oil and remaining 3 tablespoons butter. Cook, covered, over very low heat about 1½ hours or till tender, turning meat carefully several times. If necessary, add a little water to keep meat moist. Remove from heat. Chill overnight. Slice thinly to serve. Makes 10 servings.

Veal in Aspic

To cut meat easily and uniformly, remove both ends from an empty soup or vegetable can. Bend the can to an oval shape and use as a pattern for cutting.

1 2-pound veal leg heel roast
2 envelopes unflavored gelatin
2 13¾-ounce cans chicken broth
½ cup dry white wine
2 slightly beaten egg whites
1 2½-ounce can deviled ham
1 tablespoon snipped parsley
2 teaspoons finely chopped onion
1 teaspoon prepared horseradish
2 hard-cooked eggs, sliced

Place meat on rack in shallow roasting pan. Insert meat thermometer. Roast in 325° oven about 80 minutes or till thermometer registers 170°. Chill meat. In saucepan soften gelatin in broth; add wine and egg whites. Bring to boiling, stirring constantly. Remove from heat and strain through cheese-cloth. Cool to room temperature. Pour thin layer into a 9x9x2-inch pan, covering bottom. Chill till *almost* set.

Meanwhile, cut veal into twelve ⅛-inch-thick slices; trim to uniform shapes about 3¾x2½ inches (see note, right; store meat trimmings for another use). Combine deviled ham, parsley, onion, and horseradish. Spread 6 of the veal slices with ham mixture. Top with remaining slices. Arrange veal in partially set gelatin mixture. Place 2 egg slices on top of each. Carefully spoon a little of the remaining gelatin mixture over and around eggs and meat. Chill 20 minutes. Spoon remaining gelatin mixture over all. Cover pan; chill till set. Trim gelatin mixture closely around each portion of veal. Arrange on salad greens, if desired. Makes 6 servings.

Thin slices of chilled Veal a la Royale can lend an air of elegance and grace to a leisurely picnic in the park. Fresh fruit and a bottle of wine are all you need to complete the mood.

Beef Roast with Vegetable Stuffing

In some parts of the country, a beef round tip roast is known as "sirloin tip," "knuckle," "face," or "veiny."

1 pound fresh broccoli *or* 2 10-ounce packages frozen cut broccoli, thawed
4 medium carrots, sliced
1 large onion, chopped (1 cup)
1 4½-ounce jar sliced mushrooms, drained
1 teaspoon salt
¾ teaspoon dried dillweed
¼ teaspoon pepper
¼ cup shredded cheddar cheese
1 4- to 5-pound beef round tip roast
2 tablespoons cooking oil
3 tablespoons all-purpose flour
½ teaspoon kitchen bouquet (optional)
2 tablespoons butter *or* margarine

Cut fresh broccoli stalks lengthwise into uniform spears, following branching lines. Cut into 1-inch pieces. In large bowl combine fresh or frozen broccoli, carrots, and the next 5 ingredients. Remove 2 cups of the mixture; chop finely. Set remaining mixture aside. Stir cheese into chopped mixture.

Cut two horizontal slits about 2 inches apart, almost to other side, in end of roast having largest diameter. Stuff pockets with the vegetable-cheese mixture; skewer shut. Brown meat in hot oil in Dutch oven. Place roast, fat side up, in the Dutch oven; add ¾ cup *water*. Roast, covered, in 350° oven for 2½ to 3 hours or till meat is tender. Transfer meat to serving platter; keep warm. Pour pan juices into measuring cup; skim off fat. Add enough water to pan juices to make 1½ cups liquid; pour into saucepan. Blend ½ cup cold *water* into flour; stir into pan juices. Add kitchen bouquet, if desired. Cook and stir till thickened and bubbly.

Meanwhile, in large covered saucepan cook the reserved vegetable mixture in boiling salted water for 15 to 20 minutes or till crisp-tender. Drain. Add butter or margarine, stirring till melted.

Pass buttered vegetables and gravy with meat. Makes 8 servings.

Saucy Beef Sandwiches

1 3-pound boneless beef round rump roast
3 tablespoons cooking oil
1 large onion, thinly sliced
1 cup water
¼ cup tomato paste
3 tablespoons vinegar
1 tablespoon liquid beef-flavored gravy base
2 bay leaves
1 teaspoon sugar
½ teaspoon salt
½ teaspoon dried oregano, crushed
2 tablespoons cold water
2 teaspoons cornstarch
10 to 12 individual French rolls, split and toasted

Sprinkle meat with a little salt and pepper. In Dutch oven brown meat in hot oil. Add onion, the 1 cup water, tomato paste, vinegar, gravy base, bay leaves, sugar, salt, and oregano. Cover and simmer about 2 hours or till meat is tender; cool. Remove meat; slice thinly. Remove bay leaves.

Skim fat from pan juices. Add water to juices, if necessary, to make 2½ cups liquid. Blend the 2 tablespoons cold water into cornstarch; stir into juices. Cook, stirring constantly, till mixture is thickened and bubbly. Return sliced meat to sauce; heat through. Spoon meat and sauce on warm French rolls. Makes 10 to 12 sandwiches.

Roast with Barbecue Gravy

1 tablespoon all-purpose
    flour
1 4-pound boneless beef
    chuck pot roast
¾ cup bottled barbecue sauce

¼ cup orange marmalade
1 tablespoon vinegar
2 tablespoons cold water
2 tablespoons cornstarch

Place flour in an oven roasting bag; shake to coat bag. Sprinkle meat with a little salt and pepper. Slide meat into bag; place in large shallow roasting pan. Combine barbecue sauce, marmalade, and vinegar; pour over meat. Seal bag with twist tie. Punch several holes in top of bag with tines of fork. Roast in 325° oven for 2½ to 2¾ hours or till tender.

Snip off one corner of bag; drain juices into measuring cup. Spoon off excess fat. Add water, if necessary, to make 2 cups liquid. In saucepan blend the 2 tablespoons cold water into cornstarch. Add pan juices. Cook and stir till thickened and bubbly. Remove meat from bag and slice; place on serving platter. Spoon some gravy over meat; pass remaining gravy. Garnish with orange slices and parsley, if desired. Makes 8 servings.

Chinatown Chuck Roast

1 3- to 3½-pound beef chuck
    pot roast, cut 1½ inches
    thick
¼ cup cooking oil
¼ cup vinegar

3 tablespoons soy sauce
2 tablespoons honey
½ teaspoon ground ginger
1 teaspoon cornstarch

Place meat in a plastic bag; set in shallow pan. For marinade combine oil, vinegar, soy sauce, honey, and ginger; pour over meat. Close bag. Marinate several hours or overnight in the refrigerator, turning meat occasionally.

Remove meat, reserving marinade. Place meat on unheated rack in broiler pan. Broil 3 to 5 inches from heat till desired doneness, turning once (allow about 30 minutes total time for medium-rare).

Meanwhile, in saucepan blend the reserved marinade into cornstarch. Cook and stir till thickened and bubbly. Thinly slice meat diagonally across the grain; spoon marinade over slices. Garnish with green onion, if desired. Makes 6 servings.

Burgundy Beef Roast

2 tablespoons all-purpose
    flour
1 teaspoon salt
    Dash pepper
1 3- to 4-pound beef chuck
    pot roast
2 tablespoons cooking oil

1 cup shredded carrot
½ cup chopped onion
½ cup burgundy
1 clove garlic, minced
¼ cup cold water
2 tablespoons all-purpose
    flour

Combine 2 tablespoons flour, salt, and pepper. Coat meat with the flour mixture. In Dutch oven brown meat on both sides in hot oil. Remove from heat; add carrot, onion, burgundy, and garlic. Return to heat; simmer, covered, for 2½ to 3 hours or till meat is tender.

Remove meat to warm serving platter. Skim fat from pan juices. Blend cold water into 2 tablespoons flour; stir into pan juices. Cook and stir till thickened and bubbly; serve with meat. Makes 6 to 8 servings.

Corned Beef Platter

Brisket is the usual cut of beef cured or pickled in a strong salt brine for corned beef (seasonings may be added to the brine). This curing process was originally used as a method of storing meat without refrigeration.

1 3- to 4-pound corned beef brisket
4 large sweet potatoes, peeled
6 to 8 boiling onions
1 20-ounce can pineapple chunks
2 tablespoons brown sugar
1 tablespoon cornstarch

Place meat in Dutch oven; add juices and spices from package, if desired. Add water to cover meat. Bring to boil. Reduce heat; simmer, covered, about 2¼ hours or till nearly tender. Cut potatoes in 1-inch pieces; add to pan. Add onions. Cover; cook 20 minutes. Drain pineapple; reserve syrup. Add pineapple to pan; cook 10 minutes or till potatoes are tender.

In saucepan mix sugar and cornstarch; stir in reserved syrup. Cook and stir till bubbly. Arrange vegetables and pineapple around meat on platter. Spoon glaze over. Garnish with snipped parsley, if desired. Serves 6 to 8.

Corned Beef with Wine Sauce

If desired, use this sauce with a packaged corned beef for oven roasting. Follow the package directions for preparing the roast.

1 3- to 4-pound corned beef brisket
½ cup dry red wine
2 teaspoons cornstarch
1 8-ounce can whole cranberry sauce
¼ cup orange marmalade
1 teaspoon lemon juice

Place brisket on rack in shallow roasting pan; add pickling juices and spices from package, if desired. Add 2 cups *water*. Cover pan with foil. Roast in 325° oven about 3 hours or till tender. Remove meat to platter. In saucepan blend wine into cornstarch. Add cranberry sauce and marmalade. Cook and stir till thickened and bubbly. Stir in lemon juice. Spoon some sauce over meat; pass remaining sauce. Makes 6 to 8 servings.

Macaroni-Stuffed Brisket

¾ cup elbow macaroni
1 slightly beaten egg
⅓ cup milk
½ cup shredded Swiss cheese
¼ cup grated parmesan cheese
2 tablespoons snipped parsley
2 tablespoons chopped pimiento
¼ teaspoon salt
¼ teaspoon poultry seasoning
1 3½- to 4-pound fresh beef brisket
1 teaspoon dry mustard
1 tablespoon worcestershire sauce
¼ cup all-purpose flour
1 3-ounce can sliced mushrooms

Cook macaroni in boiling salted water for 8 to 10 minutes or till tender; drain. Combine the next 8 ingredients and dash *pepper*; stir in macaroni.

Trim excess fat from meat. Butterfly brisket by slicing meat horizontally to within 1 inch of one edge. Spread open. Spoon macaroni mixture onto bottom half of meat. Fold other half over; skewer shut. Combine dry mustard, 1½ teaspoons *salt*, and ¼ teaspoon *pepper*; rub mixture on both sides of meat. Place in shallow roasting pan. Combine worcestershire sauce and ½ cup *water*; pour over meat. Cover and roast in 325° oven for 3 to 4 hours or till tender. Place meat on serving platter; remove skewers. Keep warm.

Skim fat from pan juices. Add water to juices, if needed, to make 1¼ cups liquid. Pour into a saucepan. Blend ½ cup cold *water* into flour; stir into pan juices. Add *undrained* mushrooms. Cook and stir till bubbly. Spoon a little gravy over meat; pass remainder. Makes 10 to 12 servings.

Vary tradition by serving Corned Beef Platter with sweet potatoes, onions, and pineapple.

T-Bone Steaks with Sautéed Vegetables

2 beef T-bone steaks, cut
   1 inch thick
2 tablespoons butter
¼ teaspoon dried oregano,
   crushed
¼ teaspoon garlic powder

1 small sweet red pepper
1 small green pepper
1 small onion, sliced and
   separated into rings
½ cup sliced fresh
   mushrooms

Trim excess fat from steaks. Rub some of the trimmings over surface of large heavy skillet; heat till skillet is very hot. Add steaks; keep temperature very hot. Pan-broil steaks till desired doneness; turn once (allow 10 minutes total time for rare; 13 to 14 minutes for medium; 20 minutes for well-done). Sprinkle with some salt and pepper after turning.

Meanwhile, in saucepan melt butter. Stir in oregano, garlic powder, and ¼ teaspoon *salt*. Cut peppers into rings; halve large rings. Add peppers, onion, and mushrooms to pan. Cover and cook about 5 minutes or till vegetables are just tender. Spoon over steaks. Makes 2 servings.

If your meat market features only the larger-than-one-serving-size steaks, plan to serve two from each steak. Cooking times will be about the same for steaks of the same thickness. (Adjust timing for thinner steaks.) For hints on carving steaks so each person will receive some of the tenderloin, see beef porterhouse steak, page 171.

Mushroom-Stuffed Steaks

4 beef top loin steaks, cut
   1 inch thick
2 cups sliced fresh mushrooms
¼ cup chopped onion
¼ cup chopped celery

2 tablespoons butter
⅛ teaspoon salt
⅛ teaspoon dried thyme,
   crushed
Dash worcestershire sauce

Cut a 2-inch-wide slit horizontally in fat side of each steak. Insert knife in slit; make pocket by "fanning" knife. In saucepan cook mushrooms, onion, and celery in hot butter about 5 minutes; stir occasionally. Stir in salt, thyme, worcestershire, and ⅛ teaspoon *pepper*. Fill each steak pocket with about ¼ cup of the mushroom mixture. Place steaks on unheated rack in broiler pan. Broil 4 inches from heat till desired doneness; turn once (allow 16 to 18 minutes total time for medium-rare). Serves 4.

Seafood-Steak Roll-Ups

1½ pounds boneless beef
   sirloin steak, cut
   ¼ inch thick
½ cup dry red wine
¼ cup finely chopped celery
1 tablespoon butter
1 7½-ounce can minced clams

1 4½-ounce can shrimp
½ teaspoon worcestershire
   sauce
½ teaspoon prepared
   horseradish
6 slices bacon, partially
   cooked

Cut meat into 6 pieces. Place in shallow dish; pour wine over. Cover; marinate 2 hours at room temperature, turning occasionally. Cook celery in butter 10 minutes. Drain clams and shrimp; mash shrimp. Add clams and shrimp to celery. Stir in worcestershire and horseradish. Drain meat well; reserve wine. Pat out ¼ cup clam mixture atop each piece of meat; roll up jelly roll-style. Wrap a bacon slice around each; secure with wooden picks. Brush with reserved wine. Place on unheated rack in broiler pan. Broil 4 to 5 inches from heat till desired doneness (allow 10 to 12 minutes for rare). Turn occasionally. Remove picks. Serves 6.

T-Bone Steaks with Sautéed Vegetables features slices of peppers, mushrooms, and onion. If your skillet isn't large enough to pan-broil the steaks, check the broiling chart on page 23.

Deviled Blade Steak Broil

2 1-pound beef chuck blade steaks, cut ¾ inch thick
Instant unseasoned meat tenderizer
2 tablespoons dry mustard
2 tablespoons catsup
2 tablespoons water
2 tablespoons worcestershire sauce
2 tablespoons butter
2 teaspoons sugar
1½ teaspoons salt
¾ teaspoon paprika
¼ teaspoon pepper

Sprinkle meat on both sides with meat tenderizer according to label directions. For sauce, in small saucepan combine dry mustard, catsup, water, worcestershire sauce, butter, sugar, salt, paprika, and pepper. Heat, stirring constantly, till butter melts; keep warm.

Place blade steaks on unheated rack in broiler pan. Broil meat 3 to 5 inches from heat for 6 to 7 minutes; brush with mustard sauce and turn. Broil 6 to 7 minutes more for medium-rare, brushing with sauce after 4 minutes. Remove to serving platter; spoon remaining sauce over steaks. Garnish with parsley, if desired. Makes 4 servings.

Steak au Poivre

Crack whole pepper using a mortar and pestle. Wooden, ceramic, and glass sets are available. Or, use a metal spoon to press pepper against the side of a metal mixing bowl.

2 to 4 teaspoons whole black pepper
4 beef top loin steaks, cut 1 inch thick (2 pounds)
¼ cup butter *or* margarine
¼ cup chopped shallot *or* green onion
1 teaspoon instant beef bouillon granules
3 tablespoons brandy

Coarsely crack pepper (see note, left). Slash fat edge of steaks at 1-inch intervals; place 1 steak on waxed paper. Sprinkle with ¼ to ½ teaspoon of the cracked pepper. Rub over meat; press in with heel of hand. Turn steak; repeat on other side. Repeat with remaining steaks and pepper.

In 12-inch skillet melt *half* the butter. Cook steaks in butter over medium-high heat till desired doneness, turning once (allow 11 to 12 minutes total time for medium). Season steaks on both sides with a little salt. Remove steaks to warm platter; keep hot. In same skillet cook shallot or green onion in remaining butter about 1 minute or till tender but not brown. Add bouillon granules and ⅓ cup *water;* boil rapidly over high heat 1 minute, scraping up browned bits from pan. Stir in brandy; cook 1 minute more. Pour over steaks. Makes 4 servings.

Tahiti Beef and Lobster Kabobs

1 8-ounce can pineapple slices
¼ cup sauterne
2 tablespoons cooking oil
¼ teaspoon ground ginger
1 1-pound beef sirloin steak
1 8-ounce frozen lobster tail
1 medium green pepper
8 preserved kumquats

Drain pineapple, reserving ¼ cup syrup. Quarter each pineapple slice; set aside. For marinade stir together reserved pineapple syrup, sauterne, cooking oil, and ginger. Cut steak into 1½x1-inch pieces; add to marinade. Cover; refrigerate 4 to 6 hours or overnight. Drain, reserving marinade.

Thaw lobster. Remove meat from tail in one piece; cut into 8 pieces. Cut pepper into 1-inch squares. On 4 long skewers or 8 medium skewers alternately thread steak, lobster, pineapple, pepper, and kumquats. Grill over *hot* coals till meat is desired doneness (allow 15 to 17 minutes total time for medium-rare). Turn often; brush with reserved marinade. Serves 4.

Thickness	1 inch	1½ inches	2 inches
	(approximate total time in minutes)		
Rare	8 to 10	14 to 16	20 to 25
Medium	12 to 14	18 to 20	30 to 35
Well-Done	18 to 20	25 to 30	40 to 45

Broiling Beef Steaks

To test a broiled or grilled steak for doneness, slit the center of the steak and note the inside color: red—rare; pink—medium; gray—well-done.

Choose a beef porterhouse, T-bone, top loin, sirloin, or tenderloin steak cut 1 to 2 inches thick. Without cutting into the meat, slash the fat edge at 1-inch intervals. Place steak on unheated rack in broiler pan.

Broil 1- to 1½-inch-thick steaks so surface of meat is 3 inches from heat. Broil 2-inch cuts 4 to 5 inches from heat. (Check range instruction booklet.) Broil on one side for about half of the time indicated in chart for desired doneness. Season with a little salt and pepper, if desired. Turn with tongs and broil till desired doneness. Season again.

Thickness	1 inch		1½ inches
Temperature of Coals	Medium-hot	Medium	Medium-hot
	(approximate total time in minutes)		
Open Grill **Rare**	12 to 18	20 to 25	18 to 20
Medium	15 to 20	25 to 30	20 to 25
Covered Grill **Rare**	8 to 10	15 to 18	10 to 15
Medium	10 to 15	18 to 22	15 to 18

Grilling Beef Steaks Outdoors

Choose beef porterhouse, T-bone, or sirloin steaks. Slash the fat edge at 1-inch intervals to keep steaks flat on grill. To estimate temperature of coals, hold hand, palm side down, about 4 inches above coals. Count seconds "one thousand one, one thousand two," and so on. When you can hold your hand comfortably over the coals for only 2 to 3 seconds, they have a temperature of *medium-hot;* 3 to 4 seconds indicates *medium.* Grill steaks for about half of the time indicated in the chart for desired doneness. Flip steaks using tongs and pancake turner (piercing with fork wastes good meat juices); grill till desired doneness.

Steak with Chicken Livers

4 ounces chicken livers
2 tablespoons butter
¼ cup chopped green onion
1 cup sliced fresh mushrooms
½ cup dry white wine
¼ teaspoon salt
Dash pepper
1 2- to 2½-pound beef sirloin steak, cut 1 to 1½ inches thick

Slice chicken livers (should have about ½ cup). In skillet quickly cook livers in hot butter; remove from pan. In same skillet cook onion till almost tender; add mushrooms and cook 1 to 2 minutes more. Return livers to skillet. Stir in wine, salt, and pepper. Keep warm; *do not boil.*

Grill steak over *medium* coals, turning once (allow 20 to 25 minutes total time for medium-rare). Spoon some of the chicken liver mixture over steak. Garnish with parsley and hot peppers, if desired. Makes 4 servings.

London Broil

Scoring helps to tenderize the meat. For help in how to do it, see page 164.

1 1-pound beef flank steak
⅓ cup cooking oil
1 teaspoon vinegar
1 small clove garlic, minced

Score steak on both sides. Place steak in plastic bag; set in shallow pan. For marinade combine oil, vinegar, and garlic; pour over steak. Close bag. Let stand at room temperature 2 to 3 hours, turning meat occasionally.

Remove steak from marinade; place on unheated rack in broiler pan. Broil 3 inches from heat, turning once and sprinkling with salt and pepper (allow 8 to 10 minutes total time for medium-rare). Sprinkle with more salt and pepper. Carve diagonally across grain into very thin slices. Serves 4.

Beef Fondue

Instead of cooking oil, you may use peanut oil. Neither one will affect the flavor of the cooked meat.

Or, use a mixture of 3 parts cooking oil to 1 part clarified butter. (Cool melted butter and use only the oily top layer; discard bottom layer.) This mixture has a buttery aroma.

1 pound trimmed beef tenderloin *or* sirloin, cut in ¾-inch cubes
Cooking oil
1 teaspoon salt
Green Goddess Sauce, Olive Sauce, and/or Horseradish Sauce

Bring meat to room temperature. Choose a deep, heavy metal fondue cooker that is smaller at the top than the bottom (this shape helps prevent spattering). Pour in oil to no more than half capacity or to depth of 2 inches. Heat oil-filled cooker over range to 425°. Add salt (helps reduce the spattering). Transfer cooker to fondue burner; keep hot.

Spear meat with fondue fork or bamboo skewer; fry in hot oil till desired doneness (allow 15 seconds for rare; up to 1 minute for well-done). Transfer meat to dinner fork and dip in sauce. Makes 4 servings.

Green Goddess Sauce: In bowl combine two 3-ounce packages softened *cream cheese* and 3 tablespoons *milk.* Stir in 2 tablespoons finely snipped *chives,* 1 tablespoon snipped *parsley,* 2 teaspoons *anchovy paste,* and 1 teaspoon finely chopped *onion.* Makes about 1 cup.

Olive Sauce: In bowl combine ½ cup dairy *sour cream* and one 3-ounce package softened *cream cheese.* Stir in 2 tablespoons chopped pimiento-stuffed *olives,* 1 tablespoon finely chopped *onion,* and 1 teaspoon snipped *parsley.* Makes about 1 cup.

Horseradish Sauce: Whip together one 8-ounce package softened *cream cheese* and 2 to 3 tablespoons prepared *horseradish* till fluffy. Blend in 2 tablespoons *milk.* Makes about 1⅓ cups.

Fire up the grill and choose a thick sirloin when you want to serve Steak with Chicken Livers.

Saucy Steak and Vegetable Platter

1 1-pound beef flank steak
½ cup dry white wine
¼ cup cooking oil
1½ cups whole fresh mushrooms
1 small onion, sliced
3 tablespoons chopped green onion
1 clove garlic, minced
¼ cup butter *or* margarine
¾ cup beef broth
⅓ cup dry white wine
1 cup light cream
2 tablespoons cornstarch
2 10-ounce packages frozen broccoli spears
1 15-ounce can sliced potatoes
Garlic salt

Partially freeze steak; thinly slice across grain into bite-size strips. Place in shallow pan. Combine the ½ cup wine and oil; pour over meat. Cover; marinate at room temperature 2 hours, stirring occasionally. Drain meat well; set aside. Discard marinade. In skillet cook mushrooms, onion, green onion, and garlic in butter till tender. Add broth, the ⅓ cup wine, and ¼ teaspoon *salt*. Blend cream into cornstarch; add to skillet. Cook and stir till bubbly. Pour into bowl; keep warm. Cook broccoli according to package directions; drain and keep warm. Heat potatoes. In hot skillet cook and stir meat about 1½ minutes; sprinkle with garlic salt. Arrange broccoli, potatoes, and meat on platter. Spoon sauce atop. Serves 4.

German Cheese Schnitzel

In Germany and Austria, "schnitzel" refers to a thin veal cutlet that is coated with seasoned flour, then dipped in egg and crumbs and fried quickly in butter.

1½ pounds veal leg round steak *or* veal leg sirloin steak	⅓ cup all-purpose flour
2 tablespoons lemon juice	6 tablespoons butter
2 eggs	¾ cup chicken broth
2 tablespoons cooking oil	½ cup dairy sour cream
½ cup fine dry bread crumbs	1 tablespoon all-purpose flour
⅓ cup grated parmesan cheese	¼ teaspoon dried dillweed

Cut veal into 6 pieces; pound with meat mallet to ¼-inch thickness. Sprinkle both sides with lemon juice. Cover; let stand at room temperature 30 minutes. Sprinkle meat with some salt and pepper. Blend eggs, oil, and 2 tablespoons *water*. Mix crumbs and parmesan. Coat meat with ⅓ cup flour; dip in egg mixture. Hold meat up by tongs to allow excess to drip off. Coat meat with crumb mixture; let stand 15 minutes or till coating dries.

In skillet cook meat, a few pieces at a time, in hot butter about 3 minutes or till brown. Turn and brown second side; remove and keep warm.

Pour broth into skillet, scraping to loosen crusty drippings. Combine sour cream, 1 tablespoon flour, and dillweed; stir into broth. Cook and stir till thickened; *do not boil.* Pass with meat. Makes 6 servings.

Veal Cordon Bleu

The literal translation of this French recipe title is "blue ribbon veal." The Italians have a similar dish called Saltimbocca ("jump in the mouth"). It is characterized by the addition of sage to the bread crumbs.

2 slices boiled ham	1 tablespoon snipped parsley
2 slices Swiss cheese	⅛ teaspoon pepper
1 pound veal leg round steak, cut ¼ inch thick	¼ cup all-purpose flour
⅔ cup fine dry bread crumbs	1 slightly beaten egg
	¼ cup butter *or* margarine

Quarter ham and cheese slices. Cut veal into 4 pieces; pound with meat mallet to ⅛-inch thickness (each about 8x4 inches). Halve veal pieces crosswise. On one half, place two quarters *each* of ham and cheese; trim or fold to fit. Cover with second piece of veal; seal edges. Repeat with remaining meats and cheese. Combine bread crumbs, parsley, pepper. Dip meat in flour, then in beaten egg, then in crumb mixture.

In skillet cook meat in hot butter over medium-high heat about 4 minutes per side or till golden brown. Serve at once. Makes 4 servings.

Veal Scallopini with Wine

The term "scallopini" refers to thin slices of meat, usually veal. Technically, these slices must be cut from the leg. Kosher scallopini must be cut from the leg of the forequarter. For this recipe, you may use 1 pound veal cutlets instead of the round steak.

1 pound veal leg round steak, cut ¼ inch thick	1 4-ounce can sliced mushrooms, drained
3 tablespoons butter	2 tablespoons sliced pitted ripe olives
¼ cup dry white wine	2 tablespoons snipped parsley
1 tablespoon lemon juice	
1 teaspoon instant chicken bouillon granules	

Cut veal into 4 pieces; pound with meat mallet to about ⅛-inch thickness. In large skillet cook veal in hot butter, a few pieces at a time, about 1 minute per side. Remove; keep warm. To skillet add wine, lemon juice, bouillon granules, ½ cup *water*, and ⅛ teaspoon *pepper*. Boil rapidly 3 to 4 minutes or till liquid is reduced to about ⅓ cup. Stir in mushrooms, olives, and parsley. Pour over veal. Serves 4.

Lemon slices and fresh dill garnish thin veal slices in German Cheese Schnitzel.

Steak and Bean Pot

4 beef cubed steaks
½ cup chopped onion
1 clove garlic, minced
2 tablespoons cooking oil
2 21-ounce cans pork and
  beans in tomato sauce

1 teaspoon chili powder
¼ teaspoon dried oregano,
  crushed
1 medium tomato, sliced
¼ cup shredded sharp
  American cheese

Cut steaks in bite-size strips; quickly brown meat, onion, and garlic in hot oil. Add beans, chili powder, and oregano. Turn into a 2-quart casserole.

Bake in 350° oven for 45 minutes. Remove from oven; stir. Halve tomato slices; place atop meat. Bake 15 minutes more. Top with cheese; bake 2 to 3 minutes or till cheese melts. Makes 6 servings.

Autumn Chowder

1 pound beef round steak, cut
  in ½-inch cubes
2 tablespoons cooking oil
3 medium potatoes, peeled
  and chopped (3 cups)
1 medium rutabaga, peeled
  and chopped (2 cups)
2 cups chopped cabbage
3 medium carrots, chopped

2 medium onions, chopped
2 tablespoons snipped
  parsley
1 tablespoon vinegar
1½ teaspoons salt
1 teaspoon sugar
¼ teaspoon pepper
1 bay leaf

In Dutch oven brown about half the meat at a time in hot oil. Stir in potatoes, rutabaga, cabbage, carrots, onions, parsley, vinegar, salt, sugar, pepper, and bay leaf. Add 6 cups *water*. Bring mixture to boiling; reduce heat. Cover and simmer for 1 to 1¼ hours or till meat and vegetables are tender. Remove bay leaf. Makes 6 servings.

Crockery cooker directions: Brown meat in hot oil as above. Place vegetables in electric slow crockery cooker; place browned meat atop. Add parsley, vinegar, salt, sugar, pepper, and bay leaf. Add 4 cups *water*. Cover and cook on low-heat setting for 8 hours.

To make beef jerky, *remove and discard all fat from 1 pound beef top **round steak;** freeze steak till icy. Cut in very thin strips, cutting across the meat grain for crisp jerky and with the grain for chewy jerky. Place some strips in bowl or crock in ½-inch-thick layer. Sprinkle with some **salt, pepper,** and **liquid smoke.** Repeat layers till all meat is used. Weight down meat with plate or heavy object; cover and refrigerate overnight. Drain meat; pat dry with paper toweling. Arrange meat on rack in shallow baking pan. Bake in 250° oven for 3½ to 4 hours or till desired dryness. Cool. Store in airtight plastic bags or jar with tight-fitting lid in the refrigerator or at cool room temperature. Makes about ½ pound jerky.*

1 2-pound beef round steak
¼ cup all-purpose flour
1 teaspoon salt
½ teaspoon paprika
¼ cup cooking oil
¾ cup chopped onion
1 clove garlic, minced
2 tablespoons all-purpose
 flour
1 10½-ounce can condensed
 beef broth

¼ cup dry white wine
1 teaspoon worcestershire
 sauce
1 8-ounce can tomato sauce
½ cup dairy sour cream
¼ cup snipped parsley
 Hot cooked noodles
¼ cup chopped green pepper
¼ teaspoon dried oregano,
 crushed
¼ cup grated parmesan
 cheese

Two-Dinner Round Steak

One 2-pound beef round steak and a basic sauce let you prepare two different main dishes at one time. Serve the Round Steak Stroganoff *today—and have the* Saucy Swiss Steak *ready for tomorrow.*

Trim excess fat from steak. Divide steak in half. Cut one portion into 4 pieces for *Saucy Swiss Steak*. Cut other portion into bite-size strips for *Round Steak Stroganoff*. Combine ¼ cup flour, salt, and paprika; use to coat all of the meat. Pound the 4 steak pieces with meat mallet till about ⅛ inch thick. Brown pieces in *2 tablespoons* of the oil about 1½ minutes per side; arrange in 8x8x2-inch baking dish. Cover; refrigerate.

In same skillet brown beef strips, adding remaining oil as needed. Remove meat and set aside. Cook onion and garlic in meat drippings till onion is tender but not brown. Blend in the 2 tablespoons flour. Add beef broth, wine, worcestershire sauce, and *2 tablespoons* of the tomato sauce. Cook, stirring constantly, over medium-high heat till bubbly. Remove ¾ cup of the onion mixture for *Saucy Swiss Steak*; set aside.

For *Round Steak Stroganoff* blend sour cream and parsley into the remaining onion mixture in skillet. Return browned beef strips to skillet. Heat through; *do not boil*. Serve over hot cooked noodles. Makes 4 servings.

For *Saucy Swiss Steak* combine the reserved ¾ cup onion mixture, remaining tomato sauce, green pepper, and oregano. Pour over browned steaks in baking dish. Cover; chill overnight. Before serving, bake, covered, in 350° oven for 50 to 60 minutes. Place meat on platter. Skim fat from sauce; pour sauce over meat. Sprinkle with parmesan. Makes 4 servings.

Spinach Beef Roll

2 tablespoons all-purpose
 flour
½ teaspoon salt
¼ teaspoon garlic salt
⅛ teaspoon pepper
1 2-pound beef round steak,
 cut ¾ inch thick
½ of a 10-ounce package
 frozen chopped spinach,
 cooked and well drained

¾ cup soft bread crumbs
 (1 slice)
⅓ cup grated parmesan
 cheese
2 tablespoons chopped onion
¼ teaspoon ground sage
¼ teaspoon dried thyme,
 crushed
2 tablespoons shortening
⅔ cup dry red wine

Combine flour, salt, garlic salt, and pepper; sprinkle on meat and pound with meat mallet till meat is about ¼ inch thick. Cut meat in half lengthwise. Combine spinach, bread crumbs, cheese, onion, sage, and thyme; spread half over each piece of meat. Roll up jelly roll-style, starting from shorter side. Skewer or tie to secure. In skillet brown meat slowly on all sides in hot shortening. Transfer to 12x7½x2-inch baking dish. Pour wine over meat. Cover; bake in 350° oven for 45 minutes. Uncover; bake 15 minutes more or till tender. Slice meat; pass juices with the meat. Serves 8.

Stir-Fried Beef

1 pound beef round steak, cut ¼ inch thick
¼ cup chopped onion
3 tablespoons soy sauce
1 teaspoon instant beef bouillon granules
1 teaspoon worcestershire sauce
1 clove garlic, minced
2 medium carrots, bias-sliced
1 small head cauliflower, broken into flowerets (about 2 cups)
2 tablespoons cooking oil
1 cup sliced fresh mushrooms
1 6-ounce package frozen pea pods, partially thawed
1 tablespoon cornstarch

Partially freeze meat; thinly slice across grain into bite-size strips. For marinade blend onion, soy, bouillon granules, worcestershire, garlic, ⅔ cup *water*, ½ teaspoon *salt*, and dash *pepper*. Add meat; stir to coat. Cover; let stand at room temperature 1 hour. Stir once or twice. Drain well; reserve marinade.

Cook carrots and cauliflower in boiling salted water 3 minutes; drain. In large skillet or wok brown meat in hot oil. Remove meat with slotted spoon. Add mushrooms to skillet; cook and stir 1 minute. Add pea pods and partially cooked carrots and cauliflower. Cook and stir 2 minutes or till crisp-tender. Add meat. Blend reserved marinade and ¼ cup cold *water* into cornstarch; add to skillet. Cook and stir till bubbly. Serves 4 or 5.

Spanish-Style Round Steak

1½ pounds beef round steak, cut in ¼-inch strips
1½ teaspoons salt
¼ teaspoon pepper
2 tablespoons cooking oil
½ cup chopped onion
1 clove garlic, minced
1 12-ounce can (1½ cups) vegetable juice cocktail
1 10½-ounce can condensed beef broth
1⅓ cups long grain rice
1 10-ounce package frozen peas
¼ cup chopped pimiento

Sprinkle meat with salt and pepper. In 10-inch skillet brown half the meat at a time in hot oil. Add onion and garlic; cook till onion is tender. Add vegetable juice, beef broth, and 1⅓ cups *water*. Bring to boil; reduce heat. Cover; simmer 30 minutes. Add *uncooked* rice, frozen peas, and pimiento. Return to boil. Reduce heat; simmer about 20 minutes more or till meat is tender and rice is done. Makes 6 to 8 servings.

Beef Rolls and Kraut

2 pounds beef round steak, cut ½ inch thick
6 smoked sausage links
2 tablespoons cooking oil
1 16-ounce can tomatoes
½ cup chopped onion
1 teaspoon caraway seed
1 16-ounce can sauerkraut
2 tablespoons all-purpose flour

Cut meat in 6 pieces; pound with meat mallet to 5-inch squares. Season with salt and pepper. Wrap meat around sausage; secure with wooden picks. In skillet brown meat in hot oil; drain. Cut up tomatoes; *do not drain*. Add tomatoes, onion, and caraway. Cover; simmer 1 hour. Rinse sauerkraut; drain. Add to skillet; cook 15 minutes. Remove meat. Blend ¼ cup *water* into flour; add. Cook and stir till bubbly. Serve with meat. Serves 6.

Ordinary vegetables and round steak take on an Oriental flavor in colorful Stir-Fried Beef.

Summer Swiss Steak

1½ pounds beef round steak,
    cut ¾ inch thick
2 tablespoons all-purpose
    flour
1 teaspoon salt
⅛ teaspoon freshly ground
    black pepper
½ cup chopped onion

2 tablespoons shortening
½ cup water
1 teaspoon instant beef
    bouillon granules
1 cup sliced zucchini
1 cup whole kernel corn
½ cup chopped green pepper
2 large tomatoes

Cut meat in 6 pieces. Mix flour, salt, and pepper; pound into meat using meat mallet. In 12-inch skillet brown meat and onion in hot shortening. Blend water and bouillon granules; pour over meat. Cover; simmer 1 hour.

Place zucchini slices atop meat; add corn and green pepper. Sprinkle vegetables with additional salt and pepper. Cover; simmer 10 minutes. Peel and slice tomatoes over bowl to catch tomato juice; add slices and juice to meat mixture. Simmer 10 minutes more. Makes 6 servings.

Moussaka Sandwiches

1 pound beef round steak, cut
    ½ inch thick
¼ cup cooking oil
¾ teaspoon salt
¼ teaspoon garlic powder
⅛ teaspoon pepper
2 cups cubed peeled eggplant
    (½ medium eggplant)
½ cup chopped onion

2 medium tomatoes, peeled
    and chopped
1 3-ounce can sliced
    mushrooms
⅓ cup chili sauce
8 individual French rolls,
    split, toasted, and
    buttered
4 slices mozzarella cheese

Partially freeze meat; thinly slice across grain into bite-size strips. In large skillet brown meat in hot oil. Sprinkle with salt, garlic powder, and pepper. Push meat to one side of skillet. Add eggplant and onion; cook 5 minutes. Stir in tomatoes, *undrained* mushrooms, and chili sauce; cover and simmer 25 to 30 minutes, stirring occasionally. Spoon mixture into rolls. Cut cheese into quarters; place 2 atop each sandwich. Makes 8 sandwiches.

Steak and Oyster Pie

2 pounds beef round steak
⅓ cup all-purpose flour
1 cup thinly sliced onion
1 cup sliced fresh mushrooms
¼ cup shortening
½ pint shucked oysters *or*
    1 8-ounce can oysters

1½ teaspoons salt
⅛ teaspoon pepper
2 cups thinly sliced potato
1 package piecrust mix
    (for 2-crust pie)
Milk

Partially freeze beef; thinly slice across grain into bite-size strips. Coat with flour. In Dutch oven brown beef, onion, and mushrooms in hot shortening. Drain oysters; reserve liquid. Set oysters aside. Add enough water to reserved liquid to make 2½ cups; stir into beef with salt and pepper. Cover; simmer 1½ hours. Add potato; cook 20 minutes. Stir in oysters. Prepare pastry according to package directions. On floured surface roll out ⅔ of the pastry to 13-inch circle; pat into a 2-quart casserole. Fill with beef mixture. Roll out remaining pastry; place atop. Cut slits in top crust; trim ½ inch beyond edge. Tuck top crust under edge of bottom crust; flute edge. Brush top with milk. Bake in 450° oven about 20 minutes. Serves 6 to 8.

Oxtail-Vegetable Soup

2 pounds oxtails, cut in
  1½-inch lengths
3 tablespoons all-purpose
  flour
2 tablespoons cooking oil
1 medium onion, chopped
1 16-ounce can tomatoes
1 10½-ounce can condensed
  beef broth
½ cup dry red wine
1 teaspoon sugar
½ teaspoon salt
½ teaspoon dried thyme,
  crushed
1 bay leaf
4 medium carrots
4 medium parsnips, peeled
½ cup frozen peas

Trim fat from oxtails; coat with flour. In Dutch oven brown meat in hot oil. Add onion, *undrained* tomatoes, broth, wine, sugar, salt, thyme, bay leaf, ½ cup *water,* and ¼ teaspoon *pepper.* Bring to boil; reduce heat. Cover; simmer 2 hours. Skim fat. Cut carrots and parsnips in strips; add to soup. Cover; cook 25 minutes. Add peas; cook 5 minutes. Makes 4 servings.

Wined Short Ribs

½ cup dry red wine
1 teaspoon dried thyme,
  crushed
½ teaspoon garlic salt
½ teaspoon lemon pepper
2 pounds beef short ribs

In Dutch oven mix wine, thyme, garlic salt, lemon pepper, and ½ cup *water;* add ribs. Cover; simmer 1¼ to 1½ hours. Drain; reserve liquid. Grill over *slow* coals 15 to 20 minutes. Turn often; brush on reserved liquid. Serves 4.

Short Ribs and Limas

Beef short ribs can be cut from the chuck, plate, or rib. See page 7 for more information.

3 pounds beef short ribs
2 tablespoons cooking oil
2 10-ounce packages frozen
  lima beans
1 11-ounce can condensed
  beef soup with vegetables
  and barley
1 soup can (1¼ cups)
  water
1 envelope *regular* onion
  soup mix
1 3-ounce can sliced
  mushrooms

In Dutch oven brown ribs in hot oil; add frozen limas. Combine soup, water, dry soup mix, and *undrained* mushrooms; pour over meat and limas. Cover; simmer 1½ to 2 hours. Spoon off fat. Serves 6.

Crockery cooker directions: Brown ribs as above; place in electric slow crockery cooker. Place frozen limas atop. Combine remaining ingredients; add. Cover; cook on low-heat setting 10 hours. (Or, cook on high-heat setting 5 hours.) Skim off fat. (For thicker sauce turn cooker to high-heat setting. Remove meat. Cover; heat cooking liquid to boiling. Blend ¼ cup *water* into 1 to 2 tablespoons all-purpose *flour;* add to boiling liquid. Cook and stir till bubbly. Serve with meat.)

Deviled Beef Bones

For types of beef ribs to try in this recipe, see page 7.

4 pounds beef ribs
1 tablespoon paprika
2 teaspoons chili powder
¾ teaspoon salt
¼ teaspoon dry mustard
¼ teaspoon garlic powder

Place single layer of ribs, meaty side down, in two shallow roasting pans. Roast in 450° oven 30 minutes; drain. Combine remaining ingredients and ⅛ teaspoon *pepper;* sprinkle evenly on all sides of ribs. Reduce oven to 350°. Roast ribs, meaty side up, 45 to 60 minutes more. Makes 4 servings.

Osso Bucco

This Italian dish, featuring veal shanks or knuckles, is a specialty of Milan. Literally, osso bucco means "bone with a hole" or "hollow bone." The inside marrow is considered by many to be the best part.

2 pounds veal shanks, sawed
   into 2½-inch pieces
   (4 to 6 pieces)
2 tablespoons cooking oil
⅓ cup chopped onion
¼ cup chopped carrot
¼ cup chopped celery
1 small clove garlic, minced
1 8-ounce can tomatoes,
   cut up
½ cup water
¼ cup dry white wine
1 tablespoon snipped parsley
1 small bay leaf

½ teaspoon salt
½ teaspoon instant beef
   bouillon granules
¼ teaspoon dried basil,
   crushed
¼ teaspoon dried thyme,
   crushed
Dash pepper
¼ cup cold water
2 tablespoons all-purpose
   flour
Hot cooked noodles *or* rice
Gremolada

In heavy skillet slowly brown meat in hot oil; remove. Add onion, carrot, celery, and garlic to skillet; cook till onion and celery are tender. Drain off excess fat. Return meat to skillet; add *undrained* tomatoes, water, wine, parsley, bay leaf, salt, bouillon granules, basil, thyme, and pepper. Cover; simmer about 1 hour or till meat is tender. Remove meat; keep warm. Blend cold water into flour; stir into broth mixture. Cook and stir till thickened and bubbly. Arrange meat on noodles or rice. Pour on some broth mixture; pass the remainder. Sprinkle meat with Gremolada. Serves 4.

   Gremolada: Lightly mix together 2 tablespoons snipped *parsley;* 1 small clove *garlic,* minced; and 1 teaspoon finely shredded *lemon peel.*

Sensational Veal Stew

2 to 2½ pounds boneless veal,
   cut in 1-inch cubes
6 tablespoons butter
16 small whole onions
4½ cups sliced fresh mushrooms
1 clove garlic, minced
1 teaspoon salt
⅛ teaspoon freshly ground
   black pepper
⅓ cup all-purpose flour
1 10½-ounce can condensed
   chicken broth

¾ cup dry white wine
1 leek, sliced
1 carrot, halved
1 stalk celery, halved
2 sprigs parsley
1 bay leaf
¼ teaspoon dried thyme
3 tablespoons lemon juice
2 egg yolks
¾ cup whipping cream
Grated nutmeg
Lemon wedges

In Dutch oven simmer veal in butter over low heat about 10 minutes (do not brown). Add onions, mushrooms, garlic, salt, and pepper; cook 10 minutes more. Sprinkle flour over meat; stir till blended. Add chicken broth, wine, leek, carrot, and celery. Tie parsley, bay leaf, and thyme in cheesecloth bag; add to mixture.

   Cover; simmer about 30 minutes or till meat is tender, stirring occasionally. Remove and discard cheesecloth bag, carrot, and celery. Stir in lemon juice. Beat together egg yolks and cream. Stir about 1 cup of the hot mixture into egg yolk mixture; return to hot mixture, stirring constantly. Heat till slightly thickened and bubbly. Transfer to serving bowl; sprinkle with nutmeg. Pass lemon wedges. Makes 6 to 8 servings.

Easy Beef-Vegetable Soup

1½ pounds beef shank cross
    cuts
5 cups water
1 16-ounce can tomatoes,
    cut up
1 10-ounce package frozen
    mixed vegetables
1 cup frozen loose-pack hash
    brown potatoes

½ of an envelope (¼ cup)
    regular onion soup mix
¼ cup sliced celery
1 teaspoon sugar
1 teaspoon seasoned salt
½ teaspoon worcestershire
    sauce
Dash bottled hot pepper
    sauce

In 3-quart saucepan simmer beef shanks in water, covered, for 1½ to 2 hours or till meat is tender. Chill beef and broth till layer of fat forms; remove and discard fat. Cut meat into bite-size pieces.

In saucepan combine meat and *3 cups* of the broth (chill remaining broth for another use). Stir in *undrained* tomatoes, mixed vegetables, potatoes, dry soup mix, celery, sugar, seasoned salt, worcestershire, hot pepper sauce, and ⅛ teaspoon *pepper*. Bring to boiling; reduce heat. Cover; simmer 15 to 20 minutes or till vegetables are tender. Makes 6 servings.

Beef-Barley Stew

2 pounds beef shank cross
    cuts
2 tablespoons cooking oil
1 18-ounce can tomato juice
    (2¼ cups)
1½ cups water
2 cups sliced carrot
    (4 medium)
1 cup sliced celery

⅔ cup quick-cooking barley
⅓ cup bottled barbecue sauce
1 4-ounce can mushroom
    stems and pieces
2 cloves garlic, minced
2 teaspoons sugar
1 teaspoon salt
½ teaspoon chili powder
¼ teaspoon pepper

In 4-quart Dutch oven brown meat in hot oil. Add tomato juice, water, carrot, celery, *uncooked* barley, barbecue sauce, *undrained* mushrooms, garlic, sugar, salt, chili powder, and pepper. Cover and bring to boiling, stirring occasionally. Reduce heat and simmer 1½ to 2 hours or till meat and vegetables are tender; stir occasionally. Remove meat; cut from bones. Chop meat and return to mixture. Heat through. Makes 6 to 8 servings.

Special Hungarian Goulash

⅓ cup all-purpose flour
1 teaspoon salt
    Dash pepper
1 pound boneless veal, cut
    in ½-inch cubes
1 pound boneless pork, cut
    in ½-inch cubes
3 tablespoons cooking oil
¼ cup chopped onion

2 tablespoons catsup
2 teaspoons instant chicken
    bouillon granules
2 bay leaves
1 teaspoon paprika
½ cup dairy sour cream
1 27-ounce can sauerkraut
1 teaspoon caraway seed
6 hot boiled potatoes

In paper or plastic bag combine flour, salt, and pepper; add meat cubes, shaking to coat. In skillet brown meat in hot oil; add onion. Stir in catsup, bouillon granules, bay leaves, paprika, and 2¼ cups *water*. Cover and simmer 1 hour. Remove bay leaves; blend in sour cream. Drain sauerkraut; rinse, if desired. Heat sauerkraut and caraway; transfer to platter and top with meat mixture. Pass hot potatoes. Makes 6 servings.

Beef Borscht Stew

If fresh beets are not available, substitute one 16-ounce can shredded beets, drained.

1½ to 2 pounds beef shank
    cross cuts
1 pound fresh beef brisket,
    cut in small cubes
1¼ cups chopped onion
¼ cup chopped celery
1½ teaspoons salt
¼ teaspoon pepper
1 bay leaf
1½ cups chopped carrot
1 8-ounce can tomatoes,
    cut up
3 tablespoons sugar
3 tablespoons lemon juice
1 teaspoon paprika
3 cups coarsely shredded
    cabbage
1½ cups chopped fresh beets
Dairy sour cream

In Dutch oven combine meats, ¼ *cup* of the onion, celery, salt, pepper, bay leaf, and 8 cups *water*. Cover; simmer 1½ hours. Remove shanks. Skim fat from broth. Cut up shank meat; return to broth. Add carrot, *undrained* tomatoes, sugar, lemon juice, paprika, and remaining 1 cup onion. Cover; simmer 15 to 20 minutes. Stir in cabbage and beets; simmer, covered, 10 minutes. Remove bay leaf. Top each serving with sour cream. Serves 8 to 10.

Leek and Beef Stew

1½ pounds beef stew meat, cut
    in 1-inch cubes
1 clove garlic, minced
2 tablespoons cooking oil
1 16-ounce can tomatoes
½ cup dry red wine
2 tablespoons snipped parsley
1 teaspoon sugar
4 carrots, bias-sliced
1 rutabaga, peeled and
    chopped
1 pound leeks, cut in 1-inch
    slices
4 teaspoons cornstarch

In large saucepan cook meat and garlic in hot oil till meat is brown; add 1 teaspoon *salt* and ¼ teaspoon *pepper*. Stir in *undrained* tomatoes, wine, parsley, sugar, and 1 cup *water*. Cover; simmer 1¼ to 1½ hours. Add carrots and rutabaga; cover and simmer 10 minutes. Add leeks; cover and simmer 10 to 15 minutes more or till vegetables are tender. Skim off *excess* fat. Blend 2 tablespoons cold *water* into cornstarch; stir into stew. Cook and stir till thickened and bubbly. Cook 2 minutes more. Makes 6 servings.

Cranberry Beef Stew

2 pounds beef stew meat, cut
    in 1-inch cubes
2 tablespoons cooking oil
1 clove garlic, minced
1 bay leaf
2 teaspoons salt
1 teaspoon worcestershire
    sauce
½ teaspoon paprika
⅛ teaspoon pepper
6 carrots, sliced (1 pound)
1 pound small whole onions
1 16-ounce can whole
    cranberry sauce
½ teaspoon kitchen bouquet
2 tablespoons cornstarch

Brown meat on all sides in hot oil; add garlic, bay leaf, salt, worcestershire, paprika, pepper, and 3 cups *water*. Cover; simmer 1¼ hours, stirring occasionally. Remove bay leaf. Add carrots, onions, and cranberry sauce. Cover and cook 30 to 45 minutes more or till meat and vegetables are tender. Blend ¼ cup cold *water* and kitchen bouquet into cornstarch; stir into stew. Cook and stir till thickened and bubbly. Makes 8 servings.

Using both beef shank cross cuts and fresh beef brisket makes this a meaty Beef Borscht Stew.

Basic Beef and Broth

This one preparation makes enough cooked beef and broth for 1 recipe of Stew, 1 recipe of Soup, and 1 recipe of Goulash. Or, make 1 recipe of Soup and 2 recipes of either Stew or Goulash.

5 pounds beef stew meat, cut in 1-inch cubes	2 cups water
⅓ cup all-purpose flour	1 14-ounce can (1¾ cups) beef broth
1½ teaspoons salt	1 large onion, chopped
Dash pepper	¼ cup soy sauce
¼ cup cooking oil	2 cloves garlic, minced

Coat meat with mixture of flour, salt, and pepper. In 5-quart Dutch oven brown one-fourth of the meat at a time in hot oil. Return all meat to pan. Stir in water, broth, onion, soy, and garlic. Bring to boil; reduce heat. Simmer, covered, 45 minutes. Cool. Drain meat; reserve broth. Divide meat into 1½- or 3½-cup containers; cover and chill, or label and freeze. Divide broth into 1-, 1½-, or 3-cup containers; chill or freeze. Makes about 8½ cups cooked beef and 5½ cups broth. Use in stew, soup, or goulash.

	Stew	Soup	Goulash
Basic Beef cubes	3½ cups	1½ cups	3½ cups
Basic Beef broth	1½ cups	3 cups	1 cup
Additional liquid	*(tomato juice, beer, dry red or white wine, or additional Basic Beef broth)*		
	1 cup	2 cups *and* 1 cup water	¾ cup
Vegetables	*(carrot, celery, onion, potato, rutabaga, cauliflower, broccoli, corn, peas, green beans) Use any combination for a total of:*		
	6 cups, cut in chunks	5 cups, chopped	2 cups, finely chopped
Crushed dried herbs	*(basil, oregano, marjoram, thyme) Use one or two types for a total of:*		
	1 teaspoon	1 teaspoon	1 teaspoon
Optional meat	*(cooked bulk pork sausage or sliced brown-and-serve sausage links or crisp-cooked and crumbled bacon) Add one, if desired.*		
	4 ounces *or* 4 slices	4 ounces *or* 4 slices	4 ounces *or* 4 slices
	In 4-quart Dutch oven combine beef, broth, additional liquid, vegetables, and herbs. Stir in one 8-ounce can *tomato sauce*, ⅓ cup *vinegar*, and ¼ cup packed *brown sugar*. Simmer, covered, about 30 minutes or till vegetables are almost tender. Add optional meat; simmer 10 minutes more. Season to taste with salt and pepper. Blend ¼ cup cold *water* into 2 tablespoons *cornstarch*; stir into stew. Cook and stir till bubbly. Serves 8 to 10.	Cut beef in smaller pieces. In 4-quart Dutch oven combine beef, broth, additional liquid, vegetables, and herbs. Bring to boiling; reduce heat. Cover and simmer 30 minutes. Add 1 cup uncooked medium *noodles* and optional meat. Simmer 15 minutes more. Season to taste with some salt and pepper. Makes 10 servings.	In 4-quart Dutch oven combine beef, broth, additional liquid, vegetables, and herbs. Simmer, covered, 10 minutes. Add optional meat; simmer 10 minutes. Season with salt and pepper. Blend ¼ cup cold *water* into 2 tablespoons all-purpose *flour;* add to meat. Cook and stir till bubbly. Blend about 1 cup of hot mixture into ½ cup dairy *sour cream* or plain *yogurt*. Return all to pot. Heat through; *do not boil.* Serve over hot cooked *noodles*. Makes 6 servings.

Rio Grande Stew

2 pounds beef stew meat,
  cut in 1½-inch cubes
2 tablespoons cooking oil
1 10½-ounce can condensed
  beef broth
½ cup chopped celery
½ cup chopped onion
2 cloves garlic, minced
2 bay leaves
1 tablespoon dried oregano,
  crushed
1 tablespoon ground
  coriander
2 teaspoons ground cumin
1½ teaspoons salt

3 medium carrots, cut in
  chunks
2 fresh ears corn, cut in
  1-inch pieces
1 15-ounce can garbanzo
  beans
8 cabbage wedges
1 16-ounce can tomatoes,
  cut up
½ cup finely chopped onion
1 4-ounce can green chili
  peppers, rinsed, seeded,
  and chopped
¼ cup snipped parsley
1 clove garlic, minced

In large Dutch oven brown half the meat at a time in hot oil. Add beef broth, celery, ½ cup chopped onion, 2 cloves garlic, bay leaves, oregano, coriander, cumin, salt, and 3 cups *water*. Bring to boiling; reduce heat. Cover and simmer about 2 hours or till meat is almost tender. Skim off fat. Stir in carrots, corn, and *undrained* garbanzo beans; arrange cabbage atop. Simmer, covered, 20 to 30 minutes or till meat and vegetables are done. Remove bay leaves. Season to taste with salt and pepper.

Meanwhile, combine *undrained* tomatoes, ½ cup finely chopped onion, chili peppers, parsley, 1 clove garlic, and ½ teaspoon *salt*. Serve stew in bowls; pass tomato mixture to spoon atop. Makes 8 servings.

Chinese Beef Casserole

Cut your own stew meat from round steak or pot roast. Trim and discard excess fat, and remove any bones (use for **Basic Beef Stock**, page 168). Cut meat into cubes, keeping them as uniformly shaped as possible so they'll cook evenly.

1½ pounds beef stew meat, cut
  in 1-inch cubes
2 tablespoons cooking oil
¼ cup soy sauce
¼ cup dry sherry
2 tablespoons cornstarch
1 teaspoon sugar
⅛ teaspoon ground ginger

4 cups sliced Chinese
  cabbage (8 ounces)
1 5-ounce can water
  chestnuts, drained and
  sliced
¼ cup chopped green onion
½ of a 3-ounce can (about 1
  cup) chow mein noodles

In skillet brown half the meat at a time in hot oil. In 2-quart casserole combine beef, soy sauce, and 1½ cups *water*. Cover; bake in 350° oven for 1 hour 45 minutes. Combine sherry, cornstarch, sugar, and ginger; stir into casserole. Fold in cabbage, water chestnuts, and green onion. Return to oven; bake, covered, 10 minutes more. Top with noodles. Makes 6 servings.

Fruited Beef with Bulgur

2 pounds beef stew meat, cut
  in 1-inch cubes
2 tablespoons cooking oil
1 cup chopped onion
1 cup bulgur wheat

3 cups beef broth
⅓ cup dried apricots,
  finely snipped
¼ cup raisins
1 teaspoon curry powder

Brown meat in hot oil. Drain; reserve 2 tablespoons drippings. Transfer meat to 2-quart casserole. Cook onion in reserved drippings till tender. Stir in bulgur. Add broth, apricots, raisins, curry, and 1 teaspoon *salt;* bring to boil. Pour over meat. Bake, covered, in 325° oven 1½ hours. Serves 6 to 8.

Burgundy Beef Casserole

4 slices bacon	1 clove garlic, minced
3 pounds beef stew meat, cut in 1-inch cubes	1 pound small whole onions
¼ cup all-purpose flour	2 cups burgundy
1 teaspoon salt	1 sprig parsley
¼ cup cognac	1 bay leaf
1 cup finely chopped carrot	1½ cups water
¼ cup finely chopped onion	1 6-ounce package long grain and wild rice mix
1 leek, finely chopped (optional)	3 cups sliced fresh mushrooms

In large skillet cook bacon till crisp. Drain; reserve drippings in pan. Crumble bacon; set aside. Coat meat with mixture of flour and salt. Brown half of the meat at a time in the hot drippings. Transfer meat to a 4-quart casserole. Warm cognac in a small saucepan just till hot; *do not boil.* Ignite; pour over meat in casserole. Allow flame to burn out.

In same skillet cook carrot, chopped onion, leek, and garlic till vegetables are tender; add a little cooking oil if necessary. Stir into meat in casserole. Add small whole onions and bacon. Stir in burgundy, parsley, and bay leaf. Bake, covered, in 350° oven for 1½ hours. Stir in water and rice mix. Bake, covered, for 30 minutes. Stir in mushrooms. Return to oven and bake, covered, 30 minutes more. If desired, sprinkle with 2 tablespoons snipped parsley. Makes 8 to 10 servings.

Texas Chili Pie

3 pounds beef stew meat, cut in ½-inch cubes	1 teaspoon ground cumin
2 cups chopped onion	2 15½-ounce cans red kidney beans, drained
1 28-ounce can tomatoes, cut up	½ cup yellow cornmeal
2 cups water	½ cup all-purpose flour
1 6-ounce can tomato paste	1 tablespoon sugar
1 4-ounce can green chili peppers, rinsed, seeded, and chopped	1½ teaspoons baking powder
	¼ teaspoon salt
3 cloves garlic, minced	1 beaten egg
2 tablespoons chili powder	2 tablespoons milk
2 teaspoons salt	2 tablespoons cooking oil
	1 8-ounce can cream-style corn

Divide meat and onion between two ungreased 2½-quart casseroles. In bowl combine *undrained* tomatoes, water, tomato paste, *half* of the chili peppers, garlic, chili powder, the 2 teaspoons salt, and ground cumin. Divide between the two casseroles.

Bake, covered, in 350° oven for 2 hours. Stir in the drained beans. Increase oven temperature to 400°. Cover and bake 15 minutes longer.

Meanwhile, combine cornmeal, flour, sugar, baking powder, and ¼ teaspoon salt. Add egg, milk, and oil. Stir in corn and the remaining chili peppers. Remove casseroles from oven; spoon half of the cornmeal mixture over the hot mixture in each casserole. Bake, uncovered, 25 to 30 minutes or till topping is golden brown. Makes 2 casseroles, 8 servings each.

Roasts from the Shoulder

The pork shoulder includes the Boston shoulder from the upper area and the arm picnic or arm shoulder from the lower area.

Shoulder Arm Roast A square-shaped roast that is cut from the upper portion of the Arm Picnic. Contains the round arm bone. *Roast.*

Shoulder Arm Picnic The round arm bone identifies this roast from the lower shoulder area. It is less tender than the upper Blade Boston Roast. May be sold boned, rolled, and tied. Also called fresh picnic. *Roast.* When cured and smoked, it is labeled **Smoked Arm Picnic** or simply smoked picnic. This is often confused with ham, and is prepared similarly. May be labeled "fully cooked" or "cook-before-eating." *Bake or cook in liquid.*

Shoulder Blade Boston Roast
A square-shaped roast with identifying blade bone from the upper shoulder. Sometimes called Boston butt. Also sold with bone removed, rolled, and tied. *Roast.* When cured and smoked, it is labeled **Smoked Pork Shoulder Roll.** *Bake or cook in liquid.*

Ribs (also see pages 56-59)

Include the meaty **Country-Style Ribs,** the **Loin Back Ribs,** and the mostly bone **Spareribs.** *Roast, braise, cook in liquid,* or *broil slowly (often broiled on outdoor grill).*

Since the pork carcass is smaller than the beef, it is halved but not quartered. Wholesale cuts include the shoulder, the loin, the leg (ham), and the side, as shown. The loin is the most tender area with tenderness decreasing as cuts are made closer to the shoulder and to the leg.

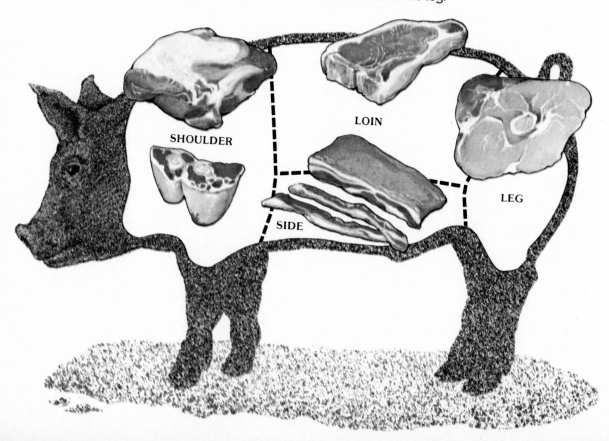

SHOULDER

LOIN

LEG

SIDE

Steaks from the Shoulder

Shoulder Arm Steak Cut from the Arm Picnic. Contains the identifying round arm bone. *Braise or panfry.*

Shoulder Blade Steak Cut from the Blade Boston Roast. Contains blade bone. *Braise, broil, panbroil, or panfry.*

Cubed Steak Any boneless piece of pork which has been put through a tenderizing machine. *Braise, broil, panbroil, or panfry.*

Roasts from the Loin

Cuts from the loin are the most tender and usually the most expensive of all pork cuts.

Center Loin Roast Cut between Loin Blade Roast and Sirloin Roast. Includes a portion of the tenderloin. May be smoked. With tenderloin removed, it is a **Loin Center Rib Roast.** Two rib roasts tied together make a **Crown Roast.** *Roast.*

Boneless Top Loin Roast Flat-shaped loin eye muscle. May have two roasts tied, flat sides together, in a roll shape. *Roast.* Becomes **Canadian-Style Bacon** when shaped into compact roll, then cured and smoked. *Bake, broil, panbroil, or panfry.*

Sirloin Roast Cut from the loin section nearest the leg. Usually 5 to 7 inches in length. Contains the backbone and hip bone. *Roast.*

Loin Blade Roast Includes the first 5 to 7 rib bones. May have the blade bone removed. *Roast.*

Pork Tenderloin Small tapering muscle that extends through part of the loin. Usually weighs 1 pound or less. Also comes cured and smoked. *Roast, braise, or broil.*

Chops from the Loin

Sliced from loin roasts.

Sirloin Chop Cut from the loin section nearest the leg. Contains section of backbone and/or hip bone. May be smoked. Also called sirloin steak. *Braise, broil, panbroil, or panfry.*

Loin Blade Chop Cut from the first 5 to 7 ribs. May have the blade bone removed. *Braise, broil, panbroil, or panfry.*

Loin Rib Chop Tender rib eye muscle. May be smoked, boneless, and/or butterflied. When cut thicker, with pocket, it is known as **Loin Rib Chop for Stuffing.** *Braise, broil, panbroil, or panfry.*

Loin Chop Cut between Loin Rib Chop and Sirloin Chop. Includes a portion of tenderloin as well as the loin eye muscle. *Braise, broil, panbroil, or panfry.*

Sirloin Cutlet Boneless lean piece from the wedge-shaped area above the hip bone. Also called pork cutlet. *Braise, broil, panbroil, or panfry.*

Top Loin Chop From center loin section. Tenderloin removed; chine bone chipped. May be boneless and/or butterflied. *Braise, broil, panbroil, or panfry.*

Cuts from the Side and Other Areas

Pork Cubes for Kabobs Cut from the shoulder or leg (smoked ham). *Broil, braise, panfry, or roast.*

Pork Jowl Square piece in front of shoulder. Often smoked; may be sliced. *Broil, panbroil, panfry, or cook in liquid.*

Pork Hock Cut from shank (lower) end of arm or leg (ham). Mostly bone and cartilage with little meat. May be fresh, cured and smoked, or pickled. *Braise or cook in liquid.*

Fresh Side Pork Whole piece removed from side. May be sliced. Called salt pork when salt is rubbed on pieces. *Roast, broil, panbroil, panfry, or cook in liquid.* Cured and smoked to make **Slab Bacon**; also may be sliced. *Bake, broil, panbroil, or panfry.*

Pigs Feet May be fresh, smoked, or pickled. *Cook in liquid or braise.*

Ham

According to USDA standards, all meat labeled "ham" must come from the hind leg of a pig. It may be fresh, but is usually cured and smoked. Curing may be done by simply rubbing salt over the surface and storing in a cool place (dry salt cure). Or a salt solution may be pumped into the meat, left for a certain time, then rinsed away (brine cure). The ham is then cooked and, sometimes, smoked. All may be fully-cooked or require cooking before eating (see Ham Terminology below for cooking information).

Whole Ham Pear-shaped cut containing leg and shank bones. Usually weighs 10 to 18 pounds. *Bake.*

Center Slice Nearly round, meaty cut from center of whole ham. Contains small round leg bone, which may be removed. *Bake, broil, panbroil, or panfry.*

Shank Half Lower half of whole ham that includes shank bone and part of leg bone. Has lower proportion of meat to bone than rump half.

Rump Half Upper half of whole ham. Has more meat to bone than shank half. Called **Rump Portion** when center slice is removed.

Country-Style Ham

Distinctively-flavored ham that is dry cured. Usually saltier and firmer than smoked hams. Many types; must be processed in Smithfield, Va. to be labeled a Smithfield ham.

Follow label directions (usually must be scrubbed, soaked, and simmered before baking).

Boneless Ham

All of the bones and most of the interior and exterior fat are removed. Remaining lean meat is then shaped inside a casing or placed into a can and processed. A whole ham averages 7 to 10 pounds, but it is usually cut into halves,

quarters, or pieces. Also referred to as a rolled, shaped, formed, or sectioned and formed ham. Usually fully-cooked; some require cooking before eating.

Partially Boned Ham

One or two of the three bones (shank, aitch, leg) in a whole ham are removed. Called a **Shankless Ham** when the shank bone is removed. Called a **Semi-Boneless Ham** when both the shank and aitch bones are removed, leaving only the round leg bone. Usually cut into two smaller pieces. All may be fully-cooked or require cooking before eating.

Canned Ham

Usually consists of boneless cured ham pieces that are placed in a can, then vacuum sealed and fully-cooked. A small amount of dry gelatin is added before sealing to absorb the natural ham juices while the ham cooks. Traditional pear-shaped canned hams range in weight from 1½ to 10 pounds. All canned hams are ready-to-eat. Most are labeled "perishable—keep refrigerated." Some may be shelf stable. Check the label.

Ham Terminology

Cured and Smoked
Describes the curing and smoking processes. May need additional baking to finish cooking and develop flavors. Should be refrigerated.
Fully Cooked Cured and smoked pork products which are completely cooked. Ready-to-eat but may be heated. Refrigerate.
Cook Before Eating
Indicates that the ham was not completely cooked during the smoking process. To serve, bake to an internal temperature of 160°.
Water Added Hams which retained water during the curing process so that they weigh more than they did before processing. Added moisture cannot exceed 10% of the weight of the fresh ham.

Pork Loin with Curry-Horseradish Sauce

1 teaspoon curry powder
½ teaspoon salt
½ teaspoon pepper
1 4- to 5-pound boneless
pork loin roast
Milk
½ cup chopped onion

2 to 3 teaspoons curry
powder
2 tablespoons butter
2 tablespoons all-purpose
flour
½ cup dairy sour cream
1 tablespoon prepared
horseradish

Mix the 1 teaspoon curry, salt, and pepper, rub onto meat. Place meat on rack in shallow roasting pan. Insert meat thermometer. Roast in 325° oven 2½ to 3 hours or till thermometer registers 170°. Remove meat; keep warm. Skim fat from pan juices; measure juices. Add milk to make 1¼ cups liquid; set aside. Cook onion and 2 to 3 teaspoons curry in butter till onion is tender. Stir in flour and ¼ teaspoon *salt*; add milk mixture. Cook and stir till bubbly. Stir in sour cream and horseradish; heat through; *do not boil*. Spoon some over roast; pass remainder. Serves 10 to 12.

If desired, garnish this roast with fresh mint and poached apple slices.

Orange-Sauced Pork Roast

1 2-pound boneless pork
shoulder roast
2 tablespoons butter *or*
margarine
½ cup chopped onion
1 teaspoon grated orange peel
⅔ cup orange juice

⅓ cup dry sherry
2 tablespoons sugar
2 tablespoons lemon juice
1½ teaspoons salt
1 bay leaf
1 tablespoon cold water
1 tablespoon cornstarch

In large skillet brown meat in butter; remove meat. Add onion; cook till tender. Stir in orange peel, juice, sherry, sugar, lemon juice, salt, bay leaf, and dash *pepper*. Return meat; cover. Simmer 1¼ to 1½ hours or till tender. Transfer meat to hot platter; slice. Remove bay leaf. Skim fat from juices. Measure juices; add enough water to make 1½ cups. Blend cold water into cornstarch; stir into orange mixture. Bring to boil. Cook and stir 1 to 2 minutes. Pass with meat. Serves 6 to 8.

Harvest Pot Roast

1 4-pound pork shoulder
roast
2 tablespoons cooking oil
1 medium onion, cut in thin
wedges
2 teaspoons salt
1 teaspoon dried dillweed

½ teaspoon pepper
1 acorn squash
6 to 8 small potatoes,
peeled
3 large carrots, sliced
¼ cup all-purpose flour
½ teaspoon kitchen bouquet

In Dutch oven brown meat in hot oil. Spoon off fat. Add onion, salt, dillweed, pepper, and 2 cups *water*. Bring to boil; reduce heat. Simmer, covered, 1 hour or till meat is nearly tender. Cut squash crosswise into 1-inch-thick slices; discard seeds. Halve slices. Add squash slices, potatoes, and carrots to meat. Simmer 30 minutes more or till meat and vegetables are tender; remove to warm platter. Skim fat from juices; reserve 1½ cups juices. Blend ½ cup cold *water* into the flour; stir into reserved juices. Cook and stir till thickened and bubbly. Stir in kitchen bouquet; simmer 2 to 3 minutes, stirring occasionally. Season to taste with salt and pepper. Pass with meat. Serves 6 to 8.

Pork Crown Roast with Apricot Stuffing

Normally, a rib crown roast isn't found in the meat section of your supermarket. You'll have to call ahead and place an order to have it specially cut for you. Make sure the fat is trimmed from the center of the roast.

1 5½- to 6-pound pork rib crown roast (12 to 16 ribs)
1 tablespoon sugar
1 teaspoon instant chicken bouillon granules
¾ cup hot water
¼ cup snipped dried apricots
4 cups dry whole wheat bread cubes (5½ slices)
1 large apple, peeled, cored, and chopped

½ teaspoon finely shredded orange peel
½ teaspoon salt
½ teaspoon ground sage
¼ teaspoon ground cinnamon
⅛ teaspoon pepper
½ cup chopped celery
¼ cup chopped onion
¼ cup butter *or* margarine
¼ cup orange juice
1 tablespoon light corn syrup
½ teaspoon soy sauce

Place roast, bone tips up, on rack in shallow roasting pan. Season with a little salt and pepper. Make a ball of aluminum foil and press into cavity to hold open. Wrap bone tips with foil. Insert meat thermometer, making sure bulb does not touch bone. Roast in 325° oven 2½ hours.

Meanwhile, prepare stuffing. Dissolve sugar and bouillon granules in hot water; pour over apricots. Let stand 5 minutes. In large bowl combine bread cubes, apple, orange peel, salt, sage, cinnamon, and pepper. Cook celery and onion in butter or margarine till tender; add to bread mixture. Add apricot mixture; toss lightly to moisten. (If desired, add ¼ cup additional water for a moister stuffing.)

Remove all foil from roast. Pack stuffing lightly into center of roast, mounding high. Combine orange juice, corn syrup, and soy sauce; spoon some over meat. Roast, uncovered, 45 to 60 minutes more or till thermometer registers 170°; baste occasionally with orange juice mixture. Carefully transfer to warm platter. Garnish with canned apricot halves, if desired. Slice between ribs to serve. Serves 12 to 16.

Fruit-Stuffed Pork Rib Roast

1 4-pound pork loin center rib roast, backbone loosened
1 20-ounce can pie-sliced apples
1 pound ground pork

9 slices dry raisin bread, cut in ½-inch cubes
1 teaspoon ground cinnamon
¾ teaspoon salt
½ teaspoon ground cardamom
¼ teaspoon ground allspice

Place roast, rib side down; cut pockets between rib bones. Season with salt and pepper. Drain apples, reserving juice; finely chop apples. Add water to reserved juice to make 1 cup liquid; set aside.

In skillet cook ground pork till browned; drain off excess fat. Stir in bread cubes, cinnamon, salt, spices, chopped apple, and dash *pepper*. Add reserved apple liquid; toss to moisten. Spoon about ½ cup stuffing into each pocket of roast; insert meat thermometer in meat so it doesn't touch bone. Spoon remaining stuffing into 1-quart casserole; set aside. Roast meat in 325° oven for 1½ hours or till meat begins to brown. Cover loosely with foil to prevent stuffing from over browning. Roast 1 to 1½ hours more or till meat thermometer registers 170°. Bake stuffing in casserole, uncovered, with roast during last 40 minutes of cooking time. Serves 8.

Pork Crown Roast with Apricot Stuffing *is a star attraction for your next dinner party.*

Tenderloin Pinwheels

1 1-pound pork tenderloin
1½ cups finely chopped fresh mushrooms (4 ounces)
1 tablespoon butter *or* margarine
1 cup frozen peas
1 beaten egg
1 cup soft bread crumbs (1¼ slices)

½ cup finely chopped fully cooked ham
¼ teaspoon salt
Dash pepper
½ teaspoon instant beef bouillon granules
¼ cup hot water
1 tablespoon butter *or* margarine

Split tenderloin lengthwise, cutting to, but not through, opposite side; open out flat. Working out from the center, pound tenderloin lightly with meat mallet to about 10x6-inch rectangle. Sprinkle with a little salt. Cook mushrooms in 1 tablespoon butter or margarine about 3 minutes or till tender, stirring occasionally. Spread evenly over tenderloin. Cook peas according to package directions; drain well. Mash slightly with a fork. Add egg, bread crumbs, ham, salt, and pepper. Toss lightly. Spoon atop mushroom layer. Roll up jelly roll-style, beginning at narrow end. Tie meat with string, first at center, then at 1-inch intervals.

Place meat on rack in shallow roasting pan. Dissolve bouillon granules in hot water. Stir in 1 tablespoon butter till melted; brush some over meat. Roast, uncovered, in 325° oven about 1½ hours or till meat is tender; brush occasionally with remaining bouillon mixture. Transfer meat to warm platter. Remove strings; slice. Serves 4.

Breaded Pork Tenderloin

If you want to serve these in a bun for sandwiches, cut the tenderloin into 6 slices and prepare the same way.

1 1-pound pork tenderloin, cut crosswise in 4 slices
¼ cup all-purpose flour
¼ teaspoon salt
⅛ teaspoon pepper
1 beaten egg

1 tablespoon milk
¾ cup fine dry bread crumbs (3 slices)
2 tablespoons finely chopped green onion
2 tablespoons cooking oil

Pound pork slices with meat mallet flattening to ¼-inch thickness. Combine flour, salt, and pepper; set aside. Combine egg and milk; pour into a pie plate. Combine bread crumbs and green onion. Dip each pork slice in flour mixture, then in egg mixture, then in crumbs to coat. In large skillet cook 2 slices in hot oil over medium-high heat for 2 to 3 minutes per side or till done. Remove to platter; keep warm. Repeat with remaining slices, adding more oil, if necessary. Makes 4 servings.

Asparagus-Sauced Pork Tenderloin

2 1-pound pork tenderloins, each cut crosswise in 4 slices
2 tablespoons butter
1 10¾-ounce can condensed cream of asparagus soup

¼ cup milk
½ cup chopped onion
1 2½-ounce jar sliced mushrooms, drained
½ teaspoon curry powder
Dash pepper

Pound pork slices with meat mallet to flatten to ¼-to ½-inch thickness. In skillet brown pork in butter; remove pork and set aside. In same skillet blend together soup and milk; stir in onion, mushrooms, curry powder, and pepper. Return meat to skillet. Cover and simmer 40 to 45 minutes or till tender. Serve soup mixture atop meat. Makes 8 servings.

Roasting Fresh Pork

Carve meat across the grain. For carving tips, see pages 170-171. For gravy-making tips, see page 168.

Cut	Approx. Weight (pounds)	Internal Temperature on removal from oven	Approx. Cooking Time (total time)
Roast meat at constant 325° oven temperature.			
Center Loin Roast	3 to 5	170°	2½ to 3 hours
Sirloin Roast	5 to 7	170°	3½ to 4¼ hours
Loin Blade Roast	3 to 4	170°	2¼ to 2¾ hours
Boneless Top Loin Roast	3 to 4	170°	2½ to 3 hours
Tenderloin	1	170°	¾ to 1 hour
Shoulder Blade Boston Roast	4 to 6	170°	3 to 4 hours
Boneless Shoulder Blade Boston Roast	3 to 5	170°	2 to 3 hours
Shoulder Arm Picnic Roast	5 to 8	170°	3 to 4 hours
Leg (fresh ham)	10 to 16	170°	4½ to 6 hours
Leg (fresh ham) rump portion	5 to 7	170°	3½ to 4½ hours

Roasting Directions: Sprinkle meat with some salt and pepper. Place meat, fat side up, on rack in shallow roasting pan. Insert meat thermometer into center of roast so bulb reaches the thickest part of the lean meat. Make sure bulb doesn't rest in fat or touch bone. Do not cover, add water, or baste. Roast in 325° oven till thermometer registers 170°. To check, push thermometer into meat a little farther. If temperature drops, continue roasting. Let meat stand 15 minutes for easier carving.

Roast Pork with Brussels Sprouts Sauté

1 3- to 4-pound pork roast
2 pints fresh brussels sprouts
2 medium onions, cut in thin wedges
2 tablespoons butter
2 teaspoons snipped fresh basil
½ teaspoon salt
⅛ teaspoon pepper

Roast meat according to chart above. Just before roast is done, prepare vegetables. Trim stems of fresh brussels sprouts. Halve large sprouts. In covered saucepan combine brussels sprouts, onions, butter, basil, salt, and pepper. Cook, stirring occasionally, 8 to 10 minutes or till sprouts are tender. Serve with meat. Makes 6 to 8 servings.

If fresh brussels sprouts or fresh basil aren't available, make these substitutions. Use two 10-ounce packages frozen brussels sprouts, thawed. Use ½ teaspoon dried basil, crushed.

Pork Steaks with Apple Stuffing

These steaks may vary in diameter. If you buy the largest ones, you'll probably need to use two pans.

6 pork shoulder blade steaks, cut ½ inch thick
2 tablespoons shortening
3 cups plain croutons
1½ cups finely chopped unpeeled apple
½ cup raisins
½ cup finely chopped celery

½ cup finely chopped onion
¾ teaspoon salt
½ teaspoon poultry seasoning
Dash pepper
1¼ teaspoons instant beef bouillon granules
⅔ cup hot water

Slowly brown *3* of the steaks on both sides in hot shortening. Season with a little salt and pepper. Place in a 15x10x1-inch baking pan. Repeat with remaining steaks. Combine croutons, apple, raisins, celery, onion, salt, poultry seasoning, and pepper. Dissolve bouillon granules in hot water; toss with crouton mixture. Pack some into ½ cup measuring cup and unmold on one steak; repeat. Cover; bake in 350° oven about 1 hour. Makes 6 servings.

Skillet Pork Chops and Hot Slaw

If desired, use trimmings from the pork chops for browning instead of the 2 tablespoons shortening. Trim excess fat from chops; heat in skillet till 2 tablespoons accumulate. Discard trimmings.

6 pork chops, cut ½ inch thick
2 tablespoons shortening
¼ cup vinegar
1 tablespoon all-purpose flour
1 tablespoon sugar
1 tablespoon prepared mustard

2 teaspoons worcestershire sauce
1 teaspoon salt
½ teaspoon celery seed
5 cups coarsely shredded cabbage
1 cup shredded carrot
½ cup chopped onion
½ cup chopped green pepper

In skillet brown chops on both sides in hot shortening. Season with a little salt and pepper. Add 2 tablespoons *water;* cover immediately. Simmer 20 minutes. Remove chops; keep warm. Blend together the vinegar, flour, sugar, mustard, worcestershire, salt, celery seed, and ¼ cup *water.* Stir into pan drippings. Add vegetables. Cook and stir till mixture thickens; top with chops. Simmer, covered, 5 minutes more. Makes 6 servings.

Smoky Pork Skillet

1¼ cups dried whole green peas
4 cups cold water
1 13¾-ounce can chicken broth
½ cup chopped onion
1 teaspoon dried basil, crushed

½ teaspoon salt
5 smoked pork chops, cut ½ inch thick
2 tablespoons shortening
1 tablespoon all-purpose flour

In saucepan bring peas, water, and broth to boiling. Reduce heat; simmer 2 minutes. Remove from heat; cover and let stand 1 hour. (Or, add peas to the cold water; soak overnight.) Add onion, basil, and salt. Cover; simmer 3 to 3½ hours or till peas are tender but still retain their shape. Drain, reserving ¾ cup liquid.

In large skillet brown chops in hot shortening. Remove chops. Pour off all but 1 tablespoon drippings. Blend in flour. Stir in reserved pea liquid. Cook and stir till mixture thickens. Stir in peas; arrange chops atop. Cover and cook over low heat 5 minutes or till heated through. Makes 5 servings.

Chutney Chops with Pineapple

6 pork chops, cut ½ inch
   thick
2 tablespoons cooking oil
1 20-ounce can pineapple
   slices
½ cup chutney, chopped
2 teaspoons salt

2 to 3 teaspoons curry
   powder
1 teaspoon instant beef
   bouillon granules
1 7-ounce package (2¼ cups)
   quick-cooking rice

In 12-inch skillet cook chops in hot oil over medium heat 15 to 20 minutes, turning once. Remove chops from skillet; set aside. Drain pineapple slices, reserving syrup. Set 3 slices aside; chop remaining slices. Add enough water to reserved syrup to make 2¼ cups liquid.

In same skillet combine the syrup mixture, chutney, salt, curry powder, and bouillon granules; bring to boiling. Stir in *uncooked* rice and chopped pineapple. Place browned pork chops atop rice. Quarter reserved pineapple slices; arrange over chops. Cover; reduce heat and simmer for 5 minutes more or until rice is cooked. Makes 6 servings.

Chili Barbecued Pork Chops

For help in determining the temperature of the coals, see page 23.

½ cup chopped onion
1 clove garlic, minced
2 tablespoons cooking oil
½ cup chili sauce
¼ teaspoon finely shredded
   orange peel

¼ cup orange juice
1 tablespoon brown sugar
½ teaspoon salt
   Dash bottled hot pepper
   sauce
6 pork loin butterfly chops

In small saucepan cook onion and garlic in hot oil till tender but not brown. Stir in chili sauce, orange peel, orange juice, brown sugar, salt, and pepper sauce; mix well. Bring to boiling; remove from heat.

Sprinkle pork chops with a little salt and pepper. Grill chops over *medium* coals about 15 minutes. Turn meat; brush with some of the chili sauce mixture. Grill 15 to 20 minutes more, brushing with remaining chili sauce mixture. Makes 6 servings.

Grilled Rice-Stuffed Pork Chops

½ cup cold water
¼ cup long grain rice
1 teaspoon instant chicken
   bouillon granules
½ teaspoon dry mustard
¼ teaspoon ground sage
¼ teaspoon salt

¼ teaspoon pepper
2 tablespoons chopped green
   onion
1 2½-ounce jar chopped
   mushrooms, drained
4 pork rib chops, cut 1 inch
   thick

In saucepan combine cold water, rice, bouillon granules, mustard, sage, salt, and pepper; cover with tight-fitting lid. Bring to boil; reduce heat. Simmer 10 minutes (do not lift cover). Remove from heat; let stand, covered, 10 minutes. Stir in green onion and mushrooms.

Cut pocket in each chop by cutting from fat side almost to bone edge. Season cavity with a little salt and pepper. Spoon about ¼ cup rice mixture into each pocket. Securely fasten pocket opening with wooden picks. Grill chops over *medium* coals 20 minutes; turn and grill 10 minutes more. Before serving, remove the picks. Makes 4 servings.

Pork Chops with Anise-Corn Stuffing

For 3 cups toasted bread cubes, cut up 6 bread slices and place in a shallow pan. Toast the cubes in a 350° oven for 15 to 20 minutes, shaking the pan occasionally.

For easier turning when preparing these on the grill, use a wire grill basket.

1 medium green pepper, chopped (¾ cup)
½ cup chopped onion
3 tablespoons butter
3 cups toasted bread cubes (see note, left)
1 tablespoon snipped chives
½ teaspoon salt
¼ teaspoon aniseed, crushed
1 8¾-ounce can whole kernel corn
12 thinly sliced pork chops

Cook green pepper and onion in butter till tender. Remove from heat; add bread cubes, chives, salt, aniseed, and dash *pepper*. Drain corn; reserve 3 tablespoons liquid. Stir corn and reserved liquid into onion mixture; toss lightly. Season chops with some salt and pepper. Spoon a generous ½ cup onion mixture atop each of 6 chops; top with remaining chops. Grill stacked chops over *medium* coals 45 to 50 minutes or till done, carefully turning once, using a wide spatula and guiding with a long-tined fork. (Or, place stacked chops in shallow baking pan; cover with foil. Bake in 325° oven about 1¼ hours or till done.) Sprinkle with paprika, if desired. Serves 6.

Skewered Pork and Vegetable Bundles

1 pound lean boneless pork, cut 1 inch thick
⅓ cup soy sauce
2 tablespoons brown sugar
¼ teaspoon ground ginger
4 large carrots, cut into 3-inch-long sticks
1 bunch green onions
2 tablespoons butter *or* margarine, melted

Partially freeze meat; cut thinly across grain into strips at least 3 inches long. In bowl combine soy, brown sugar, and ginger; add meat. Cover; marinate at room temperature for 2 to 3 hours, stirring occasionally. Cook carrots in boiling salted water 4 to 5 minutes or till just tender. Drain well; cool. Cut each onion into 3-inch lengths, splitting bulb in half. Wrap *half* the meat strips around bundles of 4 carrot pieces. Wrap remaining meat strips around bundles of 4 onion lengths. Secure with wooden picks. Thread bundles ladder-fashion on two parallel skewers (see photo, right). Brush with melted butter. Grill over *medium* coals about 4 minutes. Turn and grill 3 to 4 minutes more; brushing occasionally with melted butter. (Or, broil 3 to 5 inches from heat for 4 to 5 minutes per side.) Serves 4 or 5.

Use your broiler if you don't have a barbecue grill. Set the oven temperature to "Broil"; preheat, if desired (check range instruction booklet). Broil pork 2 to 3 inches from heat for half the suggested time. Season with salt and pepper. Turn meat with tongs; cook till done. Season again. Use suggested grilling times in recipe or follow these guidelines: rib or loin chops (¾ to 1 inch thick) 20 to 25 minutes total time, shoulder steaks (½ to ¾ inch thick) 20 to 22 minutes; and pork kabobs (pieces about 1 inch square) 22 to 25 minutes.

Moist, tender pork grills to perfection in hearty Pork Chops with Anise-Corn Stuffing, Skewered Pork and Vegetable Bundles, *and* Pork and Fruit Kabobs *(see recipe, page 54).*

Pork and Fruit Kabobs

(pictured on page 53)

1 8-ounce can pineapple slices
⅓ cup orange marmalade
2 tablespoons soy sauce

1½ pounds lean boneless pork, cut in 1-inch pieces
2 medium cooking apples, cored and cut in 6 wedges each

Drain pineapple; reserve 2 tablespoons syrup. Quarter each slice; set aside. In saucepan combine reserved syrup, marmalade, and soy. Heat till marmalade melts. Thread six skewers alternately with pork, pineapple, and apples. Grill over *medium* coals about 15 minutes, turning and brushing often with marmalade mixture. Serves 6.

Pork Chop Suey

If you check prices, you may find it is more economical to cut your own pork cubes from lean boneless pork. Some larger cuts to choose from are sirloin end of loin, boneless shoulder roasts, boneless loin roasts, or loin blade roasts.

1 pound boneless pork, cut in ¾-inch cubes
1 clove garlic, minced
1 tablespoon cooking oil
¼ cup soy sauce
2 teaspoons instant chicken bouillon granules
1½ cups bias-sliced celery
1 medium onion, cut in wedges
2 cups fresh bean sprouts *or* 1 16-ounce can bean sprouts, drained

1 8-ounce can water chestnuts, drained and thinly sliced
1 6-ounce package frozen pea pods, thawed and halved crosswise
½ cup thinly sliced fresh mushrooms
2 tablespoons cornstarch
Hot cooked rice *or* chow mein noodles, warmed
Soy sauce

In large skillet brown pork and garlic in hot oil. Add the ¼ cup soy sauce, bouillon granules, and 1½ cups *water*. Simmer, covered, for 30 minutes. Add celery and onion; cook for 5 minutes, stirring occasionally. Add bean sprouts, water chestnuts, pea pods, and mushrooms. Blend 2 tablespoons *water* into cornstarch; stir into meat mixture. Cook and stir till vegetables are crisp-tender and mixture is thickened and bubbly. Serve with rice or chow mein noodles. Pass additional soy sauce. Makes 4 to 6 servings.

Stir-Fried Pork and Rice

3 slightly beaten eggs
3 tablespoons cooking oil
1 pound pork cubed steaks, cut in ½- to ¾-inch strips
1 medium unpeeled cucumber, thinly sliced
1 cup bias-sliced celery

¼ cup chopped green onion
1 small clove garlic, minced
2 cups cooked brown *or* long grain rice
¼ cup soy sauce
2 medium tomatoes, each cut into eighths

In large skillet cook eggs in *1 tablespoon* of the oil till set, stirring just enough to break egg into bite-size pieces; remove from skillet and set aside. In same skillet heat 1 tablespoon of the remaining oil. Cook meat strips, half at a time, till browned; remove from skillet and set aside. In same skillet cook and stir cucumber, celery, onion, and garlic in remaining oil over medium-high heat about 4 minutes or till tender. Stir in cooked rice, the ¼ cup soy sauce, browned pork, and cooked eggs. Arrange tomatoes on top; cover and cook about 3 minutes or just till tomatoes are hot. Pass additional soy sauce, if desired. Makes 4 servings.

Jicama and Pork

Jicama (hick-a-ma) is a Mexican vegetable with a texture similar to water chestnuts.

1 pound lean boneless pork
½ cup cold water
2 tablespoons soy sauce
2 tablespoons dry sherry
1 tablespoon cornstarch
1 clove garlic, minced
1 teaspoon grated gingerroot
2 tablespoons cooking oil
¼ teaspoon salt

2 cups chopped Chinese cabbage *or* fresh spinach
1 green pepper, cut in thin strips
1 small jicama, peeled and cubed (¾ cup)
2 tablespoons sliced green onion
Hot cooked rice

Partially freeze meat; slice thinly across grain. Cut into bite-size strips. Blend cold water, soy, and sherry into cornstarch; set aside. In large skillet cook and stir garlic and gingerroot in hot oil about 30 seconds. In same skillet cook and stir pork, half at a time, about 5 minutes or till browned. Return all meat to skillet; sprinkle with salt. Add cabbage or spinach, pepper, jicama, and onion. Cook and stir 1 minute more. Pour soy mixture over vegetables; cook and stir till thick and bubbly. Serve with rice. Serves 4.

Pork in Sweet-Sour Sauce

1½ pounds lean boneless pork, cut in ½-inch cubes
2 tablespoons cooking oil
¼ cup chopped onion
1 15¼-ounce can pineapple chunks
¼ cup packed brown sugar

2 tablespoons cornstarch
¼ teaspoon ground ginger
¼ cup vinegar
3 tablespoons soy sauce
1 medium green pepper, cut in 1-inch squares
Hot cooked rice

In large skillet brown the pork, half at a time, in hot oil. Return all meat to skillet. Add onion and ¼ cup *water*. Cover and simmer for 30 to 35 minutes.

Drain pineapple, reserving juice. Combine brown sugar, cornstarch, ginger, and ¼ teaspoon *salt*. Blend in reserved pineapple juice, vinegar, and soy sauce. Add to pork mixture along with green pepper; cook and stir till thick and bubbly. Stir in pineapple; heat through. Serve over rice. Serves 6.

Microwave cooking directions: In 2-quart nonmetal casserole combine brown sugar, cornstarch, salt, and ginger. Stir in water, vinegar, and soy sauce. Add pork cubes, undrained pineapple, and onion; stir to coat pork. Cover with lid, waxed paper, or clear plastic wrap. Cook in countertop microwave oven 14 minutes, stirring once after 7 minutes. Stir in green pepper; cover and micro-cook 1 minute more. Serve over hot rice.

Microwave cooking works for most meat cuts but you will probably notice a difference in color and tenderness from the conventionally roasted, broiled, and baked meat you are used to. Defrosting meat in the microwave oven can be a dinner-saver when you forget to thaw meat or when unexpected company arrives. Speed up barbecuing by micro-cooking ribs or other cuts about ¾ done and then grilling. Microwave ovens vary with the manufacturer so check your owner's manual for specific suggestions and recommendations.

Spiced Orange-Apricot Ribs

1 teaspoon salt	4 pounds pork loin back ribs
1 teaspoon ground ginger	*or* spareribs
1 teaspoon ground	Hickory chips
coriander	½ cup apricot preserves
½ teaspoon paprika	¼ cup orange juice
¼ teaspoon pepper	3 tablespoons soy sauce
	1 tablespoon lemon juice

Combine salt, ginger, coriander, paprika, and pepper; rub onto meaty side of ribs. Cover and refrigerate for 2 hours. About an hour before cooking time, soak hickory chips in enough water to cover.

Lace ribs accordion-style on spit rod. Secure the ribs with holding fork. Arrange *hot* coals on both sides of a shallow foil drip pan. Drain hickory chips; sprinkle some over coals. Attach spit; position drip pan under meat. Turn on motor; lower the grill hood or cover with foil tent. Grill ribs over *hot* coals about 1 hour or till done. Sprinkle the coals with dampened hickory chips every 20 minutes.

Combine apricot preserves, orange juice, soy sauce, and lemon juice. Brush ribs frequently with orange juice glaze during the last 15 minutes of cooking. Heat and pass the remaining glaze. Garnish ribs with orange slices, if desired. Makes 4 servings.

Mustard-Glazed Country Ribs

Country-style ribs are the meatiest of all pork ribs. They're cut from the front (shoulder) end of the back ribs, then split open.

4 pounds pork country-	2 cloves garlic, minced
style ribs	2 teaspoons celery seed
½ cup sugar	2 teaspoons salt
½ cup vinegar	1 teaspoon ground turmeric
⅓ cup prepared mustard	1 medium onion, thinly sliced
¼ cup chopped onion	

In large saucepan or Dutch oven pour enough water over ribs to cover. Bring to boiling; reduce heat. Cover; simmer for 45 minutes. Drain well.

Meanwhile, in small saucepan combine sugar, vinegar, mustard, chopped onion, garlic, celery seed, salt, and ground turmeric. Bring to boiling, stirring till sugar dissolves. Place ribs, meaty side up, in shallow roasting pan. Brush some of the mustard mixture over ribs. Roast, uncovered, in 350° oven about 15 minutes. Top with sliced onion and some additional sauce. Roast 15 minutes more, brushing occasionally with mustard sauce. Transfer ribs to warm platter. Reheat remaining sauce and pass with ribs. Serves 4 to 6.

Grilling over the coals. Pork retains its moistness best when cooked over medium coals. Use these timings as a guide on a covered grill: loin chops (1½ inches thick) 25 to 30 minutes total time; blade steaks (¾ inch thick) 15 to 20 minutes; and loin back ribs or spareribs (5 to 6 pounds) 1¼ to 1½ hours.

Grilled Spiced Orange-Apricot Ribs and meaty, roasted Mustard-Glazed Country Ribs make out-of-the-ordinary dining. The brush-on glazes put these ribs in a class by themselves.

Oriental Spareribs

3 pounds meaty pork
  spareribs, sawed in half
  across bones
¼ cup soy sauce
¼ cup dry sherry
  Five Spice Powder
1 tablespoon vinegar
½ teaspoon salt

⅛ teaspoon pepper
1 beaten egg
¼ cup cornstarch
¼ cup all-purpose flour
  Cooking oil for
    deep-fat frying
  Sweet and Pungent Sauce
  Hot cooked rice

Cut meat into 2-rib portions. Simmer, covered, in enough boiling water to cover for 30 minutes; drain. Place ribs in a 12x7½x2-inch baking dish. For marinade combine soy, sherry, Five Spice Powder, vinegar, salt, and pepper; pour over ribs. Let stand at room temperature for 30 minutes, turning once. Drain spareribs, reserving marinade.

Combine egg, reserved marinade, cornstarch, and flour; beat till smooth. Dip spareribs in egg mixture. Fry ribs, a few at a time, in deep hot oil (365°) 1 to 2 minutes or till golden brown. Drain on paper toweling. Keep warm in oven. Spoon some Sweet and Pungent Sauce over hot ribs to glaze. Serve with rice. Pass remaining sauce. Makes 4 or 5 servings.

Five Spice Powder: In small bowl combine 1 teaspoon ground *cinnamon,* 1 teaspoon crushed *aniseed,* ¼ teaspoon crushed *fennel seed,* ¼ teaspoon freshly ground *pepper* or ¼ teaspoon crushed *Szechwan pepper,* and ⅛ teaspoon ground *cloves.*

Sweet and Pungent Sauce: Drain one 8¼-ounce can *pineapple chunks,* reserving ⅓ cup syrup. In saucepan combine the reserved syrup, 2 tablespoons *brown sugar,* 4 teaspoons *cornstarch,* and ⅛ teaspoon *salt.* Stir in 1 8-ounce can undrained *tomatoes,* ¼ cup finely chopped *onion,* 1 tablespoon *vinegar,* and 1 tablespoon *soy sauce.* Cook and stir till thickened and bubbly. Add pineapple chunks and 1 small *green pepper,* cut in 1-inch squares. Heat through. Makes 2½ cups sauce.

Plantation Spareribs

Pork spareribs come from the rib cage. A thin covering of meat surrounds and attaches the ribs. A large portion of the weight is bone.

½ cup sorghum *or* molasses
¼ cup prepared mustard
¼ cup vinegar
2 tablespoons worcestershire
  sauce

½ teaspoon salt
½ teaspoon bottled hot
  pepper sauce
3 pounds pork spareribs

For sauce blend sorghum or molasses into mustard; stir in vinegar, worcestershire, salt, and hot pepper sauce. Bring to boiling; set aside. Place ribs, meaty side down, in shallow roasting pan. Roast in 450° oven for 30 minutes. Remove meat from oven; drain off excess fat. Turn ribs meaty side up; sprinkle with some salt. Reduce oven temperature to 350°; continue roasting for 1 hour or till tender. During last 30 minutes of roasting, baste frequently with sauce. Cut into serving-size pieces. Makes 4 servings.

Microwave cooking directions: Cut spareribs into serving-size pieces. Season with a little salt. Arrange in a 12x7½x2-inch nonmetal baking dish. Cover with waxed paper or clear plastic wrap. Cook in countertop microwave oven 10 minutes. Drain well; rearrange ribs in dish.

In 2-cup glass measure blend sorghum or molasses into mustard. Stir in vinegar, worcestershire, salt, and hot pepper sauce. Micro-cook about 2 minutes or till mixture boils. Spoon mixture over ribs. Micro-cook, covered, for 18 to 20 minutes or till ribs are done. Rearrange ribs in dish and baste with sorghum mixture every 5 minutes.

Portuguese Marinated Ribs

1 cup water
¾ cup vinegar
½ teaspoon finely shredded
    lemon peel
3 tablespoons lemon juice
1 clove garlic, minced
1 dried red chili pepper,
    seeded and crushed

2 teaspoons cumin seed,
    crushed *or* 1 teaspoon
    ground cumin
1 teaspoon salt
¼ teaspoon pepper
4 pounds pork spareribs,
    cut in serving-size
    pieces

Place large plastic bag in large bowl. In bag combine all ingredients except ribs; mix well. Add ribs and close bag tightly. Refrigerate 6 hours or overnight, turning bag several times to distribute seasonings. Drain ribs; discard seasoning mixture. Place meat in deep roasting pan. Roast, uncovered, in 450° oven for 25 minutes. Drain off fat. Reduce oven to 350°. Roast, covered, 30 minutes. Uncover and roast 30 minutes more. Serves 4 to 6.

Spanish Spareribs

8 ounces pork sausage links
2½ to 3 pounds meaty pork
    spareribs, cut in 2-rib
    portions
3 slices bacon, cut up
½ cup chopped onion
1 clove garlic, minced
1 16-ounce can tomatoes

1 10½-ounce can condensed
    beef broth
½ cup sliced pimiento-stuffed
    olives
2 tablespoons snipped parsley
½ cup cold water
¼ cup all-purpose flour
Hot cooked noodles

In Dutch oven brown sausage links. Remove; drain off fat. In same pan brown ribs, half at a time; remove. Add bacon, onion, and garlic; cook till bacon is crisp and onion is tender. Return meats to pan. Add *undrained* tomatoes, beef broth, olives, and parsley. Cover and simmer 1 hour or till ribs are tender. Remove meats; keep warm. Skim off fat; measure sauce. Add water, if necessary, to make 2½ cups liquid; return to pan. Blend cold water into flour; stir into liquid. Cook and stir till thickened and bubbly. Serve meat over hot cooked noodles. Pass sauce. Makes 6 servings.

Smoked Pineapple Pork Ribs

Hickory chips
1 teaspoon salt
½ teaspoon paprika
½ teaspoon ground turmeric
6 pounds pork loin back ribs
    or spareribs

1 8-ounce can crushed
    pineapple
½ cup packed brown sugar
3 tablespoons prepared
    mustard
2 tablespoons lemon juice

About an hour before cooking time, soak hickory chips in enough water to cover. Combine salt, paprika, and turmeric; rub onto meaty side of ribs. Place ribs, bone side down, over *slow* coals. Close hood or cover with foil tent; drain hickory chips. Cook ribs 30 minutes on each side sprinkling coals with dampened hickory chips every 20 minutes. (If thin end of spareribs cooks too quickly, place foil under end piece and continue cooking.)

    In saucepan combine *undrained* pineapple, brown sugar, mustard, and lemon juice. Heat and stir till sugar is dissolved. Brush some on ribs; cook 10 to 15 minutes more. Heat remainder; serve with ribs. Serves 6.

Pork loin back ribs contain rib bones from the rib area of the loin. The thicker layer of meat covering the ribs comes from the loin eye. These are often smoked.

German Pork and Sauerkraut

4 slices bacon
2 pounds pork stew meat, cut in 1-inch cubes
1 cup chopped onion
2 cloves garlic, minced
1 27-ounce can *or* 2 16-ounce cans sauerkraut, drained
1 cup dry white wine
½ cup water

6 whole black peppercorns
6 juniper berries (optional)
1 bay leaf
1 teaspoon salt
½ teaspoon instant chicken bouillon granules
½ teaspoon dried thyme, crushed

In large skillet cook bacon till crisp; drain, reserving 2 tablespoons drippings. Crumble bacon; set aside. In same skillet cook meat, onion, and garlic in drippings till meat is browned and onion is tender. Remove from heat. Stir in sauerkraut, wine, water, remaining ingredients, and bacon. Turn into a 3-quart casserole. Bake, covered, in 325° oven for 1¾ to 2 hours or till pork is tender. Remove bay leaf. Makes 6 servings.

Pork and Brew

⅓ cup all-purpose flour
½ teaspoon salt
⅛ teaspoon pepper
2 pounds pork stew meat, cut in 1-inch cubes
3 tablespoons cooking oil
3 medium onions, sliced
1 12-ounce can beer

1 teaspoon instant chicken bouillon granules
¼ teaspoon salt
¼ teaspoon dried thyme, crushed
¼ cup cold water
Hot cooked rice

In paper or plastic bag combine flour, the ½ teaspoon salt, and the pepper. Add pork cubes, a few at a time, shaking to coat. Reserve 1 tablespoon of the remaining flour mixture. In large skillet brown meat on all sides in hot oil. Stir in onions, beer, bouillon granules, the ¼ teaspoon salt, and thyme. Cover and simmer about 1 hour or till meat is tender. Blend cold water into the 1 tablespoon reserved flour mixture; stir into meat mixture. Cook, stirring constantly, till thickened and bubbly. Serve over hot cooked rice. Makes 6 servings.

Pork and Cabbage Soup

1 pound pork stew meat, cut in ½-inch cubes
1 tablespoon cooking oil
1 10¾-ounce can condensed tomato soup
1 10½-ounce can condensed beef broth
2 soup cans (2½ cups) water
¼ cup dry sherry

1 small head cabbage, shredded (4 cups)
½ cup chopped onion
1 bay leaf
1 teaspoon salt
½ teaspoon paprika
Dash pepper
Dairy sour cream
Snipped parsley *or* chives

In 4½-quart Dutch oven brown pork in hot oil. Drain off excess fat. Blend in tomato soup, beef broth, water, and sherry. Stir in cabbage, onion, bay leaf, salt, paprika, and pepper. Bring to boiling. Reduce heat; cover and simmer about 40 minutes or till meat is tender. Season to taste with salt and pepper. Remove bay leaf. Top each serving with a dollop of sour cream. Garnish with parsley or chives. Makes 5 or 6 servings.

South American Pork Soup

1½ pounds pork stew meat, cut in ½-inch cubes
2 tablespoons cooking oil
1 small onion, finely chopped
1 clove garlic, minced
1 teaspoon paprika
2 medium potatoes, peeled and cut in small cubes
2 small sweet potatoes, peeled and cut in small cubes
2 medium carrots, chopped
1 cup chopped peeled winter squash
1 tomato, peeled and chopped
1 8½-ounce can whole kernel corn
2 teaspoons salt
¼ teaspoon pepper
2 cups torn fresh spinach

If fresh spinach isn't available, substitute ½ of a 10-ounce package frozen chopped spinach.

In 4-quart Dutch oven brown half of the meat in hot oil; remove from pan. Brown the remaining meat with onion, garlic, and paprika. Return all meat to pan. Add 3 cups *water.* Bring to boil; reduce heat. Cover and simmer for 1¼ hours. Stir in potatoes, sweet potatoes, carrots, squash, tomato, *undrained* corn, salt, and pepper. Cover; simmer 15 to 20 minutes more or till meat and vegetables are tender. Stir in spinach; simmer 3 to 5 minutes more. Season to taste with salt and pepper. Makes 8 servings.

Zesty Pork Chili

1 pound pork stew meat, cut in ¾-inch cubes
2 tablespoons shortening
1 cup water
4 to 6 teaspoons chili powder
½ teaspoon salt
1 clove garlic, minced
2 medium potatoes, peeled and cut in 1-inch cubes (2 cups)

In large saucepan brown half the meat at a time in hot shortening. Drain off excess fat; return all meat to pan. Stir in water, chili powder, salt, and garlic. Cover and simmer for 35 minutes. Stir in cubed potatoes. Cover and simmer 20 to 25 minutes more or till meat and potatoes are tender. Serves 4.

Pork and Vegetable Stew

¼ cup all-purpose flour
2 teaspoons salt
1 teaspoon ground sage
Dash pepper
2 pounds pork stew meat, cut in 1-inch cubes
3 tablespoons shortening
2 cups water
2 teaspoons instant chicken bouillon granules
1 bay leaf
4 medium carrots, cut in ½-inch pieces
3 medium potatoes, peeled and sliced
1 10-ounce package frozen lima beans
½ teaspoon salt
⅛ teaspoon pepper
2 tablespoons cold water
1 tablespoon all-purpose flour

In paper or plastic bag combine ¼ cup flour, 2 teaspoons salt, sage, and dash pepper. Add meat, a few pieces at a time, shaking to coat. Brown meat on all sides in hot shortening; drain off excess fat. Stir in water, bouillon granules, and bay leaf. Cover and simmer for 40 minutes. Stir in carrots, potatoes, lima beans, ½ teaspoon salt, and ⅛ teaspoon pepper; simmer about 25 minutes or till vegetables are tender. Remove bay leaf. Blend cold water into 1 tablespoon flour; stir into meat and vegetables. Cook and stir till thickened and bubbly. Makes 8 servings.

Oven-Baked Pork Stew

1½ pounds pork stew meat, cut in 1-inch cubes
2 tablespoons cooking oil
3 tablespoons all-purpose flour
1 16-ounce can tomatoes, cut up
¼ cup water
1 clove garlic, minced
1 bay leaf
1 teaspoon sugar
1 teaspoon instant beef bouillon granules
½ teaspoon salt

½ teaspoon dried thyme, crushed
½ teaspoon dried oregano, crushed
¼ teaspoon bottled hot pepper sauce
4 medium sweet potatoes, peeled and sliced ¾ inch thick (4 cups)
1 large onion, cut in wedges
1 medium green pepper, cut in thin strips
1 10-ounce package frozen peas, thawed

In large skillet brown meat, half at a time, in hot oil. Remove meat from skillet, reserving drippings. Blend flour into drippings. Add *undrained* tomatoes, water, garlic, bay leaf, sugar, bouillon granules, salt, thyme, oregano, and pepper sauce. Cook and stir till thickened and bubbly.

In a 3-quart casserole combine meat, sweet potatoes, onion, and green pepper. Add tomato mixture. Bake, covered, in 350° oven about 1½ hours or till meat and vegetables are tender, stirring occasionally. Remove bay leaf. Stir in peas. Bake 5 to 10 minutes more. Makes 6 servings.

Pork Stroganoff For a Crowd

Be sure to use imitation sour cream in this recipe. Dairy sour cream tends to break down and water out during the baking.

3 pounds pork stew meat, cut in ½-inch cubes
2 tablespoons cooking oil
1 cup chopped onion
1 cup water
1 clove garlic, minced
8 ounces medium noodles (6 cups)
2 10½-ounce cans condensed old-fashioned vegetable soup
1 10¾-ounce can condensed cream of mushroom soup

2 8-ounce cans imitation sour cream (2 cups)
1 8-ounce can mushroom stems and pieces, drained
2 teaspoons poppy seed (optional)
¼ teaspoon pepper
2 16-ounce cans cut green beans, drained
1½ cups soft bread crumbs (2 slices)
2 tablespoons butter *or* margarine, melted

In 10-quart Dutch oven brown meat, ⅓ at a time, in hot oil. Return all meat to Dutch oven. Add onion, water, and garlic. Cover; simmer about 1¾ hours or till meat is tender. Meanwhile, cook noodles in large amount of boiling salted water 7 to 8 minutes or till tender; drain. Stir vegetable and mushroom soups, imitation sour cream, mushrooms, poppy seed, and pepper into meat; fold in drained noodles and green beans. Divide mixture between two 2-quart casseroles. Toss bread crumbs with melted butter or margarine; sprinkle atop casseroles. Bake in 375° oven about 35 minutes or till heated through. Makes 2 casseroles, 6 to 8 servings each.

Especially for busy days, Oven-Baked Pork Stew can be popped into the oven and ignored for an hour and a half. Chock-full of vegetables and meat cubes, it's a satisfying meal in itself.

Planked Ham

To season a nonvarnished wooden plank, brush it with cooking oil and heat it in a 325° oven for about 1 hour.

1 3-pound canned ham
1½ teaspoons finely shredded orange peel
¾ cup orange juice
¼ cup light corn syrup
½ teaspoon ground nutmeg

5 hot cooked sweet potatoes (2½ pounds)
1 egg
3 tablespoons butter *or* margarine
Cooking oil
2 oranges

Place ham on rack in shallow baking pan. Bake in 325° oven for 35 minutes. Meanwhile, for glaze combine ½ *teaspoon* of the orange peel, ½ *cup* of the orange juice, corn syrup, and nutmeg. Bring to boiling. Spoon some of the glaze over ham and continue baking 20 to 25 minutes more, basting occasionally with glaze.

In bowl beat together sweet potatoes, the remaining 1 teaspoon orange peel, the remaining ¼ cup orange juice, the egg, and *1 tablespoon* of the butter. Place ham on a seasoned plank (see note, left). Using pastry bag with large star tip, pipe border of sweet potatoes around ham. Melt the remaining 2 tablespoons butter; drizzle over potatoes. Brush the exposed wood with oil. Peel and slice oranges; cut slices in half and arrange atop ham. Brush with the remaining glaze. Return to oven and bake about 30 minutes or till heated through. Makes 10 servings.

Barbecue-Glazed Ham and Pineapple

1 20-ounce can pineapple slices
½ cup chili sauce
¼ cup sugar
2 tablespoons lemon juice

2 teaspoons worcestershire sauce
½ teaspoon chili powder
1 3-pound canned ham
2 tablespoons cold water
1 tablespoon cornstarch

Drain pineapple; reserve ¼ cup syrup. For sauce combine reserved syrup, chili sauce, sugar, lemon juice, worcestershire, and chili powder. Place ham on rack in shallow baking pan. Arrange pineapple around ham. Pour sauce over all. Bake in 325° oven about 1½ hours, basting frequently with sauce. Remove ham and pineapple to warm platter; keep warm. Measure pan juices. Add enough water to make 1¼ cups liquid. Blend 2 tablespoons cold water into cornstarch; stir into pan juices. Cook and stir till bubbly. Serve with ham and pineapple. Makes 8 to 10 servings.

Microwave cooking directions: Place ham in 12x7½x2-inch non-metal baking dish. Cook, covered with waxed paper, in countertop microwave oven for 10 minutes, giving dish half-turn after 5 minutes. Meanwhile, drain pineapple; reserve syrup. Combine ¼ *cup* of the reserved syrup, chili sauce, sugar, lemon juice, worcestershire, and chili powder. Turn ham over; spoon on sauce. Micro-cook, uncovered, about 10 minutes or till ham is hot, giving dish a half-turn and brushing with sauce after 5 minutes. Remove ham; keep warm. Pour pan juices into 2-cup glass measure; add enough water to make 1¼ cups liquid. Blend 2 tablespoons cold water into cornstarch; stir into juices. Micro-cook, uncovered, 2 to 2½ minutes or till thickened and bubbly, stirring every 30 seconds; keep warm.

Place pineapple slices and remaining pineapple syrup in baking dish. Micro-cook, covered, about 3 minutes or till hot, turning dish once. Arrange pineapple slices and ham on platter. Spoon some of the chili sauce mixture atop; pass the remainder.

1 2-pound smoked pork
  shoulder roll
¼ cup sugar
1 tablespoon cornstarch
¼ teaspoon ground allspice
½ cup orange juice

¼ cup honey
¼ cup butter *or* margarine
1 17-ounce can sweet
  potatoes, drained
1 orange, peeled and
  sectioned

Place shoulder roll on rack in shallow baking pan. Insert meat thermometer. Roast in 325° oven for 1 hour. Meanwhile, in small saucepan combine sugar, cornstarch, and allspice; blend in orange juice and honey. Cook and stir till thickened and bubbly. Cook 1 minute more; stir in butter or margarine. Arrange sweet potatoes and orange sections around roast; spoon orange juice mixture over all. Bake about 30 minutes more or till thermometer registers 170°. Makes 8 servings.

Orange-Glazed Smoked Shoulder

A smoked pork shoulder roll is not a ham, although it has a similar flavor and is prepared in much the same way. It is actually a boneless pork shoulder blade boston roast that is cured and smoked. It should be cooked before eating.

1 3- to 4-pound fully cooked
  boneless smoked ham
2 egg whites
2 tablespoons sugar

2 tablespoons dry mustard
⅓ to ½ cup fine dry bread
  crumbs

Trim fat from ham; place ham on rack in shallow baking pan. Insert meat thermometer. Bake in 325° oven about 1¼ hours. Combine egg whites, sugar, and mustard; brush *half* over top and sides of ham. Sprinkle with *half* the bread crumbs, patting them on the sides. Repeat with remaining egg white mixture and crumbs. Bake ham 15 to 20 minutes more or till thermometer registers 140°. Serve hot or cold. Makes 10 to 12 servings.

Scandinavian Jul Ham

1 8-ounce package (2 cups)
  dried apples
1 3-pound smoked ham, rump
  portion
6 cups water

4 teaspoons instant chicken
  bouillon granules
2 tablespoons dark brown
  sugar
Dumplings

Cover apples with boiling water; let stand till cool. Drain. Trim fat from ham; place ham in 6-quart Dutch oven. Add water and bouillon granules. Bring to boiling; reduce heat. Simmer, covered, for 1½ hours or till ham is tender. Remove ham. Skim fat from broth. Slice ham ¼ inch thick; cut into cubes. Return ham to Dutch oven; add drained apples and brown sugar. Bring to boiling, stirring to dissolve sugar. Reduce heat; simmer 15 to 20 minutes. Meanwhile, prepare Dumplings. Drop in 6 or 8 spoonfuls onto simmering broth. Cover tightly; simmer 10 minutes more. Remove Dumplings to serving dish; pour ham mixture around Dumplings. Makes 6 to 8 servings.

Dumplings: Combine 1½ cups all-purpose *flour,* 2 teaspoons *baking powder,* and ¼ teaspoon *salt.* Cut in 2 tablespoons *butter or margarine* till mixture resembles coarse meal. Add 1 cup *milk;* beat vigorously till smooth.

German Ham and Dumplings

A smoked ham that is not labeled "fully cooked" must be cooked thoroughly before eating.

Thoroughly scrub and rinse a *country-style ham.* Soak in water overnight; drain. Place in large kettle; cover with water. Bring to boil; reduce heat and simmer for 20 to 25 minutes per pound. When just cool enough to handle, remove skin from ham and trim fat. Stud fat side with whole *cloves;* sprinkle with *brown sugar.* Bake in 350° oven about 20 minutes. Slice thinly.

Country-Style Ham

Baking Smoked Pork

If you like, prepare a glaze for hams or other smoked pork roasts. At the last 20 to 30 minutes of baking time, spoon fat from the baking pan. Spoon the glaze over meat. Continue baking till the meat thermometer registers the desired internal temperature, basting occasionally with glaze.

Cut	Approx. Weight (Pounds)	Internal Temperature on Removal from Oven	Approx. Cooking Time (Total Time)
Bake meat at constant oven temperature of 325°.			
Ham (cook before eating)			
whole	10 to 14	160°	3¼ to 4 hours
half	5 to 7	160°	2 to 2½ hours
shank or rump portion	3 to 4	160°	2 to 2¼ hours
Ham (fully cooked)			
whole	10 to 14	140°	2½ to 3½ hours
whole, boneless	8 to 10	140°	2 to 2¼ hours
half	5 to 7	140°	1¾ to 2¼ hours
half, boneless	4 to 5	140°	1½ to 2 hours
Arm Picnic Shoulder (cook before eating)	5 to 8	170°	3 to 4 hours
Arm Picnic Shoulder (fully cooked)	5 to 8	140°	2½ to 3¼ hours
Canadian-Style Bacon	2 to 4	160°	1¼ to 2¼ hours

Baking directions: Place meat, fat side up, on a rack in a shallow baking pan. *Do not* cover or add water. Score ham fat in diamonds, cutting only ¼ inch deep. Insert whole cloves, if desired. Insert meat thermometer into center of thickest portion of meat, making sure bulb does not rest in fat or touch bone. Bake meat in 325° oven till meat thermometer registers the desired internal temperature. To check doneness, push the thermometer into meat a little farther. If the temperature drops, continue baking the meat to the desired temperature.

Spicy Strawberry Glaze

For a simple glaze, brush baked ham with a mixture of ¼ cup dry red wine and 2 tablespoons honey as soon as it's removed from the oven.

½ cup strawberry preserves
1 tablespoon cornstarch
3 tablespoons lemon juice
⅛ teaspoon ground cinnamon
⅛ teaspoon ground cloves

In small saucepan combine strawberry preserves and cornstarch; add lemon juice, cinnamon, and cloves. Cook and stir till mixture is thickened and bubbly. Spoon over smoked pork roast during last 20 to 30 minutes of baking time.

Curried Cranberry Glaze

½ cup chopped onion
4 teaspoons curry powder
¼ cup butter *or* margarine
1 16-ounce can whole cranberry sauce
2 tablespoons light corn syrup

Cook onion and curry powder in butter or margarine till onion is tender but not brown. Stir in cranberry sauce and corn syrup; heat through. Spoon some over smoked pork roast during the last 20 to 30 minutes of baking time. Reheat remaining and pass with roast. Makes about 1¾ cups.

Quick Raisin Sauce

½ cup packed brown sugar
½ teaspoon dry mustard
¼ teaspoon ground ginger
1 22-ounce can raisin pie filling
2 tablespoons lemon juice

In saucepan combine brown sugar, mustard, and ginger. Blend in pie filling, lemon juice, and 2 tablespoons *water*. Simmer, covered, for 5 minutes. Serve with smoked pork roast. Makes 2½ cups sauce.

Curry-Sauced Ham

For a change of pace, serve the curried ham mixture on baked refrigerator biscuits or in baked frozen patty shells.

1 10-ounce package frozen mixed vegetables
½ cup chopped celery
⅓ cup chopped onion
3 cups cubed fully cooked ham
1 10¾-ounce can condensed cream of mushroom soup
1 10¾-ounce can condensed cream of potato soup
1 tablespoon curry powder
½ cup dairy sour cream
2 tablespoons milk
3 tablespoons all-purpose flour
Hot cooked rice

In large saucepan combine frozen mixed vegetables, celery, and onion; stir in 1 cup *water*. Bring to boiling; reduce heat. Cover; simmer for 10 minutes. Stir in ham, soups, and curry powder. Simmer, covered, for 20 minutes. Combine sour cream and milk; blend into flour. Add to ham mixture; cook and stir till thickened; *do not boil*. Serve over hot cooked rice. Serves 6 to 8.

Crockery cooking directions: In electric slow crockery cooker combine frozen mixed vegetables, celery, and onion; stir in 1 cup *water*. Stir in ham, soups, and curry. Cover and cook on low-heat setting 4 to 6 hours (*or* on high-heat setting 1½ to 2 hours). Turn to high-heat setting. Combine sour cream and milk; blend into flour. Add to ham mixture; cook and stir till thickened; *do not boil*. Serve as above.

Ham and Egg Pie

¼ cup sliced green onion
¼ cup butter *or* margarine
¼ cup all-purpose flour
¼ teaspoon salt
⅛ teaspoon pepper
2 cups milk
8 hard-cooked eggs, sliced
2 cups chopped fully cooked ham

Cook green onion in butter or margarine till tender but not brown. Blend in flour, salt, and pepper; add milk all at once. Cook and stir till thickened and bubbly. In bottom of an 8x1½-inch round baking dish, arrange *a third* of the egg slices; top with *a third* of the ham. Repeat to make a total of 6 layers. Pour onion mixture over all. Bake in 350° oven about 30 minutes or till heated through and lightly browned. Makes 4 to 6 servings.

Fruit-Glazed Ham Slice

This cut is usually from the center of a whole ham. If available, an off-center slice should cost less and taste equally good.

1 2-pound fully cooked ham
    slice, cut 1 inch thick
¾ teaspoon ground ginger
⅛ teaspoon pepper
1 16-ounce can pear halves
5 teaspoons cornstarch

¾ teaspoon ground ginger
½ cup red grapes, halved
    and seeded
½ cup dry white wine
1 tablespoon butter *or*
    margarine

Slash edge of ham slice to prevent curling. Rub meat with mixture of ¾ teaspoon ginger and pepper. Place on rack in shallow baking pan. Bake in 350° oven for 40 minutes. Meanwhile, drain pears, reserving ¾ cup syrup. Slice pears. In saucepan combine cornstarch and ¾ teaspoon ginger; blend in the reserved pear syrup. Cook and stir till thickened and bubbly. Cook 1 minute more. Add pear slices, grapes, wine, and butter or margarine. Stir till butter melts and fruit is hot. Spoon some of the sauce over meat on platter; pass remaining sauce. If desired, garnish meat with pear halves, frosted grapes, and parsley. Makes 6 to 8 servings.

Ham Caribbean

1 2-pound fully cooked
    center-cut ham slice,
    cut 1 inch thick
½ cup orange juice
1 tablespoon whole cloves
⅓ cup packed brown sugar

1 tablespoon cornstarch
2 tablespoons honey
2 tablespoons rum
6 medium bananas, halved
    crosswise

Slash edge of ham slice; place on rack in shallow baking pan. Bake in 350° oven for 30 minutes. Meanwhile, in saucepan combine orange juice and whole cloves; bring to boiling. Simmer 5 minutes; remove cloves. Combine brown sugar and cornstarch; blend in honey and rum. Stir mixture into orange juice. Cook and stir till thickened and bubbly. Place the halved bananas around ham. Pour orange juice mixture over ham and fruit. Return to oven; heat 5 minutes more. Transfer ham to platter. Arrange bananas around ham. Spoon orange juice mixture over all. Garnish with orange slices and parsley, if desired. Makes 6 servings.

Layered Ham Florentine

2 ¾- to 1-pound fully cooked
    center-cut ham slices,
    cut ½ inch thick
2 10-ounce packages frozen
    chopped spinach, thawed
    and drained

¼ cup finely chopped onion
¼ cup finely snipped parsley
½ cup dairy sour cream
½ cup mayonnaise *or* salad
    dressing
1 tablespoon prepared
    mustard

Slash edge of each ham slice to prevent curling. Place one of the slices on rack in shallow baking pan. Combine spinach, onion, and parsley; spoon atop ham slice, spreading mixture almost to edges. Place remaining ham slice atop spinach mixture. Bake in 350° oven for 35 to 40 minutes or till heated through. In saucepan combine sour cream, mayonnaise, and mustard; heat through but *do not boil*. Cut ham stack in slices to serve. Spoon mustard mixture over individual servings. Makes 6 servings.

Spinach and onion are the refreshing filling in Layered Ham Florentine with a mustard sauce.

Hot and Hearty Ham Soup

1 1½- to 1¾-pound meaty ham bone *or* 3 smoked pork hocks	2 large potatoes, peeled and thinly sliced (3 cups)
8 cups water	3 large carrots, thinly sliced (2 cups)
8 whole black peppercorns	1 medium onion, chopped
5 whole cloves	6 to 8 thick slices rye bread
1 clove garlic, halved	¼ cup grated parmesan cheese
½ head cabbage, coarsely chopped (3½ cups)	Swiss cheese, cut in strips

In 4½-quart Dutch oven combine ham bone, water, peppercorns, cloves, garlic, and 1 teaspoon *salt*. Bring to boiling; reduce heat. Cover and simmer 2½ hours. Remove ham bone; cool slightly. Cut off meat. Strain broth; return broth and meat to pan. Add vegetables. Cover; simmer about 40 minutes or till vegetables are tender. Season to taste with salt and pepper. Toast bread. Ladle soup into heatproof bowls. Top each with a slice of toast. Sprinkle with parmesan; top with strips of Swiss cheese. Place under broiler about 2 minutes or till Swiss cheese melts. Makes 6 to 8 servings.

Chuck Wagon Bean Soup

8 cups water	¼ cup vinegar
1 pound dry pinto beans (2½ cups)	¼ cup chili sauce
1 16-ounce can tomatoes, cut up	2 tablespoons brown sugar
	2 tablespoons worcestershire sauce
4 medium carrots, finely chopped (2 cups)	2 teaspoons prepared mustard
1 cup chopped onion	1 1-pound meaty ham bone *or* 2 smoked pork hocks

In Dutch oven combine water and beans. Bring to boiling. Simmer 2 minutes; remove from heat. Cover; let stand 1 hour. (Or, soak beans in water overnight.) Do not drain. Stir in vegetables, vinegar, chili sauce, sugar, worcestershire, mustard, and 1 tablespoon *salt*. Add ham bone. Bring to boiling. Cover; simmer 2½ to 3 hours or till beans are tender. Remove ham bone; cool slightly. Cut off meat and chop. Return meat to soup. Mash beans slightly, if desired. Makes 8 to 10 servings.

Spicy Hopping John

Actually, black-eyed peas aren't peas—they're beans. In the South, it is customary to serve this dish on New Year's Day to bring good luck. The origin of the name is the subject of many stories.

8 cups water	1 tablespoon salt
1 pound dry black-eyed peas (2 cups)	2 teaspoons chili powder
1 16-ounce can tomatoes, cut up	¼ teaspoon dried basil, crushed
1 cup chopped onion	1 bay leaf
1 cup chopped celery	1 medium smoked pork hock
	1 cup long grain rice

In Dutch oven combine water and peas. Bring to boiling; simmer 2 minutes. Remove from heat; cover and let stand 1 hour. (Or, soak peas in water overnight.) Do not drain. Stir in tomatoes, onion, celery, salt, chili powder, basil, and bay leaf. Add pork hock. Cover and simmer about 1¼ hours or till peas are tender. Remove pork hock; cool slightly. Cut off meat and chop. Return meat to pea mixture; stir in rice. Cover and cook about 20 minutes or till rice is tender. Add additional water, if desired. Remove bay leaf. Serves 12.

Spaghetti with Canadian Bacon

1 cup light cream
2 tablespoons butter *or* margarine
1 cup shredded mozzarella cheese (4 ounces)
½ cup ricotta *or* cream-style cottage cheese
1 tablespoon all-purpose flour
⅛ teaspoon ground nutmeg
  White pepper
¼ cup chopped onion
1 clove garlic, minced

1 tablespoon butter *or* margarine
1 tablespoon olive *or* cooking oil
1 cup chopped Canadian-style bacon (5 ounces)
1 cup coarsely chopped fresh mushrooms
½ teaspoon dried marjoram, crushed
2 tablespoons dry sherry
8 ounces spaghetti, cooked, drained, and buttered

In blender container combine cream and 2 tablespoons butter or margarine; add mozzarella cheese, ricotta or cottage cheese, flour, and nutmeg. Cover; blend till smooth. Pour into 1½-quart saucepan. Cook and stir till mixture thickens and cheese melts. Season to taste with white pepper and salt. Keep warm but *do not boil*.

In skillet cook onion and garlic in mixture of 1 tablespoon butter and oil till onion is tender but not brown. Stir in Canadian bacon, mushrooms, and marjoram. Cook 3 to 4 minutes, stirring occasionally. Stir in sherry; boil gently about 10 minutes or till liquid evaporates. Place hot spaghetti on large platter; top with warm cheese sauce. Spoon meat mixture over; toss. Makes 4 to 6 servings.

Hearty Brunch Casserole

1 9-ounce package frozen French toast
6 slices Canadian-style bacon
6 hard-cooked eggs, sliced

1 11-ounce can condensed cheddar cheese soup
¼ cup milk
2 tablespoons chopped pimiento

Fit toast slices into an ungreased 12x7½x2-inch baking dish. Top with Canadian bacon slices and hard-cooked egg slices. Stir together soup, milk, and pimiento; spoon over eggs. Bake, covered, in 400° oven for 30 minutes. Uncover; bake about 10 minutes more. Makes 6 servings.

Mushroom-Bacon Scramble

1 6-ounce package frozen whole mushrooms in butter sauce
16 eggs
1 cup milk
1 tablespoon snipped chives

1 teaspoon worcestershire sauce
½ teaspoon salt
2 tablespoons butter *or* margarine
8 slices Canadian-style bacon

In large skillet prepare mushrooms according to package directions. Combine eggs, milk, chives, worcestershire, salt, and dash *pepper*. In skillet with mushrooms melt butter or margarine; pour in egg mixture. Cook over medium heat, stirring occasionally, till eggs are thickened but still moist. Meanwhile, heat bacon in blazer pan of chafing dish. To serve, arrange bacon around edge of chafing dish; fill with egg mixture. Garnish with additional snipped chives, if desired. Makes 8 servings.

Cumberland-Style Bacon Rolls

Bacon is the cured and smoked side of pork. Rashers, or slices, are cut from the slab.

6 slices bacon *or* 4 slices Canadian-style bacon, cut ¼ inch thick
1 small firm banana, sliced 1 inch thick
4 small canned water chestnuts
4 pineapple chunks *or* preserved kumquats

1½ teaspoons cornstarch
1 teaspoon dry mustard
⅛ teaspoon ground ginger
¼ cup currant jelly
3 tablespoons frozen orange juice concentrate
1 tablespoon lemon juice
Dash bottled hot pepper sauce

Halve bacon slices crosswise or cut Canadian bacon slices in thirds. Partially cook bacon slices. Roll each piece of meat around a banana piece, water chestnut, pineapple chunk, or kumquat. Secure with wooden picks. Place on rack in unheated broiler pan. For sauce combine cornstarch, mustard, and ginger. Blend in jelly, orange juice concentrate, lemon juice, pepper sauce, and ½ cup *water*. Cook and stir till thickened and bubbly. Brush bacon with sauce. Broil 3 to 4 inches from heat for 3 to 4 minutes. Turn; brush with sauce. Broil 2 to 3 minutes more. Reheat remaining sauce; use for dipping. Makes 12 appetizers.

Hot Potato Salad

When buying bacon, remember to compare prices by cost per pound not cost per package. To compare the price of different size packages, divide the price of a 16-ounce package by 4; divide the price of a 12-ounce package by 3. The smaller answer indicates the better buy. If you plan to cut up the bacon, buy the less expensive packages of "ends and pieces."

4 potatoes, peeled and cubed
1 cup thinly sliced carrot
½ cup chopped celery
6 slices bacon
¼ cup chopped onion
2 tablespoons all-purpose flour

2 tablespoons sugar
½ teaspoon salt
½ cup vinegar
½ cup mayonnaise
2 hard-cooked eggs, chopped
2 tablespoons snipped parsley

Cook potatoes, carrot, and celery in boiling water about 15 minutes or till tender; drain. Cook bacon till crisp; drain, reserving 2 tablespoons drippings. Crumble bacon; set aside. Cook onion in reserved drippings till tender. Blend in flour, sugar, salt, and ⅛ teaspoon *pepper*. Stir in vinegar and ½ cup *water;* cook and stir till thickened and bubbly. Remove from heat; stir in mayonnaise, eggs, parsley, and crumbled bacon. Pour over vegetables; toss. Turn into 1½-quart casserole. Bake in 350° oven for 30 to 35 minutes or till heated through. Makes 6 servings.

***When cooking bacon**, select one of these easy methods. Canadian-style bacon: Slice ¼ inch thick; slash edges. To broil, place on unheated rack in broiler pan. Broil 3 to 4 inches from heat 1 to 2 minutes per side. To panbroil, cook in a little cooking oil 2 to 3 minutes per side.*

Bacon: To cook in the oven, place separated slices on unheated rack in shallow baking pan. Bake in 400° oven about 10 minutes. To broil, place separated slices on unheated rack in broiler pan. Broil 3 to 5 inches from heat till desired doneness, turning once and watching closely.

At a brunch or on the party appetizer scene, Cumberland-Style Bacon Rolls are a hit.

Lemon-Pepper Sandwich Loaf

1 1-pound loaf unsliced white sandwich bread	2 teaspoons poppy seed
½ cup Lemon-Pepper Butter, softened	8 slices Swiss cheese (8 ounces)
1 tablespoon prepared mustard	8 slices bacon, crisp-cooked, drained, and crumbled

Cut bread into 9 slices, cutting to, *but not through,* bottom crust. Combine ½ cup Lemon-Pepper Butter, mustard, and poppy seed; set aside 3 tablespoons of the mixture. Spread remainder on all cut surfaces of bread. Place 1 slice cheese in each cut; sprinkle bacon over cheese. Spread the reserved Lemon-Pepper Butter mixture on top and sides of loaf. Bake on ungreased baking sheet in 350° oven for 15 to 20 minutes. Makes 9 servings.

Lemon-Pepper Butter: In small mixer bowl cream 1 pound *butter or margarine* (2 cups) till light and fluffy. Add ¼ cup snipped *chives,* 1½ teaspoons finely shredded *lemon peel,* 2 tablespoons *lemon juice,* and ½ teaspoon freshly ground black *pepper.* Mix well. Store in refrigerator in tightly covered container. Makes 2 cups.

Bacon-Leek Pie

Leeks are similar to large green onions, but have a more delicate flavor. Look for crisp young leeks that have bright green tops. Trim off the tiny roots, then slice off the tops to within 2 inches of the white portion.

6 slices bacon, cut in 1-inch pieces	½ teaspoon celery seed
6 medium leeks, thinly sliced (2 cups)	¼ teaspoon pepper
1 tablespoon all-purpose flour	1⅓ cups light cream
1 teaspoon salt	3 tablespoons dry sherry
	5 slightly beaten eggs
	1 unbaked 9-inch pastry shell
	Ground nutmeg

Cook bacon till crisp; place on paper toweling and set aside. Drain fat from skillet, reserving ¼ cup drippings. Cook leeks in reserved drippings till tender but not brown, stirring occasionally. Blend in flour, salt, celery seed, and pepper. Add cream. Cook, stirring constantly, till thickened and bubbly. Stir in sherry. Gradually stir hot mixture into beaten eggs. Stir in bacon. Pour into pastry shell; sprinkle lightly with nutmeg. Bake in 400° oven for 20 to 25 minutes or till knife inserted off-center comes out clean. Let stand 5 minutes. Makes 6 servings.

Side Pork Fry

1 pound fresh side pork, sliced	½ teaspoon salt
¼ cup yellow cornmeal	⅛ teaspoon pepper
2 tablespoons all-purpose flour	⅛ teaspoon paprika
	Fried Apples

Remove the rind from side pork, if desired. Combine cornmeal, flour, salt, pepper, and paprika; coat pork slices with mixture. In skillet cook pork slices on both sides over medium heat for 18 to 20 minutes or till crisp. Serve with Fried Apples. Makes 4 servings.

Fried Apples: Core 4 tart *apples;* thinly slice into rings. In skillet melt ¼ cup *butter or margarine.* Add apple rings and ¼ cup packed *brown sugar.* Cover and cook about 10 minutes or till apples are tender and translucent, stirring occasionally. Sprinkle apple slices with ground *cinnamon, nutmeg, or cardamom.*

Leg of Lamb

Portion for roast leg of lamb comes from the hind leg. May be marketed in one piece, divided into sirloin and shank halves, or sold with roast or slices removed from the center.

Whole Leg of Lamb Whole leg consists of the full sirloin and the shank. It may also be boned, rolled, and tied. *Roast.*

American-Style Leg of Lamb is the whole leg with the shank bone removed. Meat is folded back into the pocket, squaring off the shank end. *Roast.*

Frenched-Style Leg of Lamb is the whole leg with meat trimmed off the shank bone end, making a handle for easier carving. *Roast.*

Center-Cut Leg of Lamb Roast cut from center of whole leg. *Roast.*

Leg of Lamb, Sirloin Half The half leg containing the full sirloin portion. The hip bone varies in shape throughout the cut. *Roast.*

Leg of Lamb, Shank Half The shank half or lower half of the leg. Contains the leg bone. *Roast.*

The small lamb carcass is usually divided into foresaddle (unsplit front half; includes ribs, shoulder, and breast) and hindsaddle (unsplit rear half; includes loin, flank, and legs). Usually the outer fat is covered by a natural, pinkish-red, papery layer called the fell, which may be removed if desired.

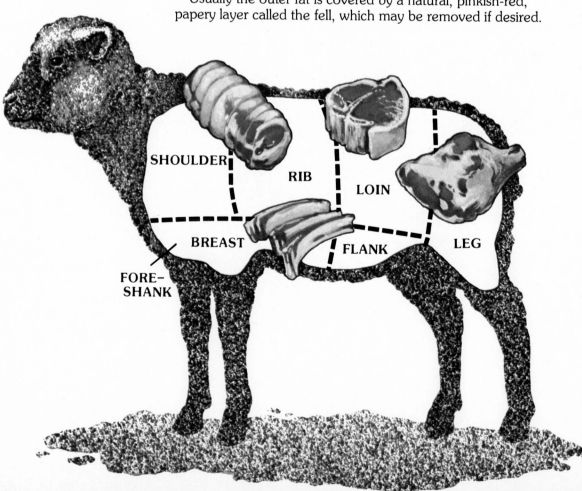

Lamb Roasts

Shoulder Blade Roast Cut from the upper shoulder area. Contains a section of blade bone, which varies in shape depending upon what part of the shoulder the roast is cut from. *Roast.*

Square-Cut Shoulder Roast Square-shaped cut with both arm bone and blade bone exposed. *Roast.*

Shoulder Arm Roast Cut from the lower shoulder area. Includes a section of the round arm bone. *Roast.*

Boneless Shoulder Roast A square-cut shoulder roast with the bones removed and the meat rolled and tied. Called a cushion roast when boned but left flat because its appearance resembles a cushion. *Roast.*

Rib Roast Cut from the rib or rack containing up to 7 rib bones. A **Rib Crown Roast** is two rib roasts, backbone removed, sewn with rib bones on the outside. Paper frills traditionally cover the bone ends when ribs are frenched. *Roast.*

Loin Roast Identified by T-shaped backbone and large top loin and smaller tenderloin muscles. *Roast.*

Lamb Chops and Steaks

Shoulder Blade Chop Cut from upper shoulder area. Contains blade bone, which varies in shape. May be boned, rolled, and skewered. *Braise, broil, panbroil, or panfry.*

Cubed Steak Mechanically tenderized boneless piece of meat. *Broil, panbroil, or panfry.*

Rib Chop From rib or rack. Has rib bone and rib eye muscle. Often frenched. *Broil, panbroil, panfry, or bake.*

Shoulder Arm Chop Lean chop from lower shoulder. Has arm bone. *Braise, broil, panbroil, or panfry.*

Leg Center Slice From the center of the leg. Identified by leg bone. *Broil, panbroil, or panfry.*

Loin Chop Cut from the loin. Identified by T-shaped backbone, large top loin or loin eye muscle, and smaller tenderloin muscle. A Loin Double Chop, often called English chop, is a cross-sectional slice from the unsplit double loin. *Broil, panbroil, or panfry.*

Leg Sirloin Chop From sirloin portion of the leg. Contains hip bone, which varies in shape. *Broil, panbroil, or panfry,*

Ribs and Shanks

Breast Spareribs Rib bones and cartilage. Most fat is trimmed off, leaving a thin covering of meat. *Braise, broil, or roast.*

Breast Riblets Made by cutting between rib bones. Alternate layers of rib bones, cartilage, lean meat, and fat. *Braise or cook in liquid.*

Lamb Shanks Cuts from the upper foreshank identified by the round arm bone. A very thin layer of fat covers the outer surface of the meat. *Braise or cook in liquid.*

Ground Lamb

Made from lean trimmings and the less tender cuts (shoulder and flank). *Bake, broil, panbroil, or panfry.*

Meat from the Breast

The breast is most often cut into riblets or stew meat, although large pieces are available for roasting.

Lamb Breast May be sold as roast for stuffing (has pocket between ribs and outer layers of meat). Also sold boned and rolled. *Braise or roast.*

Meats for Soups, Stews, and Kabobs

Lamb for Stew Lean meat cubes usually cut from the shoulder, breast, and leg areas. *Braise or cook in liquid.*

Lamb Cubes for Kabobs Boneless lean cubes from the shoulder and leg. Available in pieces or threaded on skewers. *Broil or braise.*

Crown Roast of Lamb with Rice Stuffing

1 6-ounce package long grain and wild rice mix
1 pound ground lamb
1 medium onion, chopped
¼ cup raisins
¼ cup toasted slivered almonds
¼ cup dry sherry
1 teaspoon salt
¼ teaspoon pepper

¼ teaspoon ground cloves
¼ teaspoon ground cardamom
¼ teaspoon ground ginger
⅛ teaspoon ground cinnamon
1 4-pound lamb rib crown roast, containing 2 whole rib sections and with fat trimmed from center of roast (12 to 14 ribs)
3 hard-cooked eggs, sliced

Cook rice mix according to package directions. In skillet cook ground lamb and onion till meat is browned and onion is tender. Drain excess fat. For stuffing combine cooked rice, raisins, almonds, sherry, salt, pepper, cloves, cardamom, ginger, and cinnamon. Add cooked meat and onion; toss lightly. Place roast on a small piece of foil on rack in shallow roasting pan. Spoon in stuffing till center is half full. Arrange one of the sliced eggs atop stuffing. Spoon additional stuffing atop until mixture mounds. Cover top of roast and stuffing with foil. Place remaining stuffing in a 1-quart casserole, layering another sliced egg in center of mixture.

Insert meat thermometer in meaty portion of roast, not touching bone. Roast lamb in 325° oven for 3 to 3¼ hours or till thermometer registers 175°. Uncover all but stuffing for the last 15 minutes. Bake stuffing in casserole, covered, the last 45 minutes of roasting time. Garnish with remaining sliced egg. Makes 6 or 7 servings.

Orange-Sauced Lamb Roll

1 6-pound leg of lamb, boned and butterflied
⅔ cup chopped onion
⅔ cup chopped celery
3 tablespoons butter or margarine
3 tablespoons finely shredded orange peel
1 beaten egg
4½ cups cinnamon-raisin bread cubes (6 slices)

⅓ cup packed brown sugar
2 tablespoons cornstarch
1 teaspoon salt
¾ teaspoon ground ginger
1¾ cups orange juice
2 teaspoons dried mint flakes
2 tablespoons butter or margarine
2 oranges, peeled, sectioned, and cut up

Pound lamb to ½- to ¾-inch thickness; sprinkle with some salt and pepper. Cook onion and celery in 3 tablespoons butter till tender; mix with *2 tablespoons* of the orange peel and egg. Add bread, tossing to coat. Spread over lamb; roll up jelly roll-style. Tie with string. Place on rack in shallow roasting pan. Insert meat thermometer in thickest portion of meat. Roast in 325° oven about 2½ hours or till thermometer registers 170°.

Meanwhile, in saucepan combine brown sugar, cornstarch, salt, and ginger. Stir in the remaining 1 tablespoon peel, the orange juice, and mint flakes. Cook and stir till thickened and bubbly. Stir in the 2 tablespoons butter and orange pieces. Serve with roast. Makes 12 servings.

For your next company dinner, order a boned leg of lamb for Orange-Sauced Lamb Roll. It features a cinnamon-raisin bread stuffing plus a mint-flavored orange sauce.

Lamb Shoulder Roast with Curry Sauce

1 3- to 5-pound boneless
  lamb shoulder roast
1 medium onion, sliced and
  separated into rings
1 medium cooking apple,
  cored and chopped
1 tablespoon butter

4 teaspoons all-purpose flour
1 to 2 teaspoons curry powder
2 teaspoons instant chicken
  bouillon granules
1 teaspoon lemon juice
¼ cup light raisins
  Hot cooked rice

Place meat on rack in shallow roasting pan; sprinkle with some salt and pepper. Insert meat thermometer in thickest portion of meat. Roast in 325° oven for 2 to 3 hours or till thermometer registers 160°. Let stand 15 minutes. Remove strings or netting and carve.

Meanwhile, in saucepan cook onion and apple in butter till tender. Stir in flour, curry, and ⅛ teaspoon *pepper*. Add bouillon granules, lemon juice, and 1 cup *water*. Cook and stir till slightly thickened and bubbly. Stir in raisins. Cover and simmer for 15 minutes, stirring occasionally. Serve with meat and rice. Makes 6 to 8 servings.

Rolled Lamb Shoulder with Vegetables

1 5- to 6-pound boneless lamb
  shoulder roast
1 medium onion, finely
  chopped (½ cup)
¼ cup snipped parsley
2 tablespoons lemon juice
1½ teaspoons salt
1 teaspoon dried basil,
  crushed
½ teaspoon dried marjoram,
  crushed
¼ teaspoon pepper
2 tablespoons cooking oil
1 10½-ounce can condensed
  beef broth

¾ cup dry red wine
1 bay leaf
8 to 10 tiny new potatoes
  (1½ pounds)
8 to 10 small whole onions
4 or 5 medium carrots, halved
  crosswise
4 medium zucchini, halved
  crosswise
1 medium eggplant, peeled,
  cut in 4 slices, and
  halved crosswise
  (optional)
¼ cup cold water
2 tablespoons cornstarch

Remove netting or string from rolled roast; trim excess fat. Unroll roast on board; pound slightly with meat mallet to make of even thickness. In bowl combine chopped onion, parsley, lemon juice, salt, basil, marjoram, and pepper; mix well and spread over surface of meat. Reroll roast and tie securely with string. In 6-quart Dutch oven brown meat on all sides in hot oil. Pour beef broth and red wine over meat; add bay leaf. Cover and simmer for 1½ hours.

Peel a strip from center of each potato. Add potatoes, whole onions, and carrots to Dutch oven. Cover and simmer 20 minutes more. Add zucchini and eggplant; simmer about 20 minutes more or till vegetables and meat are tender. Transfer roast to carving board. Remove strings before slicing. Transfer vegetables to large warm serving platter or bowl; cover and keep warm. Skim fat from cooking liquid. Measure 1¾ cups of the cooking liquid; return measured liquid to Dutch oven. Blend the cold water into cornstarch; stir into liquid. Cook, stirring constantly, till thickened and bubbly. Pass with meat and vegetables. Makes 8 to 10 servings.

Roasting Lamb

Plan on a little longer roasting time when the crown roast is filled with a stuffing mixture.

Cut	Approximate Weight (Pounds)	Internal Temperature on Removal from Oven	Approximate Cooking Time (Total Time)
Roast meat at constant oven temperature of 325°			
Leg, whole	5 to 9	140° (rare) 160° (medium) 170° to 180° (well-done)	2 to 3 hrs. 2½ to 3¾ hrs. 3 to 4½ hrs.
Leg, half	3 to 4	160° (medium)	1½ to 1¾ hrs.
Square Cut Shoulder	4 to 6	160° (medium)	2 to 2½ hrs.
Boneless Shoulder	3 to 5	160° (medium)	2 to 3 hrs.
Crown Roast	3 to 4	140° (rare) 160° (medium) 170° to 180° (well-done)	1¾ to 2 hrs. 2 to 2¼ hrs. 2¼ to 2¾ hrs.

Roasting directions: Season the roast by sprinkling with a little salt and pepper. Insert a meat thermometer into center of roast so that the bulb reaches the thickest part of the lean meat. Make sure the bulb does not rest in fat or touch bone. Place roast, fat side up, on a rack in shallow roasting pan. *Do not* cover, add water, or baste. Roast in 325° oven till the meat thermometer registers desired internal temperature. To check doneness, push thermometer into meat a little farther. If the temperature drops, continue cooking meat to desired temperature. Let meat stand about 15 minutes for easier carving. Remove string from rolled and tied roasts; carve meat across the grain. For further information on carving, see pages 170 and 171.

Fresh Mint Sauce

1½ teaspoons cornstarch
¼ cup snipped fresh mint leaves
3 tablespoons light corn syrup
1 tablespoon lemon juice
1 drop green food coloring (optional)

In small saucepan blend ¼ cup cold *water* into cornstarch; add mint leaves, corn syrup, and lemon juice. Cook, stirring constantly, till thickened and bubbly. Strain. Stir in green food coloring, if desired. Serve with roast lamb. Makes about ½ cup.

Cranberry-Lemon Glaze

1 8-ounce can whole cranberry sauce
½ teaspoon finely shredded lemon peel
2 tablespoons lemon juice
⅛ teaspoon dried rosemary, crushed

In saucepan combine cranberry sauce, lemon peel, lemon juice, and rosemary. Bring to boiling. Spoon some over lamb roast during the last 30 minutes of roasting time. Reheat remaining and pass with roast. Makes about 1 cup.

Pineapple-Chutney Glaze

1 20-ounce can crushed pineapple
½ cup chutney, cut up
2 tablespoons brown sugar
2 tablespoons butter
1 teaspoon salt
1 teaspoon ground ginger

Combine *undrained* pineapple and remaining ingredients. Bring to boil; reduce heat and simmer for 15 minutes. Spoon some over roast during last 30 minutes of roasting time; pass remainder. Makes about 3 cups.

Mock Gyros

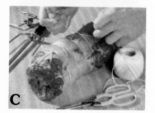

1 5- to 6-pound leg of lamb, boned and butterflied
1 2-pound boneless beef round steak, tenderized
1 tablespoon salt
2 teaspoons dried thyme, crushed
2 teaspoons ground coriander
1 teaspoon pepper
½ cup cooking oil
½ cup lemon juice
¼ cup finely chopped onion
4 cloves garlic, minced
16 to 20 pita bread rounds
2 medium tomatoes, chopped
1 cup snipped parsley
1 8-ounce carton (1 cup) plain yogurt

With meat mallet, pound both lamb and beef to 16x12-inch rectangles, about ½ to ¾ inch thick (pound lamb only on cut surface). Cut and patch meats where necessary to make surface even. Combine salt, thyme, coriander, and pepper; sprinkle *half* over the surface of each piece of meat. Pound in the seasoning mixture.

For marinade combine oil, lemon juice, onion, and garlic. Pour *half* over lamb in shallow dish; add beef and remaining marinade (see photo A). Cover and refrigerate several hours or overnight, turning occasionally.

Remove meats from marinade (most of the liquid should be absorbed). Place lamb, cut side up, on countertop or cutting board. Place beef atop lamb, fitting meat to edges (see photo B). Pound meats together. Roll up meat, beginning at narrow end. Tie securely with string, first at center, then halfway between center and each end. Tie lengthwise. Finish securing roll by tying between crosswise strings (see photo C).

Insert spit rod; adjust holding forks and test balance. Insert meat thermometer near center of meat, not touching spit rod. Place *hot* coals on both sides of a shallow foil drip pan. Attach spit so meat is over drip pan. Turn on motor and lower grill hood, or cover with foil tent. Grill for 2 to 2½ hours or till meat thermometer registers 140°. Remove from spit. Cut meat in thin slices, removing strings as you slice. Serve in bread rounds, adding tomatoes, parsley, and yogurt. Makes 16 to 20 sandwiches.

Seasoned Leg of Lamb

1 6- to 7-pound leg of lamb
Olive oil
½ cup fine dry bread crumbs
3 tablespoons finely snipped parsley
2 tablespoons butter
2 teaspoons finely shredded lemon peel
1 clove garlic, minced
1 teaspoon salt
1 teaspoon dried oregano, crushed
1 teaspoon dried basil, crushed
1 teaspoon dried rosemary, crushed

Have meatman bone leg of lamb, leaving shank bone intact. Remove fell (thin fat covering) from surface of roast. Rub inside and outside of roast with olive oil. Combine bread crumbs, parsley, butter, lemon peel, garlic, salt, oregano, basil, rosemary, and ⅛ teaspoon pepper; mix well. Spread mixture as evenly as possible over entire inside cut surface of roast. Skewer roast shut. If necessary, secure with string.

Place roast on rack in shallow roasting pan. Insert meat thermometer in thickest portion of meat. Roast lamb in 325° oven for 2 to 2½ hours or till thermometer registers 150°. Makes 12 servings.

Herbed Center-Cut Leg of Lamb

This is a roast you can cut yourself from a whole leg of lamb. See page 87 for directions.

1 2½- to 3-pound boneless center-cut leg of lamb
1 small onion, finely chopped
2 tablespoons dijon-style mustard
¼ teaspoon dried marjoram, crushed
¼ teaspoon dried rosemary, crushed
¾ cup cold water
1 teaspoon cornstarch
1 teaspoon instant chicken bouillon granules

Unroll roast; sprinkle with some salt and pepper. Combine onion, mustard, marjoram, and rosemary; spread over roast. Roll up; tie securely. Place roast, fat side up, on rack in shallow roasting pan. Insert meat thermometer in the thickest portion of meat. Roast in 325° oven for 1½ to 1¾ hours or till thermometer registers 150°. Let stand 15 minutes. Remove strings; slice. Skim fat from pan juices; measure juices and add water to make ¼ cup liquid. Blend the ¾ cup cold water into cornstarch and bouillon granules; stir into pan juices. Cook and stir till thickened and bubbly. Season with salt and pepper. Pass with meat. Makes 4 to 6 servings.

Parmesan Lamb Chops

4 lamb leg sirloin chops, cut 1 inch thick
1 tablespoon cooking oil
1 8-ounce can tomato sauce
1 tablespoon snipped parsley
1 teaspoon sugar
½ teaspoon dried oregano, crushed
¼ teaspoon dried basil, crushed
¼ cup shredded mozzarella cheese (1 ounce)
2 tablespoons freshly grated parmesan cheese
2 teaspoons cornstarch
Hot cooked noodles

Sprinkle chops lightly with some salt and pepper. In 10-inch skillet quickly brown chops on both sides in hot oil. Combine tomato sauce, parsley, sugar, oregano, basil, ¼ teaspoon *salt,* and ⅛ teaspoon *pepper;* pour over meat. Cover; simmer about 30 minutes or till meat is tender. Transfer meat to platter and sprinkle with cheeses; keep warm. Blend 1 tablespoon cold *water* into cornstarch; stir into sauce in skillet. Cook and stir till bubbly. Pass with meat and noodles. Makes 4 servings.

Lamb Stuffing Bake

4 lamb leg sirloin chops, cut ¾ inch thick
1 tablespoon shortening
1 medium orange
1 8-ounce package corn bread stuffing mix
½ cup chopped pitted dried prunes
½ teaspoon salt
½ teaspoon dried thyme, crushed
⅛ teaspoon pepper
⅓ cup chopped celery
¼ cup chopped onion
3 tablespoons butter
¾ cup water

In skillet brown lamb chops in hot shortening about 5 minutes per side. Season with some salt and pepper. Remove from skillet. Finely shred 1 teaspoon *orange peel;* set aside. Peel and section the orange over bowl to catch juice. Chop orange sections; add to juice. Add orange peel, stuffing mix, prunes, salt, thyme, and pepper. Cook celery and onion in butter till tender. Stir in water; add to stuffing mixture. Toss lightly till well mixed. Turn into an 8x1½-inch round baking dish. Arrange chops atop. Cover; bake in 350° oven for 45 to 50 minutes. Makes 4 servings.

Italian Lamb Shoulder Chops

4 lamb shoulder chops
¼ cup chopped onion
2 tablespoons cooking oil
¼ teaspoon dried basil, crushed
¼ teaspoon dried oregano, crushed
1 cup water
2 teaspoons instant chicken bouillon granules

2 medium potatoes, peeled and sliced (2 cups)
1 9-ounce package frozen Italian *or* cut green beans, partially thawed
¼ cup sliced pitted ripe olives
1 2-ounce jar chopped pimiento, drained (¼ cup)
2 teaspoons cornstarch

In large skillet brown lamb chops and onion in hot oil. Drain off excess fat. Sprinkle meat with basil, oregano, and a little pepper. Stir in water and bouillon granules. Simmer, covered, for 15 minutes. Arrange potatoes around chops; simmer, covered, about 15 minutes more or till potatoes are almost tender. Add beans, olives, and pimiento. Cover and simmer 5 to 10 minutes more or till beans are tender. Remove meat and vegetables to platter; keep warm. Blend 1 tablespoon cold *water* into cornstarch; stir into cooking liquid. Cook and stir till thickened and bubbly. Serve with meat and vegetables. Makes 4 servings.

Lemony Lamb Shoulder Chops

6 lamb shoulder chops, cut ¾ inch thick
2 tablespoons cooking oil
⅓ cup water
¼ teaspoon finely shredded lemon peel (set aside)
¼ cup lemon juice
1 tablespoon worcestershire sauce

¾ teaspoon salt
¼ teaspoon dried oregano, crushed
¼ teaspoon dried rosemary, crushed
Dash freshly ground black pepper
1 tablespoon cornstarch

In large skillet slowly brown chops on both sides in hot oil about 15 minutes. Combine water, lemon juice, worcestershire, salt, oregano, rosemary, and pepper; pour over meat. Cover; cook over low heat about 30 minutes or till tender. Remove meat to warm platter.

Pour pan juices into measuring cup; skim off fat. Add water, if necessary, to make 1 cup liquid; return to skillet. Blend 2 tablespoons cold *water* into cornstarch; stir into liquid in skillet. Add lemon peel. Cook and stir till bubbly. Pass with meat. Makes 6 servings.

Lamb Loin Chops with Walnut Glaze

4 lamb loin chops, cut ¾ inch thick
¼ cup honey
1 tablespoon lemon juice

¼ cup finely chopped walnuts
2 tablespoons snipped parsley

Place lamb chops on unheated rack in broiler pan. Broil 3 to 4 inches from heat for 5 minutes. Sprinkle with some salt and pepper. Turn; broil 5 to 6 minutes more. Blend honey and lemon juice; stir in walnuts and parsley. Spoon nut mixture over chops; broil 1 minute longer. Makes 4 servings.

Italian Lamb Shoulder Chops *is a variation on the dinner-in-a-skillet idea. A flavorful blend of potatoes, green beans, olives, and pimiento cooks with the meat.*

Broiling Lamb Chops

To check doneness, slit center of chop and note the inside color: pink—medium; gray—well-done.

Thickness	¾ inch	1 inch	1½ inches
	(approximate total time in minutes)		
Medium	10 to 12	11 to 13	15 to 18
Well-done	13 to 15	16 to 18	20 to 22

Choose lamb rib chops, loin chops, loin double chops, or leg sirloin chops. Slash the fat edge at 1-inch intervals to keep chops flat. Place chops on unheated rack in broiler pan.

Broil chops so surface of meat is 3 inches from heat (check range instruction booklet). Broil on one side for about half of the time indicated in the chart for the desired doneness. Season with a little salt and pepper, if desired. Turn with tongs and broil till desired doneness. Season again with salt and pepper.

Lamb Shish Kabobs

½ cup chopped onion
¼ cup lemon juice
2 tablespoons olive oil
1 teaspoon salt
½ teaspoon dried thyme, crushed
¼ teaspoon pepper

1½ pounds boneless lamb, cut into 1-inch pieces
Boiling water
12 large fresh mushrooms
3 medium tomatoes, quartered
2 medium green peppers, cut into 1½-inch pieces

For marinade, in bowl combine onion, lemon juice, olive oil, salt, thyme, and pepper. Add meat. Cover and refrigerate several hours or overnight. Drain meat, reserving marinade. Pour some boiling water over mushrooms; let stand 1 to 2 minutes; drain.

Thread meat on skewers alternately with tomato quarters, green pepper pieces, and mushrooms. Grill over *medium* coals for 20 to 25 minutes, brushing with marinade and turning skewers often. (For firm cooked tomatoes, grill on separate skewers for 8 to 10 minutes.) Makes 6 servings.

Chinese Curried Lamb

1 pound boneless lamb
2 egg whites
2 tablespoons cornstarch
1 clove garlic, minced
¼ cup peanut *or* cooking oil
1 8-ounce package frozen cut asparagus, thawed

1 red onion, chopped
1 green pepper, chopped
¼ cup light raisins
¼ cup dry sherry
2 tablespoons soy sauce
2 tablespoons catsup
1 tablespoon curry powder

Partially freeze meat; thinly slice across grain in bite-size strips. Combine egg whites and cornstarch; stir in meat. In wok or skillet cook and stir meat and garlic in *2 tablespoons* hot oil till meat is browned. Remove meat; set aside. Add remaining 2 tablespoons oil; heat. Add asparagus, onion, and pepper; cook and stir about 1 minute or till heated through. Combine raisins, sherry, soy, catsup, curry, ⅓ cup *water,* and ¼ teaspoon *salt;* add to wok. Stir in cooked meat; heat through. Serves 4 to 6.

Herbed Lamb Kabobs

¾ cup Russian salad dressing
3 tablespoons lime juice
½ teaspoon dried oregano, crushed
¼ teaspoon dried tarragon, crushed

1½ pounds boneless lamb, cut in 1-inch pieces
Boiling water
2 cups small fresh mushrooms
2 medium green peppers, cut in 1½- to 2-inch squares

For marinade, in bowl combine salad dressing, lime juice, oregano, and tarragon. Add lamb. Cover and let stand 2 hours at room temperature or overnight in refrigerator; stir occasionally. Drain, reserving marinade. Pour some boiling water over mushrooms; drain. Alternately thread lamb, mushrooms, and green peppers on 6 long skewers. Place on unheated rack in broiler pan. Broil 4 inches from heat for 10 to 12 minutes; turn and baste with marinade occasionally. Makes 6 servings.

Plum-Sauced Lamb Kabobs with Peaches

1 16-ounce can whole unpitted purple plums
2 tablespoons lemon juice
1 tablespoon soy sauce
½ teaspoon worcestershire sauce
¼ teaspoon dried basil, crushed

⅛ teaspoon garlic powder
1 pound boneless lamb, cut in 1-inch pieces
½ teaspoon salt
1 16-ounce can peach halves
1 to 2 tablespoons butter *or* margarine
Hot cooked rice

Drain plums; reserve ½ cup syrup. Remove pits from plums. For marinade, in blender container combine reserved syrup, plums, lemon juice, soy, worcestershire, basil, and garlic powder. Cover; blend till smooth. Pour into bowl; add lamb. Cover; marinate several hours or overnight in refrigerator. Stir occasionally. Drain meat; reserve marinade. Thread lamb on skewers; sprinkle with salt and dash *pepper*. Place on unheated rack in broiler pan. Broil 4 inches from heat for 9 to 11 minutes; turn occasionally and baste with marinade. Dot each peach with some butter; place on broiler rack with lamb. Broil 5 to 7 minutes more or till lamb is done and peaches are hot. Turn lamb occasionally and baste with marinade. Heat remaining marinade; pass with meat and peaches. Serve with rice. Serves 4.

Stretch a Leg of Lamb into Three Meals

*Making more than one meal from a leg of lamb doesn't have to mean a week of leftovers. Instead, have meatman cut (or use a saw) a 7- to 9-pound whole leg of lamb roast **before** cooking.*

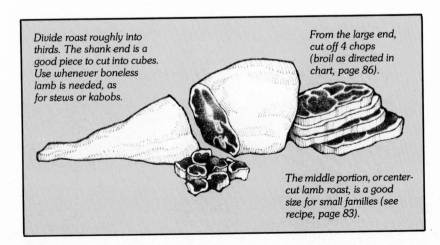

Divide roast roughly into thirds. The shank end is a good piece to cut into cubes. Use whenever boneless lamb is needed, as for stews or kabobs.

From the large end, cut off 4 chops (broil as directed in chart, page 86).

The middle portion, or center-cut lamb roast, is a good size for small families (see recipe, page 83).

Lamb Shanks Paprikash

6 lamb shanks (about
    4 pounds)
2 tablespoons cooking oil
1 16-ounce can tomatoes,
    cut up
1 large onion, chopped

2 tablespoons snipped
    parsley
1 teaspoon salt
1 teaspoon paprika
1 cup dairy sour cream
Hot cooked noodles

Sprinkle lamb shanks with a little salt and pepper. In Dutch oven brown lamb shanks on all sides in hot oil. Add *undrained* tomatoes, onion, parsley, salt, paprika, and dash *pepper*. Cover and simmer about 1½ hours or till meat is tender. Remove meat; keep warm. Skim excess fat from pan juices; measure juices. Quickly cook juices down until they measure 2 cups. Gradually stir about 1 cup of the hot juices into sour cream. Return to remaining juices in Dutch oven. Heat through but *do not boil*. Arrange lamb shanks on bed of noodles on warm platter. Spoon some sauce over meat; pass remainder. Makes 6 servings.

Curried Lamb Madras

For boneless lamb, use roasts from the leg or shoulder. Cut into uniform-size pieces for even cooking.

⅓ cup all-purpose flour
3 tablespoons curry powder
½ teaspoon salt
½ teaspoon paprika
½ teaspoon dried oregano,
    crushed
⅛ teaspoon pepper

2 pounds boneless lamb, cut
    in 1-inch cubes
1 cup chopped onion
1 cup chopped apple
½ cup butter *or* margarine
2½ teaspoons instant chicken
    bouillon granules

In paper or plastic bag combine flour, curry, salt, paprika, oregano, and pepper. Add meat; shake to coat. In Dutch oven cook onion and apple in butter or margarine till tender; remove from pan. Brown meat, about ⅓ at a time. Return onion mixture to pan; stir in bouillon granules and 2½ cups *water*. Cover and simmer about 1¼ hours or till meat is tender. Serve over hot cooked rice, if desired. Makes 6 to 8 servings.

Scotch Broth

If desired, you may substitute quick-cooking barley for the pearl barley. Cook the lamb-onion mixture for 1 hour, then add ½ cup quick-cooking barley and the vegetables. Cook, covered, about 30 minutes or till barley and vegetables are tender.

1 pound boneless lamb,
    cut in 1-inch cubes
4 cups water
1 medium onion, chopped
3 sprigs parsley
2 whole cloves
1 bay leaf
1½ teaspoons salt
¼ teaspoon pepper

¼ cup pearl barley
2 medium carrots, chopped
1 medium potato, peeled and
    chopped (1 cup)
1 stalk celery, chopped
¼ teaspoon dried thyme,
    crushed
¼ teaspoon dried rosemary,
    crushed

In large saucepan combine lamb, water, onion, parsley, cloves, bay leaf, salt, and pepper. Bring to boiling; reduce heat and simmer, covered, for 30 minutes. Remove parsley, cloves, and bay leaf. Add pearl barley; cover and cook 30 minutes more. Stir in carrots, potato, celery, thyme, and rosemary. Cover and cook about 30 minutes more or till barley and vegetables are tender. Makes 6 servings.

Paprika and dairy sour cream are the accent flavorings in Lamb Shanks Paprikash. *Common powdered paprika comes from dried, finely ground pods of sweet pepper.*

Moroccan-Style Lamb

2 teaspoons sesame seed
1 tablespoon olive oil
1 tablespoon butter
1 large onion, thinly sliced
½ teaspoon ground ginger
¼ teaspoon pepper

⅛ teaspoon saffron, crushed
2 pounds boneless lamb, cut
  in 1-inch cubes
¾ cup pitted dried prunes
1 tablespoon lemon juice
1 tablespoon honey

Sprinkle sesame seed in 15x10x1-inch shallow baking pan. Brown in 350° oven about 10 minutes, shaking occasionally; cool and set aside.

In Dutch oven heat oil and butter together. Stir in onion, ginger, pepper, saffron, and 1 teaspoon *salt*. Stir in lamb. Cover and simmer about 1½ hours or till meat is very tender, stirring occasionally. Add prunes; cover and cook 15 minutes longer. Remove meat to warm platter; arrange prunes on top and keep warm. Boil the liquid in pan over high heat till reduced to a moderately thick sauce (about ¾ cup). Stir in lemon juice and honey. Pour over lamb and prunes; sprinkle with sesame seed. Serves 8.

Spicy Lamb Stew

Cardamom is a pungent spice with a taste similar to anise and sweeter than ginger. The whole cardamom is actually a soft-shell pod containing about 20 tiny black seeds.

1½ pounds boneless lamb, cut
  in 1-inch cubes
4 whole cloves
4 whole cardamom pods,
  cracked
1 inch stick cinnamon
1 tablespoon cooking oil
1 cup chopped onion
1 small clove garlic, minced

1 teaspoon grated gingerroot
1½ teaspoons ground coriander
1 teaspoon ground turmeric
½ teaspoon ground cumin
¼ teaspoon pepper
⅛ teaspoon cayenne
1 cup plain yogurt
2 tablespoons all-purpose
  flour

In saucepan combine meat, ½ cup *water*, and ½ teaspoon *salt*. Cover; simmer 30 minutes. Meanwhile, in skillet cook and stir cloves, cardamom, and cinnamon in hot oil a few seconds. Add onion, garlic, and gingerroot; cook and stir 3 minutes more. Mix coriander, turmeric, cumin, pepper, and cayenne; stir in ¼ cup *water*. Add to onion-spice mixture. Cook and stir 10 minutes. Add onion mixture to lamb in cooking liquid. Stir in ¼ teaspoon *salt*. Cover and simmer 15 to 20 minutes more or till meat is tender. Blend yogurt and flour; stir into lamb mixture. Cook and stir just till thickened and bubbly. Serves 6.

Lamb Shanks in Pineapple-Dill Sauce

4 lamb shanks (about
  3½ pounds)
1 tablespoon cooking oil
1 6-ounce can frozen pineapple
  juice concentrate, thawed
1 tablespoon sugar

1 teaspoon dried dillweed
1 teaspoon instant chicken
  bouillon granules
½ cup hot water
2 tablespoons cornstarch
  Hot cooked rice

In 4½-quart Dutch oven brown lamb shanks on all sides in hot oil. Sprinkle with some salt and pepper. In bowl combine pineapple concentrate, sugar, and dillweed. Dissolve bouillon granules in hot water; stir into pineapple mixture. Pour over meat. Cover and simmer about 1½ hours or till meat is tender. Remove lamb shanks; keep warm. Skim fat from pan juices. Measure juices; cook over high heat till reduced to 1¾ cups. Blend ¼ cup cold *water* into cornstarch; stir into pan juices. Cook and stir till thickened and bubbly. Pass with lamb and rice. Serves 4.

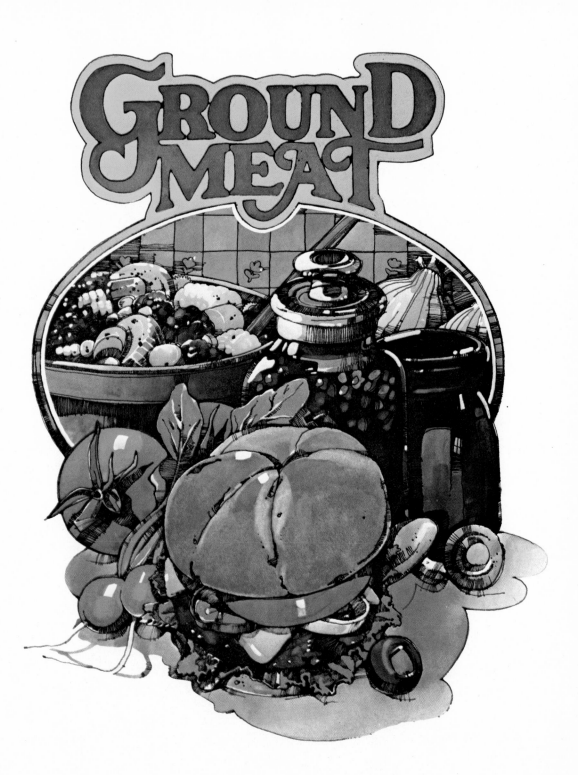

Multipurpose Meatballs

Add these frozen cooked meatballs to your favorite spaghetti, stroganoff, or sweet-sour sauce, simmer about 20 minutes, and serve. If you have a countertop microwave oven, cook the frozen meatballs just before adding to the sauce.

3 beaten eggs
½ cup milk
3 cups soft bread crumbs

½ cup finely chopped onion
2 teaspoons salt
3 pounds ground beef

In bowl combine eggs and milk; stir in crumbs, onion, and salt. Add meat; mix well. Chill. With wet hands shape meat into 72 one-inch meatballs and place in two 15x10x1-inch baking pans. Bake in 375° oven for 25 to 30 minutes. Transfer meatballs to another baking pan to cool; place in freezer just till frozen. Using 24 meatballs per package, wrap in moisture-vapor-proof bags. Seal, label, and freeze. Makes 72 meatballs.

Microwave cooking directions: Prepare meat mixture and shape as above. Arrange unbaked meatballs in baking pans; place in freezer just till frozen. Wrap, 24 per package, in moisture-vaporproof bags. Seal, label, and freeze. To cook, place 24 frozen meatballs in a layer in a 12x7½x2-inch nonmetal baking dish. Cook, covered, in countertop microwave oven 4 minutes, rearranging after each minute. Micro-cook, covered, about 6 minutes more; turn meatballs over and rearrange twice. Drain.

Oriental Meatball Salad

1 beaten egg
¼ cup milk
1½ cups soft bread crumbs
½ teaspoon onion salt
  Dash pepper
½ pound ground beef
1 tablespoon cooking oil
1 8¼-ounce can pineapple
  chunks
1 medium green pepper, cut
  in ½-inch squares

1 medium carrot, sliced
1 stalk celery, sliced
¼ cup packed brown sugar
1 tablespoon cornstarch
¼ cup dry white wine
¼ cup water
3 tablespoons vinegar
1 tablespoon soy sauce
1 medium tomato, cut in
  wedges
  Shredded lettuce

Combine egg, milk, crumbs, onion salt, and pepper; add meat and mix well. Shape into twenty 1-inch meatballs. In skillet cook meatballs in hot oil about 10 minutes or till done, turning frequently. Drain off excess fat.

Drain pineapple, reserving ¼ cup juice. In bowl combine *half* of the pineapple chunks, the green pepper, carrot, celery, and the meatballs; set aside. (Use the remaining pineapple and juice for another purpose.) In small saucepan combine brown sugar and cornstarch; stir in reserved ¼ cup pineapple juice, wine, water, vinegar, and soy. Cook and stir till thickened and bubbly. Pour hot mixture over meatball mixture. Cover and chill. To serve, carefully stir tomato wedges into meatball mixture (or reserve tomato wedges and arrange along side of serving plates). Place lettuce on plates; spoon meatball mixture atop. Makes 2 servings.

Shaping a ground meat mixture into uniform-size meatballs is a snap. Form mixture into a 1-inch-diameter roll and cut in 1-inch slices or pat the meat to a 1-inch-thick square and cut in 1-inch cubes. Then, shape meat into round meatballs.

For a refreshing summer meal serve Oriental Meatball Salad with pineapple chunks and crisp vegetables.

Up-North Gumbo

If fresh okra is not available, use one 10-ounce package frozen cut okra.

1 beaten egg
¼ cup milk
¼ cup fine dry bread crumbs
½ teaspoon salt
½ teaspoon dried oregano, crushed
1 pound ground beef
4 teaspoons instant beef bouillon granules

1 tablespoon worcestershire sauce
1 teaspoon chili powder
1 clove garlic, minced
1½ cups chopped onion
4 potatoes, peeled and chopped
2½ cups fresh *or* frozen okra, cut up

Combine egg, milk, crumbs, salt, oregano, and ⅛ teaspoon *pepper*. Add beef; mix well. Shape into 48 small meatballs. In large saucepan combine bouillon granules, worcestershire, chili powder, garlic, 4 cups *water*, and ⅛ teaspoon *pepper*. Bring to boil, stirring occasionally; add meatballs and onion. Cover; simmer 20 minutes. Add potatoes and okra; cover and simmer about 10 minutes more or till vegetables are tender. Serves 8.

Saucy Meatball Platter

Browning meatballs in a little hot oil helps prevent sticking, especially when the meats are ground pork, lamb, or veal or when the mixture contains ingredients such as bread crumbs and eggs.

2 beaten eggs
¼ cup milk
1½ cups soft bread crumbs
½ cup chopped onion
2 tablespoons snipped parsley
½ teaspoon salt
½ teaspoon dried oregano, crushed

1½ pounds ground beef
2 tablespoons cooking oil
1 11-ounce can condensed cheddar cheese soup
2 tablespoons all-purpose flour
½ cup milk
⅓ cup dry white wine
Hot cooked spaghetti

Combine eggs, the ¼ cup milk, bread crumbs, onion, parsley, salt, oregano, and dash *pepper*. Add ground beef; mix well. Shape into 30 meatballs. In large skillet brown half the meatballs at a time in hot oil. Drain off fat. Return all meatballs to skillet. Blend soup and flour; gradually stir in the ½ cup milk. Pour over meatballs in skillet. Cover; simmer 10 to 12 minutes. Stir in wine. Cover; simmer about 5 minutes. Serve over spaghetti. Makes 6 servings.

Swiss-Style Meatballs

4 beaten eggs
2 cups light cream
6 slices white bread, toasted and torn up
1 medium onion, finely chopped (½ cup)
1 teaspoon salt
½ teaspoon ground nutmeg

2 pounds ground veal *or* lean ground beef
1 pound ground pork
3 tablespoons cooking oil
1 10¾-ounce can condensed cream of celery soup
2 tablespoons all-purpose flour

Combine eggs, *1 cup* of the cream, toasted bread, onion, salt, and nutmeg. Add meats; mix well. Shape into 36 1½-inch meatballs. In large skillet brown meatballs, a few at a time, in hot oil. Place in 13x9x2-inch baking dish. Discard excess drippings. In same skillet blend soup and the remaining 1 cup cream; pour over meatballs. Cover and bake in 325° oven about 1 hour. Place meatballs in serving dish; keep warm. Skim and discard excess fat from cream sauce; pour sauce into small saucepan. Blend ½ cup cold *water* into flour; stir into sauce. Cook, stirring constantly, till thickened and bubbly. Pour sauce over meatballs. Makes 12 servings.

Fiesta Meatballs in Almond Sauce

1 beaten egg	2 tablespoons cooking oil
½ cup water	2 tablespoons chopped onion
2 cups dry bread cubes	1 clove garlic, minced
(4 slices)	½ cup tomato sauce
½ teaspoon dried oregano,	¼ cup slivered almonds,
crushed	toasted
½ teaspoon chili powder	1 tablespoon snipped parsley
¾ pound ground beef	1½ teaspoons instant chicken
¾ pound ground pork	bouillon granules
½ cup raisins	Hot cooked rice

Combine egg, water, *1½ cups* of the bread cubes, oregano, chili powder, ½ teaspoon *salt,* and ⅛ teaspoon *pepper.* Add meats and raisins; mix well. Shape into 36 one-inch meatballs. In skillet brown meatballs, a few at a time, in hot oil; set aside. Drain off fat, reserving 1 tablespoon drippings in skillet. Cook onion and garlic in reserved drippings for 5 minutes. Stir in remaining bread cubes, tomato sauce, almonds, parsley, bouillon granules, and 1½ cups *water.* Bring to boiling, stirring occasionally; add meatballs. Cover and simmer about 20 minutes. Serve over rice. Makes 6 servings.

Dilled Veal Special

1 beaten egg	1 pound ground veal
¼ cup milk	2 tablespoons cooking oil
¼ cup fine dry bread crumbs	1½ cups water
½ teaspoon salt	1½ teaspoons instant chicken
¼ teaspoon dried dillweed	bouillon granules
4 slices bacon, crisp-cooked,	2 tablespoons cold water
drained, and crumbled	4 teaspoons cornstarch

Combine egg, milk, bread crumbs, salt, and dillweed. Add bacon and ground veal; mix well. Shape into 24 1½-inch meatballs. In 10-inch skillet brown half the meatballs at a time in hot oil. Drain off excess fat. Add the 1½ cups water and the bouillon granules to skillet; stir. Return all the meatballs to skillet; bring to boiling. Simmer, covered, for 10 minutes. Transfer cooked meatballs to serving dish. Blend the 2 tablespoons cold water into cornstarch; stir into bouillon mixture. Cook, stirring constantly, till thickened and bubbly. Stir in a few drops kitchen bouquet, if desired. Pour sauce over meatballs. Makes 4 to 6 servings.

Glazed Ham-Bran Balls

1 beaten egg	½ pound ground fully cooked
⅓ cup milk	ham
1 cup raisin bran flakes	½ pound ground pork
1 tablespoon chopped onion	¼ cup packed brown sugar
⅛ teaspoon salt	¼ cup light corn syrup
⅛ teaspoon dried thyme,	1 tablespoon vinegar
crushed	½ teaspoon dry mustard

Combine egg, milk, bran flakes, onion, salt, thyme, and ⅛ teaspoon *pepper.* Add ground meats; mix well. Shape into 12 meatballs. Place in 11x7x1½-inch baking pan. Bake in 350° oven for 30 minutes. Spoon off fat. In small saucepan combine brown sugar, corn syrup, vinegar, and dry mustard; bring to boiling. Pour over ham balls. Bake about 20 minutes more, basting with the sauce occasionally. Makes 4 servings.

Double-Decker Burgers

2 pounds ground beef
1½ teaspoons seasoned salt
⅛ teaspoon pepper

8 hamburger buns, split,
   toasted, and buttered
Tomato-Cucumber Relish

Combine meat, salt, and pepper; shape into sixteen 4-inch-diameter patties. Place 8 patties on unheated rack in broiler pan. Broil 3 inches from heat till desired doneness turning once (allow 6 minutes total time for medium). Cover; keep warm. Repeat with remaining patties. For each serving, stack 2 meat patties on bottom half of each bun, spooning Tomato-Cucumber Relish between and atop patties. Top with bun tops. Makes 8 servings.

Tomato-Cucumber Relish: Combine ¼ cup *vinegar,* ¼ cup *water,* 2 tablespoons *sugar,* 1 teaspoon *salt,* and ⅛ teaspoon *pepper.* Add 1 medium *tomato,* chopped (1 cup); ½ unpeeled *cucumber,* thinly sliced; and 1 medium *onion,* chopped (½ cup). Cover and refrigerate 1 to 2 hours. Before serving, drain well; stir in ¼ cup chopped *sweet pickle.*

Spicy Apple-Pork Patties

1 beaten egg
⅓ cup cooked rice
¼ cup finely chopped onion
1 teaspoon salt
1 teaspoon worcestershire
   sauce
¾ teaspoon ground sage

1 pound ground pork
6 spiced apple rings
½ cup syrup from spiced apple
   rings
2 teaspoons cornstarch
¼ cup light corn syrup
1 tablespoon lemon juice

Combine egg, rice, onion, salt, worcestershire, and sage. Add ground pork; mix well. Shape into 6 patties; place in 13x9x2-inch baking pan. Press an apple ring into the top of each patty. Bake in 350° oven for 35 minutes. Meanwhile, in saucepan blend the ½ cup spiced syrup into cornstarch. Stir in corn syrup and lemon juice. Cook and stir till bubbly. Spoon onto meat. Bake 5 minutes more. Serve patties atop hot corn bread squares, if desired. Spoon sauce over patties. Serves 6.

Lamb Patties with Dill Sauce

6 slices bacon
1 beaten egg
¼ cup regular *or* quick-
   cooking rolled oats
¼ cup chopped onion
1½ pounds ground lamb
1 tablespoon chopped onion

1 tablespoon butter
2 tablespoons grated
   parmesan cheese
2 teaspoons all-purpose flour
½ teaspoon dried dillweed
½ teaspoon paprika
1 cup milk

Partially cook bacon, set aside. Combine egg, oats, the ¼ cup onion, 1 teaspoon *salt,* and dash *pepper.* Add lamb; mix well. Shape into 6 patties. Wrap a bacon slice around side of each patty; fasten with wooden pick. Place on unheated rack in broiler pan. Broil 5 inches from heat till desired doneness, turning once (allow 16 minutes total time for medium). Meanwhile, in saucepan cook the 1 tablespoon onion in butter till tender. Blend in parmesan, flour, dillweed, paprika, and ⅛ teaspoon *salt.* Add milk all at once. Cook and stir till bubbly; spoon over patties. Serves 6.

Ground meats, seasonings, and sauces shape up into various meat patty entrées, including Lamb Patties with Dill Sauce, Spicy Apple-Pork Patties, *and* Double-Decker Burgers.

Apricot-Ham Patties

2 beaten eggs
¾ cup milk
1½ cups soft bread crumbs
½ cup finely snipped dried apricots
¼ cup chopped onion

2 tablespoons snipped parsley
1 pound ground fully cooked ham
1 pound ground pork
⅓ cup packed brown sugar
1 teaspoon all-purpose flour

Combine eggs, milk, bread crumbs, dried apricots, onion, parsley, and dash *pepper*. Add ground ham and pork; mix well. Shape meat mixture into 8 patties. Combine brown sugar and flour; sprinkle in bottom of 15x10x1-inch baking pan. Place patties in pan. Bake in 350° oven for 40 to 45 minutes. Transfer patties to serving platter. Stir together the pan juices and spoon over meat. Makes 8 servings.

Veal Patties

1½ pounds ground veal
1 teaspoon lemon juice
½ teaspoon paprika
⅛ teaspoon ground nutmeg

1 beaten egg
2 tablespoons water
½ cup fine dry bread crumbs
2 tablespoons butter

Combine veal, lemon juice, paprika, nutmeg, 1 teaspoon *salt*, and dash *pepper*; mix well. Shape into 6 patties. Combine egg and water. Dip patties in egg mixture, then in bread crumbs. In large skillet melt butter. Add patties; cook over medium-high heat till desired doneness, turning once (allow 12 to 15 minutes total time for medium). Makes 6 servings.

Savory Lamb Burgers

⅓ cup milk
¾ cup soft bread crumbs
¼ cup chopped pimiento-stuffed olives
2 tablespoons finely chopped onion

1 tablespoon snipped parsley
¼ teaspoon dry mustard
1 pound ground lamb
1 tablespoon cooking oil
4 hamburger buns, split, toasted, and buttered

Combine milk, crumbs, olives, onion, parsley, mustard, ¼ teaspoon *salt*, and dash *pepper*. Add meat; mix well. Shape into 4 patties. Cook meat in hot oil over medium-high heat till desired doneness, turning once (allow 10 to 12 minutes total time for medium). Serve on buns. Serves 4.

Shaping patties may require a light touch, but it doesn't call for any sleight-of-hand. There's no secret to turning out uniform burgers every time when you start out with equal portions of meat. Just use a ⅓- or ½-cup measure or a large ice cream scoop to portion out the meat. You can also form the meat mixture in a roll 3 inches in diameter and cut in ½-inch slices. Or, pat out the meat mixture ½ inch thick between two sheets of waxed paper, then cut the burger with a giant cookie cutter. Use care, however, since a heavy hand will result in a burger with a compact texture.

Grilling Hamburgers Outdoors

Thickness	½ inch		¾ inch	
Temperature of Coals	Medium	Medium-hot	Medium	Medium-hot
	(approximate total time in minutes)			
Open Grill **Rare**	10 to 12	8 to 10	12 to 15	10 to 12
Medium	12 to 15	10 to 12	14 to 18	12 to 15
Covered Grill **Rare**	8 to 10	7 to 9	10 to 12	8 to 10
Medium	10 to 12	8 to 10	12 to 15	10 to 12

Shape the ground meat mixture in uniform patties (see tip, page 98). To estimate the temperature of the coals, hold your hand, palm side down, about 4 inches above the coals. Count the seconds "one thousand one, one thousand two," and so on. When you can hold your hand comfortably over the coals for only 2 to 3 seconds, the temperature is *medium-hot*; 3 to 4 seconds indicates *medium*. Grill the burgers for about half of the time indicated in the chart for the desired doneness. Then turn and grill till the burgers are done.

Taco Burgers

1 beaten egg
½ cup crushed corn chips
1 1¼-ounce envelope taco
    seasoning mix
1 pound ground beef
1 8-ounce can tomato sauce

4 hamburger buns, split,
    toasted, and buttered
1 large tomato, sliced
1 cup shredded lettuce
½ cup shredded sharp
    cheddar cheese

Combine egg, corn chips, *half* of the taco seasoning mix, and ¼ cup *water*. Add ground beef; mix well. Shape into four ½-inch-thick patties. Grill over *medium* coals, till desired doneness, turning once (allow 12 to 15 minutes total time for medium). Combine tomato sauce and the remaining taco seasoning mix. Serve patties on buns; top with some of the tomato sauce mixture. Pass tomato slices, lettuce, and cheese. Makes 4 servings.

Sour Cream-Onion Burgers

½ cup sour cream dip with
    onion
3 tablespoons fine dry bread
    crumbs

¼ teaspoon salt
1 pound ground beef
4 hamburger buns, split,
    toasted, and buttered

Combine sour cream dip, bread crumbs, salt, and dash *pepper*. Add meat; mix well. Shape into four ½-inch-thick patties. Grill over *medium* coals (*or* broil 3 to 4 inches from heat source) till desired doneness, turning once (allow 12 to 15 minutes total time for medium). Serve in buns. Makes 4.

Dilly Burgers

1 cup frozen hash brown potatoes with added onion and peppers	1 4½-ounce can deviled ham
	¼ teaspoon salt
	1 pound ground beef
1 tablespoon butter *or* margarine	½ cup dairy sour cream
	½ teaspoon dried dillweed

In small skillet cook potatoes in butter till browned. Transfer to bowl; stir in the deviled ham and salt. Add ground beef; mix well. Shape into 4 patties. Grill over *medium-hot* coals to desired doneness, turning once (allow about 10 minutes total for medium). Combine sour cream and dillweed; spoon some atop each burger. Serve on split and toasted hamburger buns, if desired. Makes 4 sandwiches.

Pinwheel Burgers

2 cups chopped fresh mushrooms (5 ounces)	1 beaten egg
½ cup finely chopped green pepper	1 teaspoon salt
	1½ pounds ground beef
¼ cup finely chopped onion	6 hamburger buns, split,
3 tablespoons butter	toasted, and buttered

In skillet cook mushrooms, green pepper, and onion in hot butter till vegetables are tender but not brown. Set aside. Combine egg and salt. Add meat; mix well. Roll or pat mixture into a 10x4-inch rectangle. Spread vegetable mixture over meat. Roll up jelly roll-style, starting from narrow end. Seal edges. Cover; chill one hour. Cut meat roll crosswise in 6 slices; place in wire grill basket. Grill over *medium-hot* coals to desired doneness, turning once (allow about 10 minutes total for medium). Serve on buns. Makes 6 sandwiches.

Burgers Florentine

A light and lively sauce plus a spinach filling highlight this low-calorie burger. Just 266 calories come with this meal-in-one patty.

1 10-ounce package frozen chopped spinach	1 teaspoon salt
	2 pounds lean ground beef
½ cup small curd cream-style cottage cheese (4 ounces)	½ of an 8-ounce can (½ cup) tomato sauce
1 tablespoon snipped parsley	¼ cup dry red wine
Dash salt	2 tablespoons chopped green pepper
1 beaten egg	
⅓ cup fine dry bread crumbs	2 tablespoons chopped onion

Cook spinach according to package directions; drain well. Stir in cottage cheese, parsley, and the dash salt; set aside.

Combine egg, bread crumbs, and the 1 teaspoon salt; add ground beef and mix well. On waxed paper, form meat mixture into 16 thin patties, each 3 inches in diameter. Place about 2 tablespoons spinach filling atop 8 of the patties; top with remaining patties and seal edges. In 12-inch skillet brown half the filled patties at a time, turning once. (If necessary, press patties at edges to reseal while cooking on first side.) Set patties aside. Drain off excess fat.

In same skillet combine tomato sauce, wine, green pepper, and onion. Return burgers to skillet; spoon some sauce atop. Cover; simmer 15 to 20 minutes. Remove burgers to serving platter; top with sauce. (If desired, boil sauce down to thicken.) Makes 8 servings.

Pita Burgers are a refreshing change from the usual burger-in-a-bun. Flat pita bread rounds are sometimes sold in the refrigerator or freezer counter as well as with the fresh bread.

Pita Burgers

2 cups shredded lettuce
1 medium cucumber, seeded
 and finely chopped
1 8-ounce carton plain yogurt
1 tablespoon sesame seed,
 toasted
1½ pounds ground beef *or*
 lamb
½ cup chopped onion

1 clove garlic, minced
1 teaspoon salt
1 teaspoon dried oregano,
 crushed
½ teaspoon dried basil,
 crushed
¼ teaspoon dried rosemary,
 crushed
6 pita bread rounds

Stir together lettuce, cucumber, yogurt, and sesame seed; set aside. Combine meat, onion, garlic, salt, oregano, basil, and rosemary; mix well. Shape into 6 thin patties, each 5 inches in diameter. Grill over *medium* coals (or broil 3 to 4 inches from heat source) to desired doneness, turning once (allow about 5 minutes total for medium). Split bread to make a pocket; place cooked meat patty inside. Spoon in lettuce mixture. Makes 6.

Meat Loaf Supreme

1 cup shredded carrot
1 cup crushed saltine
   crackers (20 crackers)
1 cup dairy sour cream
¼ cup chopped onion

1 teaspoon salt
Dash pepper
1 pound ground beef
1 pound ground pork

In bowl combine the carrot, crushed crackers, sour cream, onion, salt, and pepper. Add meats; mix well. Press into a 9x5x3-inch loaf pan. Bake in 350° oven for about 1½ hours. Let stand 10 minutes in pan for easier slicing. Makes 8 servings.

Colossal Cornburger

This Colossal Cornburger is actually a round meat loaf cooked on the grill.

1 beaten egg
1 cup whole kernel corn
½ cup coarsely crushed
   cheese crackers (8
   crackers)
¼ cup sliced green onion

¼ cup snipped parsley
1 teaspoon worcestershire
   sauce
½ teaspoon salt
½ teaspoon ground sage
2 pounds ground beef

In bowl combine the egg, corn, crackers, onion, parsley, worcestershire, salt, and sage; set aside. On sheets of waxed paper, pat half of the beef at a time to a 9-inch circle. Spoon corn mixture over one circle of meat to within 1 inch of edge. Top with second circle of meat; peel off top sheet of paper and seal edges of meat together. Invert meat onto wire grill basket; peel off remaining paper. Sprinkle with additional salt and pepper. Grill over *medium* coals to desired doneness, turning once (allow 25 to 30 minutes total time for medium). Cut in wedges. Serve with warmed catsup, if desired. Makes 6 servings.

Mexican Meat Loaf

1 beaten egg
½ cup tomato sauce
1 4-ounce can green chili
   peppers, rinsed, seeded,
   and chopped
1 3-ounce can chopped
   mushrooms, drained
⅓ cup fine dry bread crumbs

1 teaspoon salt
1 teaspoon chili powder
Dash pepper
1½ pounds lean ground beef
3 slices monterey jack
   cheese, quartered
   diagonally (3 ounces)

In bowl combine egg, tomato sauce, peppers, mushrooms, bread crumbs, salt, chili powder, and pepper. Add meat; mix well. Pat into an 8x4x2-inch loaf pan. Bake in 350° oven about 1¼ hours or till done. Let stand a few minutes then drain off excess fat. Top with cheese and return to oven to melt cheese. Let stand 10 minutes for easier slicing. Makes 6 servings.

Microwave cooking directions: Prepare meat mixture as above. Insert a 2-inch-diameter juice glass in the center of an 8-inch round nonmetal cake dish. Shape meat mixture in a ring around glass. Cover dish with waxed paper. In countertop microwave oven cook meat about 14 minutes, giving dish a quarter-turn 3 times during cooking. Remove juice glass; drain off fat. Top meat with cheese; micro-cook, uncovered, 45 to 60 seconds more. Let stand 10 minutes for easier slicing.

Elegant Meat Loaf Wellington

1 egg
¼ cup dry red wine
¼ cup water
2 cups soft bread crumbs
2 tablespoons finely chopped
  onion
1 teaspoon salt

1½ pounds lean ground beef
1 10-ounce package frozen
  patty shells, thawed
  (6 shells)
¼ cup canned liver spread
1 beaten egg
  Wine-Olive Sauce

In bowl combine the 1 egg, wine, and water; stir in bread crumbs, onion, and salt. Add beef; mix well. Pat into an 8x4x2-inch loaf pan. Bake in 350° oven for 40 minutes. Drain off excess fat. Remove meat from pan. Increase oven temperature to 400°.

On lightly floured surface, press 3 patty shells together; roll to a 10x6-inch rectangle, cutting and patching as needed. Place pastry rectangle in shallow baking pan. Carefully transfer meat loaf onto center of pastry. Spread top and sides of loaf with liver spread. Press remaining patty shells together. Roll to a 10x6-inch rectangle; place over meat. Brush edges of bottom pastry with some of the beaten egg. Seal top pastry to bottom, trimming and reserving edges. Cut decorations from trimmings; arrange atop loaf. Brush remaining beaten egg over all. Bake in 400° oven for 30 to 35 minutes. Serve with Wine-Olive Sauce. Makes 6 servings.

Wine-Olive Sauce: In saucepan melt 2 tablespoons *butter or margarine*. Blend in 4½ teaspoons *cornstarch*. Stir in 1 cup *condensed beef broth*; cook and stir till thickened and bubbly. Add ¼ cup *dry red wine* and ¼ cup sliced pitted *ripe olives*; simmer 5 minutes. Makes about 1⅓ cups.

Italian Meat Loaf

2 beaten eggs
¼ cup creamy Italian salad
  dressing
1½ cups soft bread crumbs
  (2 slices bread)
2 teaspoons instant minced
  onion
1½ teaspoons salt
1½ teaspoons Italian herb
  seasoning

¼ teaspoon pepper
2 pounds ground beef
1 cup shredded mozzarella
  cheese (4 ounces)
¼ cup snipped parsley
3 hard-cooked eggs
3 tablespoons creamy Italian
  salad dressing
1½ teaspoons prepared mustard
½ teaspoon sugar

In large bowl combine the beaten eggs, the ¼ cup salad dressing, the bread crumbs, onion, salt, herb seasoning, and pepper. Add meat; mix well. In a 12x7x2-inch baking dish, pat *half* of the meat mixture to a 9x4-inch rectangle. Top with *half* of the cheese and all the parsley, spreading to within 1 inch of all sides. Place hard-cooked eggs, end to end, lengthwise down center of meat.

On waxed paper, pat remaining meat to a 9x4-inch rectangle. Sprinkle remaining cheese to within 1 inch of all sides; press cheese into meat. Invert atop eggs. Remove paper. Shape meat mixture to form a loaf about 10 inches long; seal ends and sides well. Make shallow diagonal cuts in top of loaf to form diamond pattern.

Bake in 350° oven for 1 hour. Combine the 3 tablespoons salad dressing, the mustard, and sugar; drizzle over loaf. Bake about 15 minutes more or till done. Transfer to serving platter. Let stand 10 minutes for easier slicing. Makes 8 to 10 servings.

Lamb and Sausage Terrine

The term "terrine" refers to an earthenware dish that meat loaf-like mixtures are often cooked in.

8 slices bacon
2 cups cubed cooked lamb
½ small onion, cut up
½ clove garlic, minced
1 beaten egg
¼ cup milk
2 tablespoons brandy
¾ cup soft bread crumbs
¾ teaspoon salt
¼ teaspoon pepper
¼ teaspoon dried thyme, crushed
¼ teaspoon dried marjoram, crushed
1 pound bulk pork sausage
½ pound fully cooked ham, cut in thin slices
Leaf lettuce

Cook bacon till browned but not crisp; arrange crosswise across bottom and up sides of a 9x5x3-inch loaf pan. Grind lamb, onion, and garlic through fine blade of food chopper. In bowl combine egg, milk, and brandy; stir in bread crumbs, salt, pepper, thyme, and marjoram. Add ground lamb mixture and sausage; mix well. Pat about ⅓ of the meat mixture over bacon. Cover with half of the ham slices. Repeat layers ending with lamb mixture. Bake in 350° oven for 1¼ hours. Remove from oven; cover pan with foil. Place another 9x5x3-inch loaf pan or dish and a weight, such as a can of vegetables, on hot meat loaf. Let cool; chill at least 8 hours. Remove pan and weight; invert meat loaf onto lettuce-lined platter. If desired, garnish with parsley and cherry tomatoes. Serves 8 to 10.

Chutney Lamb Loaf

1 beaten egg
¾ cup soft bread crumbs (1 slice)
½ cup finely chopped onion
½ cup chopped chutney
¾ teaspoon celery salt
¼ teaspoon pepper
1½ pounds ground lamb

In bowl combine egg, bread crumbs, onion, chutney, celery salt, and pepper. Add lamb; mix well. Press meat mixture into an 8x4x2-inch loaf pan. Bake in 350° oven for 1 hour. Pour off excess fat; transfer meat loaf to serving platter. Serve with additional chutney, if desired. Makes 6 servings.

Pork Loaf with Olives

¼ cup finely chopped celery
¼ cup finely chopped onion
1 tablespoon cooking oil
2 beaten eggs
½ cup milk
2¼ cups soft bread crumbs (3 slices)
⅓ cup thinly sliced pimiento-stuffed olives
1 teaspoon salt
½ teaspoon dried oregano, crushed
1½ pounds ground pork
Cucumber Sauce

Cook celery and onion in hot oil about 10 minutes. Stir in eggs, milk, crumbs, olives, salt, oregano, and dash *pepper*. Add pork; mix well. Shape meat mixture into loaf shape in a 13x9x2-inch baking pan. Bake in 350° oven about 1¼ hours. Serve with chilled Cucumber Sauce. Serves 8.

Cucumber Sauce: Halve 1 medium unpeeled *cucumber;* scoop out seeds. Shred enough cucumber to make 1 cup; do not drain. Stir in ½ cup *dairy sour cream,* 1 tablespoon snipped *parsley,* 2 teaspoons grated *onion,* 2 teaspoons *vinegar,* ¼ teaspoon *salt,* and dash *pepper;* chill.

Elegant Lamb and Sausage Terrine is an excellent choice for the buffet table. The meat loaf-like mixture is baked ahead then chilled with a weight atop to form the compact loaf.

Mustard-Glazed Ham Loaf

3 beaten eggs
½ cup tomato juice
½ cup finely crushed saltine crackers (14 crackers)
2 tablespoons chopped onion
1 tablespoon prepared horseradish

½ teaspoon salt
⅛ teaspoon pepper
1½ pounds ground fully cooked ham
1 pound ground pork
Mustard Sauce

In bowl combine eggs and tomato juice; stir in cracker crumbs, onion, horseradish, salt, and pepper. Add ham and pork; mix well. In shallow baking dish shape meat mixture into a 9x5-inch loaf. Bake in 350° oven for 1¼ hours. Drain fat from ham loaf; pour Mustard Sauce over. Bake 30 minutes more, basting with sauce occasionally. Makes 8 to 10 servings.

Mustard Sauce: In bowl thoroughly combine ½ cup packed *brown sugar*, 2 tablespoons *vinegar*, and ½ teaspoon *dry mustard*.

Mini Apple-Ham Loaves

If you don't have the small fluted tube pans, use eight 6-ounce custard cups.

¾ cup finely chopped, peeled cooking apple
¼ cup chopped onion
2 tablespoons butter *or* margarine
2 beaten eggs
¼ cup milk
1 15-ounce can tomato sauce

¾ cup crushed rich round crackers (18 crackers)
1 pound ground fully cooked ham
1 pound ground pork
¼ cup packed brown sugar
1 teaspoon prepared horseradish

Cook apple and onion in hot butter till tender. Combine eggs, milk, and ¼ *cup* of the tomato sauce; stir in crackers and apple mixture. Add ham and pork; mix well. Pack mixture into six 4-inch individual fluted tube cups (six to a pan). Place on shallow baking pan. Bake in 350° oven about 30 minutes. Carefully invert pan onto shallow baking pan to remove loaves.

Combine the remaining tomato sauce, brown sugar, and horseradish; brush some over loaves. Bake 20 minutes more, basting meat several times with tomato mixture. Heat remaining sauce; pass with meat. Serves 6.

Ham-Yam Loaf

If you object to crunchy onion in your meat loaves, precook the onion in a little water or melted butter before adding.

2 beaten eggs
½ cup milk
½ cup finely chopped onion
½ cup crushed saltine crackers (14 crackers)
1 tablespoon horseradish mustard
1 pound ground pork

1 pound ground fully cooked ham
1 17-ounce can sweet potatoes, mashed
1 beaten egg
½ cup orange marmalade
½ teaspoon salt
⅛ teaspoon ground cloves

Combine the 2 eggs, milk, onion, crumbs, and mustard. Add meats; mix well. Pat *half* into a 9x9x2-inch baking pan. Combine sweet potatoes, remaining egg, *2 tablespoons* of the marmalade, salt, and cloves. Spread over meat layer in pan. Pat remaining meat mixture atop. Cover with foil; bake in 350° oven about 1 hour. Drain off excess fat. Spread with remaining marmalade. Bake, uncovered, about 30 minutes more. Makes 8 or 9 servings.

Raisin-Veal Loaf

This loaf is especially good chilled and sliced for sandwiches.

2 beaten eggs
¾ cup milk
1 cup quick-cooking rolled oats
1 cup raisins
½ cup finely chopped onion
2½ teaspoons salt
½ teaspoon poultry seasoning
¼ teaspoon pepper
2 pounds ground veal

In mixing bowl combine eggs, milk, oats, raisins, onion, salt, poultry seasoning, and pepper. Add veal; mix well. Turn mixture into an 8x4x2-inch loaf pan shaping to round top. Bake in 350° oven for about 1½ hours. Let stand 5 minutes before turning out of pan. Makes 8 to 10 servings.

Meat Loaf Potato Splits

Use your favorite firm cheese in these hot-potato-meat loaf sandwiches. Try mozzarella, Swiss, cheddar, or American for starters.

4 large baking potatoes
¼ cup butter, softened
½ teaspoon salt
½ teaspoon Italian herb seasoning
3 slices cooked meat loaf cut ½-inch-thick and quartered
3 slices cheese, quartered
Grated parmesan cheese

Scrub potatoes; prick skin with fork and bake in 425° oven for 1 hour. Reduce oven temperature to 350°. Blend together butter, salt, and Italian seasoning. Cut each potato crosswise in fourths. Place each potato on piece of foil large enough to wrap potato. Spread butter mixture on cut surfaces of potato. Sandwich meat and cheese quarters between cut edges of potatoes. Sprinkle some parmesan over each potato. Bring edges of foil together; seal securely. Bake in 350° oven 10 minutes more or till meat is hot and cheese starts to melt. Makes 4 servings.

Microwave cooking directions: Scrub potatoes; prick skin with fork. In countertop microwave oven arrange potatoes on paper toweling, leaving at least 1 inch between potatoes. Micro-cook, uncovered, 6 minutes; turn potatoes over and rearrange. Micro-cook 7 to 9 minutes more or till done. Cut each potato crosswise in fourths. Place each potato on piece of waxed paper large enough to wrap potato. Blend butter, salt, and Italian seasoning; spread on cut surfaces of potatoes. Sandwich meat and cheese quarters between cut edges of potatoes. Sprinkle parmesan atop. Bring edges of waxed paper together; fold securely. Micro-cook 1½ to 2 minutes more or till meat is hot and cheese starts to melt.

These standards are enforced in stores that grind meat under federal inspection or buy from an inspected processor. Specific state and local laws may also require these standards.

Ground beef labels *indicate the percentage of lean meat to fat. According to standards set up by the meat industry (see page 166), all ground beef should contain at least 70% lean meat. To allow for variation, labels are written "ground beef, not less than X% lean." Other requirements are that ground beef contain exclusively beef and use no other meat trimmings; and that it contain only skeletal meat (no variety meats). Oftentime, it is additionally labeled as ground (beef) chuck, ground (beef) round, or ground (beef) sirloin to indicate that all of the meat so labeled was from a specific cut. Ground round is the most lean, followed by ground sirloin, and ground chuck.*

Mexican Beef in Corn Bread *may look complicated but it's not: the corn bread-ground meat mixture bakes together as one. Top with the* Tangy Tomato Sauce.

Mexican Beef in Corn Bread

1 pound ground beef
⅓ cup chopped onion
1 clove garlic, minced
¼ cup catsup
¾ teaspoon salt

1 10-ounce package corn
   bread mix
½ cup shredded American
   cheese (2 ounces)
Tangy Tomato Sauce

Cook beef, onion, and garlic till meat is browned; drain. Stir in catsup and salt. Prepare corn bread batter according to package directions; spread *half* in a greased 8x8x2-inch baking pan. Spoon beef mixture atop; sprinkle with cheese. Spread remaining batter over. Bake in 350° oven 30 to 35 minutes. Let stand 5 minutes. Cut in squares; top with Tangy Tomato Sauce. Serves 6.

Tangy Tomato Sauce: Blend 2 tablespoons *cold water* into 2 teaspoons *cornstarch.* Stir in one 8-ounce can *tomatoes;* 2 tablespoons chopped, seeded, rinsed canned *green chili peppers;* 2 tablespoons chopped *green pepper;* and 1 teaspoon *worcestershire sauce.* Cook and stir till thickened.

Beef Crepes Florentine

1 10-ounce package frozen
chopped spinach
½ pound ground beef
½ pound bulk pork sausage
½ cup chopped onion
1 clove garlic, minced
½ teaspoon salt
2 slightly beaten eggs
1¼ cups milk

1 tablespoon cooking oil
1 cup all-purpose flour
1 15-ounce can tomato sauce
2 teaspoons sugar
1 teaspoon dried thyme,
crushed
1 cup shredded sharp
American cheese
(4 ounces)

If desired, make the crepes ahead of time and freeze for up to 4 months. Stack the unfilled crepes, placing 2 sheets of waxed paper between the crepes. Overwrap the stack in a moisture-vaporproof bag and place in a glass or plastic container. To use remove as many crepes as you need, then reseal the bag and return remaining crepes to freezer. Thaw at room temperature about 1 hour before using.

Cook spinach according to package directions; drain well. In skillet cook ground beef, pork sausage, onion, and garlic till meat is browned. Drain off excess fat. Stir in drained spinach and salt; set aside.

For crepes, in bowl combine eggs, milk, and oil; add flour. Beat with rotary beater till smooth. Lightly grease a 6-inch skillet; heat. Remove from heat. Spoon 2 tablespoons batter into skillet; lift and tilt skillet to spread batter. Return to heat; brown crepe on one side only. Invert over paper toweling; remove crepe. Repeat with remaining batter to make a total of 14 to 18 crepes.

Spoon about 3 tablespoons meat-spinach mixture down center of un-browned side of each crepe; roll up. Place seam side down in a greased 13x9x2-inch baking dish. Combine tomato sauce, sugar, and thyme; pour over crepes. Bake, covered, in 350° oven for 25 to 30 minutes. Uncover; sprinkle cheese atop. Bake 3 minutes more or till cheese melts. Serves 6.

Ham Omelet Roll

¼ cup butter *or* margarine
½ cup all-purpose flour
½ teaspoon salt
⅛ teaspoon white pepper
2 cups milk
5 egg yolks
5 egg whites
2 tablespoons chopped onion

1 tablespoon butter *or*
margarine
1 cup ground fully cooked
ham
2 tablespoons dairy sour
cream
1 teaspoon dijon-style
mustard

Grease a 13x9x2-inch baking pan, line with waxed paper, and grease again. Dust lightly with a little flour. In saucepan melt the ¼ cup butter or margarine; blend in ½ cup flour, salt, and pepper. Add milk all at once; cook and stir till thickened and bubbly. Remove from heat.

Beat egg yolks on high speed of electric mixer for about 6 minutes or till thick and lemon-colored. Gradually add milk mixture to yolks; stir constantly. Cool about 5 minutes. Wash beaters; beat egg whites to stiff peaks (tips stand straight). Fold egg whites into cooled yolk mixture; pour into prepared pan, spreading evenly. Bake in 400° oven for 25 to 30 minutes or till puffed and browned.

Meanwhile, in small skillet cook chopped onion in 1 tablespoon butter or margarine till tender but not brown. Stir in ham, sour cream, and mustard. Heat through over low heat; keep warm.

When egg mixture is done, immediately remove from oven and turn out onto clean towel. Remove waxed paper. Spread egg mixture with ham mixture. Roll up jelly roll-style, beginning with long side and using towel to help roll. Transfer to serving plate, seam side down, and slice. Makes 6 servings.

Pork-Noodle Casserole

1 pound ground pork
1 small onion, chopped
1 16-ounce can stewed
   tomatoes
4 ounces medium noodles,
   cooked and drained
1 12-ounce can whole kernel
   corn, drained

1 6-ounce can tomato paste
1 teaspoon salt
1 teaspoon chili powder
¼ teaspoon garlic powder
   Dash pepper
1 cup shredded cheddar
   cheese

In 10-inch skillet cook meat and onion till meat is browned and onion is tender; drain off excess fat. Stir in undrained tomatoes, noodles, corn, tomato paste, salt, chili powder, garlic powder, and pepper. Turn into ungreased 1½-quart casserole; cover. Bake in 350° oven for 40 minutes or till heated through. Sprinkle with shredded cheese. Bake, uncovered, 5 minutes more or till cheese melts. Makes 6 servings.

Individual Ham Souffles

¼ cup finely chopped onion
¼ cup finely chopped green
   pepper
1 tablespoon cooking oil
2½ cups ground fully cooked
   ham

1 17-ounce can sweet
   potatoes, mashed
1 5⅓-ounce can (⅔ cup)
   evaporated milk
3 well-beaten egg yolks
   Dash pepper
3 egg whites

In saucepan cook onion and green pepper in hot oil till tender but not brown. Stir in ham, sweet potatoes, evaporated milk, egg yolks, and pepper. Beat egg whites till stiff peaks form; fold into ham mixture. Spoon mixture into five 1-cup souffle dishes (or into seven 6-ounce custard cups). Place on baking sheet. Bake in 350° oven for 45 to 50 minutes or till done. Makes 5 servings.

Hearty Mexican Casserole

1 pound ground beef
1 small onion, chopped
   (¼ cup)
1 cup water
¼ cup bottled taco sauce
1 1¼-ounce envelope taco
   seasoning mix
¼ teaspoon salt

¾ cup finely chopped fully
   cooked ham
1 10-ounce package frozen
   chopped spinach
   Cooking oil
12 corn tortillas
1 cup dairy sour cream
1 cup shredded monterey
   jack cheese (4 ounces)

In skillet cook beef and onion till beef is browned and onion is tender. Drain off excess fat. Stir in water, taco sauce, *dry* taco mix, and salt. Stir in ham. Top mixture with frozen spinach. Cover and cook till spinach thaws, breaking up spinach block with a fork. Simmer, covered, for 5 minutes more. In small skillet heat some oil. Dip tortillas, one at a time, into hot oil 5 to 10 seconds or till soft and limp. Drain on paper toweling.

Spoon about ⅓ cup meat mixture down center of each tortilla; roll up. Place, seam side down, in a greased 13x9x2-inch baking dish. Bake, covered, in 350° oven for 30 to 35 minutes. Uncover; spread sour cream over tortillas. Sprinkle cheese over all. Return to oven for 5 to 10 minutes to heat sour cream and melt cheese. Makes 6 servings.

Ground Beef Curry with Custard Topping

2 pounds ground beef
1 cup chopped onion
2 tablespoons curry powder
1½ cups soft bread crumbs
½ cup milk
2 beaten eggs
½ cup raisins
½ cup chopped blanched
    almonds

2 tablespoons vinegar
4 bay leaves, crumbled
1 tablespoon sugar
1 teaspoon salt
⅛ teaspoon pepper
3 beaten eggs
⅔ cup milk
⅛ teaspoon salt
Dash pepper

In large skillet cook ground beef, onion, and curry till meat is browned. Drain off excess fat. Remove from heat. Stir in bread crumbs, the ½ cup milk, the 2 eggs, the raisins, almonds, vinegar, bay leaves, sugar, the 1 teaspoon salt, and the ⅛ teaspoon pepper. Press mixture into a 9x9x2-inch baking pan. Combine the 3 eggs, the ⅔ cup milk, ⅛ teaspoon salt, and dash pepper; beat just till blended. Slowly pour over top of meat mixture. Bake in 350° oven for 45 minutes or till top is set and lightly browned. Makes 8 servings.

Moussaka

2 medium eggplants (1½ to
    2 pounds total)
½ pound ground beef
½ pound ground lamb
1 cup chopped onion
⅓ cup tomato paste
¼ cup snipped parsley
¼ cup dry red wine
¼ cup water
2 beaten eggs
¼ cup grated parmesan cheese
¼ cup fine dry bread crumbs
¾ teaspoon salt
½ teaspoon ground cinnamon

⅛ teaspoon pepper
¼ cup butter *or* margarine
¼ cup all-purpose flour
¼ teaspoon salt
    Dash ground nutmeg
2 cups milk
2 beaten egg yolks
2 tablespoons lemon juice
    Cooking oil
¼ cup fine dry bread crumbs
2 tablespoons grated
    parmesan cheese
1 tablespoon butter *or*
    margarine, melted

Peel eggplants; cut crosswise into ¾-inch-thick slices. Sprinkle slices with a little salt; set aside. In skillet cook ground meats and onion till meat is browned and onion is tender; drain off excess fat. Stir in tomato paste, parsley, wine, and water. Simmer, uncovered, for 5 minutes; cool. Stir in the 2 eggs, the ¼ cup cheese, the ¼ cup bread crumbs, the ¾ teaspoon salt, the cinnamon, and pepper; set aside.

In medium saucepan melt the ¼ cup butter or margarine; blend in flour, ¼ teaspoon salt, nutmeg, and a dash *pepper*. Add milk; cook and stir till thickened and bubbly. Stir about 1 cup of the hot mixture into egg yolks. Return all to saucepan; cook and stir 2 minutes more. Remove from heat; gradually stir in lemon juice. Set aside.

In large skillet brown eggplant slices in hot oil, about 1½ minutes on each side. Drain on paper toweling. Grease a 12x7½x2-inch baking dish; sprinkle bottom with *2 tablespoons* of remaining crumbs. Layer with *half* of the eggplant. Pour all the meat mixture over; top with remaining eggplant. Pour milk mixture over all. Bake, covered, in 350° oven 45 minutes. Combine remaining crumbs, the 2 tablespoons cheese, and the 1 tablespoon melted butter; sprinkle over moussaka. Bake 15 minutes more. Serves 6.

Taco Casserole

1 pound ground beef
½ teaspoon garlic salt
1 9½-ounce package (6 cups) corn chips

4 or 5 slices American cheese
2 cups shredded lettuce
Homemade Taco Sauce

In skillet cook ground beef till browned. Drain off excess fat. Stir in garlic salt. Coarsely crush corn chips; place in an 8x8x2-inch baking dish or an 8x1½-inch round baking dish. Spoon hot meat over corn chips; top with cheese slices. Bake in 350° oven 10 to 12 minutes or till heated through and cheese melts. Sprinkle casserole with shredded lettuce; spoon or pour on Homemade Taco Sauce. Makes 4 to 6 servings.

Homemade Taco Sauce: In bowl stir together one 16-ounce can stewed *tomatoes,* undrained; 1 teaspoon *sugar;* ¾ teaspoon dried *oregano,* crushed; ½ teaspoon *worcestershire sauce;* ¼ teaspoon *salt;* ¼ teaspoon bottled *hot pepper sauce;* and ⅛ teaspoon *pepper.* Using edge of spoon, break up large tomato pieces. Stir in ¼ cup chopped *green pepper* and ¼ cup chopped *onion.*

Spanish Rice Skillet

1 pound ground beef
3 slices bacon, chopped
1 medium onion, chopped
¼ cup chopped green pepper
1 16-ounce can tomatoes, cut up
2 cups water

1 cup long grain rice
½ cup chili sauce
1 teaspoon salt
1 teaspoon worcestershire sauce
⅛ teaspoon pepper

In skillet cook beef, bacon, onion, and green pepper till meat is browned and vegetables are tender. Drain off excess fat. Stir in *undrained* tomatoes, water, *uncooked* rice, chili sauce, salt, worcestershire, and pepper. Bring to boil; reduce heat. Simmer, covered, 25 to 30 minutes or till liquid is absorbed and rice is tender. Makes 6 servings.

Sweet-Sour Beef 'n Cabbage

1½ pounds ground beef
½ cup chopped onion
½ cup sliced celery
½ cup chopped green pepper
2 tablespoons quick-cooking rolled oats
2 tablespoons snipped parsley
¾ teaspoon salt

¼ teaspoon garlic powder
⅛ teaspoon pepper
1 medium head cabbage
1 15-ounce can tomato sauce
¼ cup cider vinegar
3 tablespoons brown sugar
½ teaspoon salt
Dash pepper

In skillet cook ground beef, onion, celery, and green pepper till meat is browned; drain off excess fat. Sprinkle meat mixture with oats, parsley, the ¾ teaspoon salt, the garlic powder, and the ⅛ teaspoon pepper.

Core cabbage; cut in six wedges. Place atop meat. In bowl combine tomato sauce, vinegar, brown sugar, the ½ teaspoon salt, and the dash pepper; mix well. Pour over cabbage and meat. Simmer, covered, 15 to 20 minutes or till cabbage is tender. Serve at once. Makes 6 servings.

Sweet-Sour Beef 'n Cabbage is a quick and easy main dish. Since the cooked cabbage tends to water out (and so thin the sauce), it is best served as soon as it's ready.

Vegetable Burger Cups

1 beaten egg
¼ cup milk
⅓ cup coarsely crushed
    saltine crackers
    (9 crackers)
½ of a 1½-ounce envelope
    (2 tablespoons) sloppy
    joe seasoning mix
    Dash salt
1 pound lean ground beef
2 medium carrots, thinly
    sliced

1 cup fresh *or* frozen peas
¾ cup water
¼ cup chopped onion
½ teaspoon instant beef
    bouillon granules
    Dash pepper
¼ cup cold water
1 tablespoon all-purpose
    flour
½ cup shredded American
    cheese (2 ounces)

Combine egg, milk, crackers, seasoning mix, and salt. Add beef; mix well. On four squares of waxed paper, shape meat into four 5-inch patties. Press each over an inverted 6-ounce custard cup; peel off paper (leave meat on cups). Bake in shallow baking pan in 375° oven about 20 minutes.

Meanwhile, in saucepan combine carrots, peas, ¾ cup water, onion, bouillon granules, and pepper. Cook, covered, about 10 minutes or till vegetables are tender. Blend ¼ cup cold water into flour; stir into vegetables. Cook and stir till thickened and bubbly. Stir in cheese till melted. Carefully remove hot meat from custard cups. Arrange on serving platter; spoon vegetable sauce into meat cups. Garnish with raw onion rings and parsley sprigs, if desired. Makes 4 servings.

Microwave cooking directions: Prepare beef mixture; shape over custard cups as above. Place inverted cups in a 12x7½x2-inch nonmetal baking dish. Cover; set aside. In 1-quart nonmetal casserole combine carrots, peas, ¾ cup water, onion, bouillon granules, and pepper. Cook, covered with waxed paper, in countertop microwave oven about 10 minutes or till vegetables are tender; stir once. Blend ¼ cup cold water into flour; stir into vegetables. Micro-cook, uncovered, 1 minute. Stir in cheese till melted. Cover; set aside. Micro-cook meat cups, covered, 3 minutes; give dish a half turn. Micro-cook, covered, 2 minutes more or till almost done. Lift meat cups from custard cups; place on serving platter. Fill with vegetable sauce. Micro-cook, uncovered, 1 to 2 minutes or till hot.

Eggplant Roll-Ups

2 large eggplants, peeled
2 beaten eggs
⅓ cup milk
2¼ cups soft bread crumbs
⅓ cup grated parmesan cheese
2 teaspoons dried basil,
    crushed

1 teaspoon salt
¼ teaspoon pepper
⅛ teaspoon garlic powder
2½ pounds ground lamb *or*
    beef
1 32-ounce jar spaghetti
    sauce

Cut each eggplant lengthwise into twelve ¼-inch-thick slices. Cook, 8 slices at a time, in large amount of boiling salted water 3 to 4 minutes. Remove carefully; drain on paper toweling and cool. Combine eggs, milk, crumbs, cheese, and seasonings. Add *2 pounds* of the meat; mix well. Divide into 24 portions; place one in center of each eggplant slice. Wrap eggplant around meat. Place, seam side down, in a 17x12x2-inch baking pan. Brown remaining ½ pound meat; drain. Stir in spaghetti sauce; spoon over eggplant. Bake, covered, in 350° oven for 30 minutes. Uncover; bake 30 to 40 minutes more. Serve over hot cooked spaghetti, if desired. Serves 12.

Stuffed Peppers Sicilian

3 medium green peppers
3 tablespoons chopped
    onion
2 tablespoons chopped celery
1 small clove garlic, minced
1 tablespoon cooking oil

½ pound ground veal *or* beef
¼ cup canned tomato puree
¼ teaspoon salt
⅛ teaspoon pepper
1 tablespoon grated
    parmesan cheese

Slice tops from green peppers; chop tops. Scoop seeds and membrane out of pepper shells. Cook chopped green pepper, onion, celery, and garlic in hot oil till tender. Add meat; cook till browned. Drain off excess fat. Stir in tomato puree, salt, and pepper. Sprinkle a little salt inside pepper shells. Spoon in meat mixture; sprinkle with cheese. Place in shallow baking dish. Bake in 350° oven about 35 minutes. Makes 3 servings.

Beef-Stuffed Tomatoes

4 large ripe tomatoes
½ pound ground beef
1 clove garlic, minced
2 tablespoons snipped
    parsley
2 tablespoons grated
    parmesan cheese
½ teaspoon dried oregano,
    crushed

¼ teaspoon salt
¼ teaspoon dried thyme,
    crushed
⅛ teaspoon pepper
½ cup soft bread crumbs
1 tablespoon butter *or*
    margarine, melted

Cut tops from tomatoes. Scoop out centers; chop centers. Invert shells to drain. Cook beef and garlic till beef is browned. Drain off excess fat. Stir in chopped tomato, parsley, parmesan, oregano, salt, thyme, and pepper. Sprinkle a little salt inside tomato shells; place in shallow baking dish. Spoon in meat mixture. Combine crumbs and butter or margarine; sprinkle over meat. Bake in 375° oven for 20 to 25 minutes. Serves 4.

Lamb-Stuffed Grape Leaves

1 beaten egg
½ cup long grain rice
1 small onion, finely chopped
¼ cup snipped parsley
¼ cup snipped fresh mint
    leaves
¾ teaspoon salt
    Dash pepper

1 pound ground lamb
48 fresh *or* canned grape
    leaves
2 cups water
2 tablespoons butter *or*
    margarine
1 teaspoon salt
    Egg-Lemon Sauce

Combine egg, rice, onion, parsley, mint, the ¾ teaspoon salt, and pepper. Add lamb; mix well. Rinse grape leaves; drain and open flat. Place a rounded teaspoon meat mixture in center of each grape leaf. Fold in sides and roll up. Place in 3-quart saucepan, side by side, in layers. Add water, butter or margarine, and the 1 teaspoon salt. Press down with heatproof plate that fits inside saucepan. Cover and simmer about 45 minutes. Drain, reserving 1 cup of the broth for Egg-Lemon Sauce. Serve warm stuffed grape leaves with Egg-Lemon Sauce. Makes 4 servings.

Egg-Lemon Sauce: Beat 1 *egg white* to stiff peaks. Beat 1 *egg yolk* about 4 minutes or till thick and lemon-colored. Fold egg white into yolk. Slowly stir in 2 tablespoons *lemon juice*. Gradually add the 1 cup reserved broth. Cook and stir over low heat about 5 minutes or till slightly thickened and smooth. Season to taste with salt and pepper.

Pinwheel Ham

1½ cups packaged biscuit mix
⅓ cup yellow cornmeal
2 teaspoons sesame seed
½ cup milk
2 cups ground fully cooked
   ham (12 ounces)

1 4-ounce can chopped
   mushrooms, drained
1 cup dairy sour cream
2 tablespoons milk
1 to 2 tablespoons prepared
   horseradish

Combine biscuit mix, cornmeal, and sesame seed; add the ½ cup milk. Stir with fork just till dough follows fork around bowl. On lightly floured surface knead dough 10 to 12 times. Roll or pat to a 13x9-inch rectangle. Combine ham, mushrooms, and ⅓ *cup* of the sour cream; spread evenly over dough. Roll up jelly roll-style, beginning at long end; seal. Form into a ring, seam side down, on greased baking sheet; seal ends together. Make cuts at 1-inch intervals almost to center; pull sections apart and twist slightly. Bake in 400° oven for 25 to 30 minutes or till browned.

Meanwhile, combine the remaining ⅔ cup sour cream, the 2 tablespoons milk, and horseradish; mix well. Pass with meat. Makes 6 servings.

Picnic Ham Packages

1 package piecrust mix
   (for 2-crust pie)
2 cups ground fully cooked
   ham (12 ounces)
½ of a 10¾-ounce can (⅔ cup)
   condensed cream of celery
   soup
2 tablespoons catsup

2 tablespoons snipped
   parsley
1 teaspoon minced dried
   onion
1 teaspoon prepared mustard
3 slices American cheese,
   halved diagonally
3 hard-cooked eggs, sliced

Prepare piecrust mix according to package directions. On lightly floured surface roll to ¹/₁₆-inch thickness. Cut in six 7- or 7½-inch circles. Combine ham, soup, catsup, parsley, onion, and mustard; spread about ⅓ cup on half of each dough circle. Top each with cheese half and a few egg slices. Fold other half of dough over filling; seal edges with tines of fork. Prick top with fork. Bake on ungreased baking sheet in 375° oven about 40 minutes or till golden; cool and chill. Makes 6 sandwiches.

Hearty Beef Turnovers

½ pound ground beef
1 8-ounce can pizza sauce
½ teaspoon minced dried
   onion
¼ teaspoon salt
2 cups all-purpose flour

4 teaspoons baking powder
½ teaspoon salt
⅓ cup shortening
⅔ cup milk
1 cup cream-style cottage
   cheese, drained

In skillet cook meat till browned; drain off excess fat. Stir in pizza sauce, onion, and the ¼ teaspoon salt. Simmer 5 minutes; cool. Combine flour, baking powder, and the ½ teaspoon salt. Cut in shortening till mixture resembles coarse crumbs. Add milk; stir just till blended.

On floured surface roll dough to a 16x12-inch rectangle. Cut into six 8x4-inch rectangles. Spread 2 rounded tablespoons cottage cheese over half of each rectangle; top each with 3 tablespoons meat mixture. Fold over other half of rectangle to form a square; seal edges with tines of fork. Place on baking sheet. Cut slits in top for escape of steam. Bake in 400° oven for 17 to 20 minutes. Makes 6 servings.

Confetti Hamburger Salad

⅓ cup water
2 tablespoons white wine vinegar
1 0.7-ounce envelope cheese-garlic salad dressing mix
1 15½-ounce can red kidney beans, drained
1 8-ounce can whole kernel corn, drained
2 tablespoons sliced green onion
6 cups torn mixed salad greens
½ cup coarsely shredded carrot
1 pound ground beef
2 tablespoons snipped parsley
1 tablespoon white wine vinegar
3 hard-cooked eggs, cut in wedges

Blend water and the 2 tablespoons wine vinegar into *4 teaspoons* of the salad dressing mix. Add beans, corn, and green onion, stirring to coat. Cover and chill at least 2 hours, stirring several times. Line a large salad bowl with some of the salad greens. Toss together remaining greens and carrot; add to salad bowl. Cover and chill.

At serving time, brown ground beef in skillet; drain meat, reserving 2 tablespoons drippings. Stir parsley, the 1 tablespoon wine vinegar, and the remaining salad dressing mix into meat and reserved drippings; heat through. Combine salad greens, bean mixture, and beef mixture. Garnish with egg wedges. Toss gently and serve. Makes 6 servings.

Italian Soup

For beef stock recipe, see page 168. Or use 1 teaspoon instant beef bouillon granules dissolved in 1 cup hot water for each cup of beef stock. If using bouillon granules, you may wish to reduce the 1 teaspoon salt added to the soup and season to taste.

1 pound ground pork
1 teaspoon fennel seed, crushed
1 teaspoon garlic powder
½ teaspoon chili powder
¼ teaspoon salt
¼ teaspoon freshly ground black pepper
4 slices bacon
2 cups chopped onion
1 teaspoon salt
½ teaspoon garlic salt
6 cups beef stock
1 teaspoon dried oregano, crushed
4 medium potatoes, peeled and chopped (3 cups)
1 10-ounce package frozen chopped spinach

In bowl combine pork, fennel seed, garlic powder, chili powder, the ¼ teaspoon salt, and the pepper; mix well. Cover and refrigerate several hours or overnight to allow flavors to blend.

In Dutch oven cook bacon till crisp; drain, reserving drippings. Crumble bacon and set aside. Cook pork mixture, chopped onion, 1 teaspoon salt, and garlic salt in bacon drippings for 8 to 10 minutes or till meat is browned and onion is tender. Drain off excess fat. Add beef stock and oregano. Bring to boiling. Cover; reduce heat and simmer 30 minutes. Add chopped potatoes and frozen spinach. Return to boiling. Simmer, covered, 15 to 20 minutes more or till potatoes are tender. Garnish with crumbled bacon. Makes 8 to 10 servings.

Crockery cooker directions: Prepare and cook pork mixture and bacon as above; drain. Crumble bacon; set aside. In electric slow crockery cooker combine pork mixture, *only 3 cups* beef stock, oregano, and potatoes. Cover and cook on low-heat setting 8 to 10 hours (or on high-heat setting about 4 hours). Thaw spinach; drain and stir into soup. Turn to high-heat setting; cook, covered, about 15 minutes. Add bacon.

Spaghetti Pie *boasts a layer of cottage cheese plus a mozzarella topping. For a more spicy filling, substitute bulk pork or Italian sausage for the ground beef.*

Spaghetti Pie

6 ounces spaghetti
2 tablespoons butter
⅓ cup grated parmesan cheese
2 beaten eggs
1 cup cream-style
   cottage cheese
1 pound ground beef
½ cup chopped onion
¼ cup chopped green pepper

1 8-ounce can tomatoes
1 6-ounce can tomato paste
1 teaspoon sugar
1 teaspoon dried oregano,
   crushed
½ teaspoon garlic salt
½ cup shredded mozzarella
   cheese (2 ounces)

Cook spaghetti; drain. Toss with butter; stir in parmesan and eggs. Press into greased 10-inch pie plate. Top with cottage cheese. Cook meat, onion, and pepper till meat is browned; drain. Stir in remaining ingredients *except* mozzarella; heat through. Spoon over cottage cheese. Bake in 350° oven about 20 minutes. Top with mozzarella. Bake 5 minutes. Serves 6.

Creole Beef Pie

1½ pounds ground beef
1 15-ounce can tomato sauce
1 10-ounce package frozen cut okra, cooked and drained
1 teaspoon salt
¼ teaspoon dried rosemary, crushed
Few dashes bottled hot pepper sauce
Packaged instant mashed potatoes (enough for 4 servings)

In skillet brown beef; drain off excess fat. Stir in tomato sauce, okra, salt, rosemary, and pepper sauce. Turn into a 1½-quart casserole. Prepare instant potatoes according to package directions. Spoon potatoes in ring atop casserole mixture. Sprinkle with yellow cornmeal, if desired. Bake in 350° oven about 30 minutes or till bubbly. Makes 4 to 6 servings.

Tamale Pie

1 pound ground beef
1 cup chopped onion
1 cup chopped green pepper
1 clove garlic, minced
1 15-ounce can tomato sauce
1 12-ounce can whole kernel corn, drained
½ cup sliced pitted ripe olives
1 tablespoon sugar
2 to 3 teaspoons chili powder
¾ teaspoon salt
Dash pepper
1½ cups shredded sharp American cheese
¾ cup yellow cornmeal
½ teaspoon salt
2 cups cold water

In skillet cook ground beef, onion, green pepper, and garlic till meat is lightly browned and vegetables are tender. Drain off excess fat. Stir in tomato sauce, corn, olives, sugar, chili powder, ¾ teaspoon salt, and pepper. Boil gently for 20 to 25 minutes or till thickened, stirring occasionally. Add shredded cheese; stir till melted. Turn mixture into an ungreased 2-quart casserole.

In saucepan stir cornmeal and the ½ teaspoon salt into cold water. Bring to boiling; reduce heat and cook, stirring constantly, ½ to 1 minute or till thickened. Spoon over hot meat mixture. Bake in 375° oven about 40 minutes. Makes 6 servings.

Barbecue Apple-Beef Pie

1 beaten egg
¼ cup milk
1½ cups soft bread crumbs (2 slices)
1 teaspoon salt
½ teaspoon dried marjoram, crushed
¼ teaspoon pepper
1½ pounds lean ground beef
¼ cup chopped onion
2 tablespoons butter *or* margarine
½ cup packed brown sugar
½ cup catsup
2 tablespoons vinegar
1 teaspoon prepared mustard
1 20-ounce can pie-sliced apples, drained

In large bowl combine egg, milk, bread crumbs, salt, marjoram, and pepper. Add ground beef; mix well. Press meat mixture into a 9-inch pie plate to form a shell; set aside.

In saucepan cook onion in butter till tender but not brown. Stir in brown sugar, catsup, vinegar, and mustard. Fold in apples; spoon into meat shell. Bake in 375° oven for 45 to 50 minutes; remove fat from edges of pie with baster as necessary. Makes 6 servings.

Serves-a-Dozen Lasagna

If desired, layer another 8 ounces sliced mozzarella over the meat sauce before baking.

1 pound ground beef *or* bulk Italian sausage	½ teaspoon fennel seed
½ cup chopped onion	¼ teaspoon pepper
½ cup chopped celery	Dash bottled hot pepper sauce
½ cup chopped carrot	10 ounces lasagna noodles
1 clove garlic, minced	2 beaten eggs
1 16-ounce can tomatoes, cut up	2 cups ricotta *or* cream-style cottage cheese
1 6-ounce can tomato paste	½ cup grated parmesan cheese
1 teaspoon sugar	2 tablespoons snipped parsley
1 teaspoon salt	¼ teaspoon pepper
1 teaspoon dried oregano, crushed	8 ounces mozzarella cheese, thinly sliced

In 10-inch skillet cook meat, onion, celery, carrot, and garlic till meat is lightly browned. Drain off excess fat. Stir in *undrained* tomatoes, tomato paste, sugar, salt, oregano, fennel, ¼ teaspoon pepper, and hot pepper sauce. Simmer, covered, about 20 minutes, stirring occasionally.

Meanwhile, cook lasagna noodles according to package directions; drain well. Combine eggs, ricotta or cottage cheese, parmesan, parsley, and ¼ teaspoon pepper. Place *half* noodles in a greased 13x9x2-inch baking dish. Spread with *half* the cheese filling; top with all the mozzarella and *half* the meat sauce. Repeat layers of noodles, cheese filling, and meat sauce.

Bake in 375° oven about 40 minutes. Let stand 10 to 15 minutes before serving. Cut in squares to serve. Makes 12 servings.

Olive-Burger Pizza

1 pound ground beef	2 teaspoons dried oregano, crushed
1 clove garlic, minced	1 teaspoon dried basil, crushed
2 medium onions, sliced and separated into rings	1 teaspoon aniseed, crushed, *or* fennel seed, crushed
1 package active dry yeast	
¾ cup warm water (110°)	
2½ cups packaged biscuit mix	
2 cups shredded mozzarella cheese (8 ounces)	1 cup sliced pitted ripe olives
1 15-ounce can tomato sauce	½ cup grated parmesan cheese

In skillet cook beef and garlic till meat is browned; drain, reserving drippings. Cook onion rings in drippings till tender; drain off excess fat.

In bowl soften yeast in warm water. Add biscuit mix; beat vigorously for 2 minutes. Dust surface of board with additional biscuit mix. Turn dough out and knead till smooth (about 25 strokes). Divide dough in half. Pat or roll each piece to fit a greased 12-inch round pizza pan. Bake in 425° oven for 5 minutes. Sprinkle each partially-baked crust with ½ *cup* of the mozzarella.

In bowl combine tomato sauce, oregano, basil, and aniseed or fennel seed; mix well and spread half over each crust. Top each pizza with *half* the meat mixture, *half* the olives, and *half* the onion rings. Sprinkle the remaining mozzarella and parmesan over the two pizzas. Bake in 425° oven for 15 to 20 minutes or till bubbly. Makes 2 pizzas, 3 or 4 servings each.

Types of Sausages

Sausages were favorite festival meats enjoyed by the Romans who gave them their name. Later "wurstmachers" developed dry and semi-dry varieties which kept well in warm climates; or fresh and cooked varieties in the cooler northern countries. Use these descriptions as a reference for the storage and cooking requirements of the specific sausage varieties listed on the next 3 pages.

Fresh
Made from uncured, uncooked meat.
Some may be smoked.
Treat like fresh meat.
Keep refrigerated.
Use within 3 or 4 days of purchasing.
Cook thoroughly.
Allow 4 or 5 servings per pound.

Uncooked, smoked
Made from cured meat.
Smoking adds flavor and color.
Keep refrigerated.
Use within 1 week of purchasing.
Most must be thoroughly cooked unless labeled "fully cooked," "ready-to-eat," or "do not cook."
Allow 4 or 5 servings per pound.

Cooked
Made from fresh meats that may be either cured or uncured.
Keep refrigerated.
Use within 1 week of purchasing.
Ready to eat.
Generally served cold.
Allow 4 or 5 servings per pound.

Cooked, smoked
Made from fresh meats that are smoked and fully cooked.
Keep refrigerated.
Use within 1 week of purchasing (2 weeks if unopened in original vacuum package).
Ready to eat but usually served hot.
Allow 4 or 5 servings per pound.

Dry, Semi-dry
Made from cured meats that are either smoked or unsmoked.
Cured and dried through process of bacterial fermentation which develops characteristic flavor and also acts as a preservative.
Allow 8 servings per pound.

Most **dry** sausages are salamis. The casings become shriveled and texture is very firm. Cool storage recommended.
Semi-dry sausages are generally softer and include most cervelats.
Keep refrigerated.

Prepared Meats
Cured meats are often thought of as sausages.
May be smoked or unsmoked.
Keep refrigerated.
Use within 1 week of purchasing.
Ready to eat; usually served cold.
Allow 4 to 6 servings per pound.

Cooked Meat Specialties
Finely ground or pureed meat with spices and seasonings.
Government regulates percentage of non-meat ingredients, such as cereal or dried milk, which can be added.
May be cured.

Fully cooked or baked.
Keep refrigerated.
Allow 4 or 5 servings per pound.
Typically called luncheon meats.
Includes such items as olive loaf, pickle and pimiento loaf, old-fashioned loaf, honey loaf, peppered loaf and picnic loaf.

How to Cook
Fresh and uncooked sausages need to be thoroughly cooked before eating. Fully-cooked sausages may be cooked only until heated through if you want to serve them warm, or they may be served cold.

Uncooked Patties
Place in an unheated skillet. Cook slowly, uncovered, for 15 to 20 minutes or till thoroughly cooked, turning once. Drain well.
Or, arrange patties on unheated rack in a shallow baking pan. Bake in 400° oven for 20 to 25 minutes or till thoroughly cooked.

Uncooked Links
Do not prick. Place in an unheated skillet. Add ¼ cup cold water. Cover and cook slowly for 5 minutes; drain well. Uncover and cook slowly 12 to 14 minutes longer or till water has evaporated and sausages are thoroughly cooked, turning occasionally with tongs.

Fully Cooked Links
Add to boiling liquid (water, beer, or wine) in a saucepan. Reduce heat; cover and simmer for 5 to 10 minutes or till heated through.

Beerwurst *(cooked, smoked)* Pork and beef; chopped. May be all pork. Seasoning includes garlic. Natural casings or bulk pieces for slicing. Also called Beer Salami.

Berliner Sausage *(cooked, smoked)* Cured lean pork; coarsely ground. May include a small amount of beef or veal. Sugar and salt are the only seasonings. Packaged in slices or in bulk rolls for slicing. Variety known as Dutch Berliner adds bacon, eggs, onion, and spices.

Blood Sausage *(cooked)* Pork fat cooked and diced;

cooked meat, finely ground; and beef blood. Spices include allspice, cloves, onion, salt, and pepper. May be smoked or unsmoked. Natural casings or bulk pieces for slicing. Also called Blutwurst, Blood Pudding or Long Blood Sausage, Pepper Blood (links), Bloodwurst, or Biroldo. Other varieties include Black Pudding (English) with added cereal; Boudin Noir (French) with brandy; and Toscano (Italian) with raisins.

Blood and Tongue Sausage *(cooked)* Pork and/or lamb tongues are cooked and cured, then placed in center of **Blood Sausage.**

Bockwurst *(fresh or cooked)* Veal, pork, milk, chives, eggs, and parsley. Seasonings similar to frankfurters. Generally available only from January to Easter. Popular at spring sausage festivals in Germany. Highly perishable. Light colored links about 5 inches long. Also called Swiss Sausages.

Bologna *(cooked, smoked)* Beef and pork, finely ground and mildly seasoned. May also be all beef, or pork, or ham. Typical seasonings

include pepper, cloves, coriander, ginger, garlic, and nutmeg. Available in rings, chubs, and slices of varying diameters. Credited to Bologna, Italy. Many varieties depending on spices and meats used.

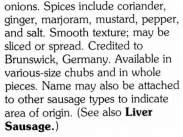

Bratwurst *(fresh or cooked)* All pork, or pork and beef, or pork and veal. Spice formulas vary with the brand. German, meaning "frying sausage." Links often 1½ inches in diameter; usually 6 or 7 links per pound.

Braunschweiger *(cooked)* Liver sausage that is smoked after cooking or includes smoked meats such as bacon. May also include milk and onions. Spices include coriander, ginger, marjoram, mustard, pepper, and salt. Smooth texture; may be sliced or spread. Credited to Brunswick, Germany. Available in various-size chubs and in whole pieces. Name may also be attached to other sausage types to indicate area of origin. (See also **Liver Sausage.**)

Cappicola *(prepared meat)* Boneless pork shoulder seasoned with ground hot or sweet peppers, paprika, salt, and sugar. Smoked.

Cervelat *(semi-dry)* Beef and pork; usually finely ground. Garlic is generally not included in the seasonings. Many varieties differentiated by grind of meat, spices used, and degree of smoking. Sliced or in rolls. Often given the general name **Summer Sausage.**

Chipolata *(fresh)* Lean pork finely chopped, plus pork fat, coarsely chopped. May include rice and rusks plus salt, pepper, coriander, pimiento, nutmeg, and thyme. Links are usually 16 to 20 per pound. Italian; popular in France. Also called

Cipollata. Name sometimes used to mean very small sausages.

Chorizo *(dry)* Pork, coarsely chopped and highly seasoned with pimiento, sweet red pepper, and sometimes garlic. Looks similar to **Italian Pork Sausage.** Spanish. Bulk and link forms.

Cooked Salami *(cooked)* Cured pork and beef, but definitely has a softer texture than dry and semi-dry salamis. Many varieties.

Cotto Salami *(cooked, smoked)* Pork and beef, coarsely ground, or all beef. Mild flavor characterized by whole peppercorns. May be smoked. Italian, meaning "cooked" salami. Sliced and in rolls.

Dried beef *(prepared meat)* Beef round is cured, smoked, dehydrated, and thinly sliced.

Farmer Cervelat *(dry)* Pork, coarsely chopped, and beef, finely chopped. Seasonings include mustard, pepper, salt, and sugar. Natural casings, usually about 2 inches in diameter. May also be called Farmer Sausage, **Cervelat,** or Bauernwurst.

Frankfurters *(cooked, smoked)* Pork and beef, ground, or all beef. Typical seasonings include coriander, garlic or onion, dry mustard, paprika, nutmeg, salt, sugar, pepper, cloves, and mace. Credited to Frankfurt, Germany. Originally used beef and pork and had more seasonings (especially garlic) than wieners. Various sizes. May be skinless or with natural casings. (See also **Wieners**)

Fresh Polish Sausage *(fresh)* Pork shoulder, coarsely chopped. Seasonings include garlic, marjoram, salt, sugar, and pepper. Usually in 10- to 14-inch links. (See also **Polish Sausage.**)

Fresh Thuringer *(fresh)* Pork or pork and veal; finely ground. May include dry milk solids, plus coriander, ginger, ground celery seed, mace, pepper, salt, and sugar. Usually in links, 3 to 5 per pound. (See also **Smoked Thuringer.**)

Frizzes *(dry)* Cured lean pork, sometimes with added cured lean beef; coarsely chopped. Some varieties made with hot spices; others with sweet spices. Irregularly shaped; natural casings.

Genoa Salami *(dry)* Usually all pork, coarsely ground; may use some beef. Garlic and wine or grape juice added. Unsmoked. Firm texture with flavor sometimes compared to aged cheese. Natural casings; about 3-inch diameter. Credited to Genoa, Italy. May be called Italian or Hard Salami. Name may be attached to other sausages to indicate area of origin.

German Salami *(dry)* Beef and pork in equal amounts; coarsely cut. Seasonings are salt, pepper, garlic, and sugar. May be lightly smoked. Sliced or chub; about 3½-inch diameter. Also called Hard Salami.

Goteborg Cervelat

(dry and semi-dry) Pork and beef, coarsely chopped. Heavily smoked. Sweet flavor from the spice, cardamom; also tends to be salty. Described as a hard cervelat. Also called Swedish Sausage.

Head Cheese *(cooked meat specialty)* Chopped, cured pork head meat in gelatin base. Seasonings often include caraway, coriander, mustard, red pepper, salt, sage, and thyme. Colorful.

Holsteiner *(dry)* Similar in flavor and texture to **Farmer Cervelat** but has larger diameter and is often ring-shaped.

Italian Pork Sausage *(fresh)* Pork, coarsely or finely chopped. May include some beef. Seasoned with fennel, garlic, coriander, nutmeg, paprika, and sometimes red pepper. Bulk, sometimes links. Also called Salsiccia.

Italian Salami *(dry or semi-dry)* Usually cured lean pork; may have some beef. Seasonings often include garlic, cinnamon, cloves, nutmeg, salt, sugar, pepper, and peppercorns. May be moistened with red wine or grape juice. Never smoked. Includes many varieties.

Kielbasa—See **Polish Sausage.**

Knackwurst *(cooked, smoked)* Beef and pork. Seasonings include coriander, garlic, nutmeg, salt, sugar, and pepper. Four-inch links usually served hot. German. Also called Knoblauch, Knochblauc, and Garlic Sausage.

Kosher Salami *(semi-dry)* Kosher beef, ground, plus cubes of fat. Seasonings include coriander, garlic, nutmeg, mustard, pepper, salt, and sugar. Meat and processing are under Rabbinical supervision.

Krakow *(cooked, smoked)* Lean pork, coarsely ground, and beef, finely chopped. Seasoned with pepper, garlic, salt, and sugar. Usually has 3-inch diameter. Polish and German. Similar to **New England Brand Sausage.**

Landjaeger Cervelat *(dry)* Beef and pork, or all beef with mustard, pepper, caraway, salt, and sugar. Heavily smoked and dried giving a black wrinkled appearance. Links are pressed to give flattened shape. Swiss.

Lebanon Bologna *(semi-dry)* Lean beef, coarsely chopped. Seasoned with cloves, coriander, garlic, ginger, pepper, salt, and sugar. Heavily smoked. Tangy flavor. Dark surface appearance. Credited to Pennsylvania Dutch in Lebanon, Pennsylvania. Sliced or in rolls.

Linguisa *(uncooked, smoked)* Pork, coarsely ground with garlic, cumin seed, and cinnamon. Cured in brine before stuffing. Portuguese.

Liver Cheese *(cooked)* Similar to **Liver Sausage** but with firmer texture. May be seasoned with coriander, ginger, mustard, onion, and pepper. Usually wrapped in white pork fat. Square shape, about 4 inches. Also called Liver Loaf.

Liver Sausage *(cooked)* Pork jowls and liver, finely ground. Smooth texture; slices or spreads easily. Seasonings include cloves, mace, marjoram, onion, salt, sugar, and pepper. Ring-shaped or in roll. Also called Liverwurst. One variety combines goose livers, diced pork tongues, and pistachio nuts.

Mettwurst *(uncooked, smoked)* Cured beef and pork, finely chopped. Seasoned with allspice, coriander, ginger, mustard, salt, pepper, and sugar. Spreading consistency. German. Also called Teawurst or Smearwurst. Name may also be given to a semi-dry, coarsely ground sausage.

Mortadella (dry) Pork, finely chopped, plus cubed pork fat. May add beef. Seasoned with anise, coriander, garlic, and peppercorns. Italian. Natural casing.

Mortadella, German-Style (cooked, smoked) Pork and beef, finely ground, plus diced pork fat and pistachio nuts. Seasoned similar to a large bologna. Natural casing.

New England Sausage (cooked, smoked) Cured lean pork, coarsely chopped. May have cloves. Ham-like flavor. Large diameter rolls. Must be labeled New England-Style or -Brand when made outside New England.

Pastrami (prepared meat) Flat pieces of lean beef are cured, then rubbed with spices including garlic and cumin; smoked.

Pepperoni

(dry) Beef and pork, coarsely chopped. Seasoned with red pepper and paprika. Sliced and in paired links, 10 to 12 inches long and about 1½ inches in diameter.

Polish Sausage (cooked, smoked) Pork, coarsely chopped, and beef, finely chopped. Seasoned with coriander, garlic, marjoram, salt, pepper, and

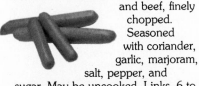

sugar. May be uncooked. Links, 6 to 14 inches long; longer ones may be tied in ring shape. Also called Kielbasa, Kolbassy, or Kobasa. (See also **Fresh Polish Sausage.**)

Pork Sausage (fresh) Ground pork seasoned with pepper, nutmeg, and sage. Sold in bulk, patties, or links. Country-Style variety is mildly cured and may be smoked or unsmoked.

Potato Sausage (fresh) Beef and pork, finely chopped; mixed with potatoes. Seasonings include ginger, mace, onion, sage, salt, sugar, and pepper. Swedish.

Prosciutto (prepared meat) Ham that is dry-cured under pressure with spices rubbed in. Slice thinly.

Salami (dry) General category of highly seasoned sausages having a characteristic fermented flavor. Pork and beef with added garlic, pepper, salt, and sugar. May or may not be smoked. Sometimes called Dry or Hard Salami to differentiate from Cooked Salami which is more perishable. See **Cooked Salami, Cotto Salami, Genoa Salami, German Salami, Italian Salami,** and **Kosher Salami.**

Scrapple (cooked meat specialty) Ground cooked pork trimmings plus cornmeal. Other flours may be added. Seasonings include pepper, sage, and salt. Available in rolls or canned. To serve, slice and fry. Pennsylvania Dutch specialty. Also called ponhaws.

Smoked Sausage Links (cooked, smoked) Beef and pork, or all pork, coarsely ground. Seasoned with pepper;

smoked. Size of links varies. Developed in Wisconsin in late 1940s.

Smoked Thuringer Links (cooked, smoked) Beef and pork, coarsely chopped. Seasonings include mustard, garlic, salt, sugar, and pepper. Usually 5 or 6 links per pound. (See also **Fresh Thuringer.**)

Souse (cooked meat specialty) Similar to **Head Cheese** but with a more sweet-sour flavor from addition of vinegar, pickles, and pimiento. Also called Sulze or Sylta.

Summer Sausage (semi-dry, dry) Properly used to describe all dry sausage, but especially refers to mildly seasoned soft cervelats such as **Thuringer Cervelat.** Originally made during the winter for summer use. Air drying removes much of the moisture giving them good keeping qualities. Typical lactic acid tartness.

Thuringer Cervelat (semi-dry) Beef and pork combination, or beef or pork alone. Mildly seasoned with coriander, pepper, cardamom, ginger, and mustard. Usually smoked. Often described as having the most tangy, fermented flavor of all cervelats. Credited to Province of Thuringia, Germany. Usually in rolls with about 2½-inch diameter. Name may be attached to other sausage varieties to indicate area of origin. (See also **Fresh** and **Smoked Thuringer.**)

Weisswurst (fresh) Pork and veal. Seasonings include mace, parsley, sage, thyme, lemon peel, salt, and sugar. Light color and delicate flavor. German, meaning "white sausage." Plump links about 4 inches long. Similar to cooked bratwurst.

Wieners (cooked, smoked) Beef, pork, and sometimes veal, finely chopped. Ratio of the meats used varies with the market price; most-used ingredient must be listed first on the label. Seasonings may include allspice, coriander, sugar, ginger, salt, and pepper. Credited to Vienna, Austria. (See also **Frankfurters.**)

Yachtwurst (cooked) Lean pork, coarsely chopped. May add beef. Includes pistachio nuts and garlic.

Make Your Own Sausage

INGREDIENTS
5 pounds untrimmed boneless
    pork shoulder, cut in
    1½-inch cubes (for Brats
    use 3 pounds boneless
    pork shoulder and
    2 pounds boneless beef
    chuck)
12 ounces pork fat
2 cups water
5 teaspoons salt
    Seasoning for Country-
    Style, Spicy Italian,
    or Brats

EQUIPMENT
Pork or beef sausage
    casings (12 to 15 feet)
Food grinder or
    processor
Sausage stuffer (use hand
    stuffer or attachment
    for electric mixer or
    grinder)

Rinse casings; soak in water at least 2 hours or overnight. With coarse blade of food grinder, grind pork and the 12 ounces pork fat together. Add the water, salt, and desired seasoning. Grind again. Attach sausage stuffer attachment to mixer or grinder. Using a 3- to 4-foot piece of casing at a time, push casing onto stuffer, letting some extend beyond end of attachment. Using coarse plate of grinder, grind mixture together, allowing it to fill casing. Fill casing till firm but not overly full, tying with string or twisting casing when links are 4 to 5 inches long. Wrap and chill. Makes 5 pounds sausage.

To cook sausages: Do not prick. Place in unheated skillet; add ¼ cup cold *water.* Cover and cook slowly for 5 minutes; drain. Uncover and cook slowly for 12 to 14 minutes, turning with tongs.

Country-Style Seasoning
2 tablespoons ground
    sage
1 tablespoon dried
    savory, crushed
1½ teaspoons pepper
1½ teaspoons cayenne
1 teaspoon ground
    nutmeg
Add to meat mixture as directed.

Spicy Italian Seasoning
8 bay leaves, finely
    crushed
5 cloves garlic, minced
2 tablespoons paprika
5 teaspoons dried thyme,
    crushed
4 dried red peppers,
    crushed
2 teaspoons fennel seed,
    crushed
1 teaspoon pepper
1 teaspoon cayenne
Add to meat mixture as directed.

Brats Seasoning
4 teaspoons sugar
4 teaspoons dried
    rosemary, crushed
1 tablespoon ground
    coriander
1 tablespoon dry mustard
1 tablespoon ground sage
1¼ teaspoons pepper
1 teaspoon paprika
1 teaspoon ground
    nutmeg
¾ teaspoon cayenne
Add to meat mixture as directed.

A food grinder or processor is one of the requirements for making sausage at home. After the meats are ground and seasoned, they're stuffed into casings. Use a hand stuffer or a stuffing attachment that fits another appliance. Then, just cook and enjoy.

Sicilian Pizza Supreme

4 to 4½ cups all-purpose flour
1 package active dry yeast
1½ cups warm water (110°)
1 beaten egg
2 tablespoons cooking oil
1 pound bulk Italian sausage
½ cup chopped onion
1 15-ounce can tomato sauce
1 teaspoon dried oregano, crushed

1 large onion, thinly sliced and separated into rings
1 4-ounce can sliced mushrooms, drained
2 cups shredded mozzarella cheese (8 ounces)
2 medium tomatoes, sliced
1 green pepper, cut in rings
½ cup grated parmesan cheese
½ teaspoon dried basil, crushed

In large mixer bowl combine *2 cups* of the flour, the yeast, and 1½ teaspoons *salt*. Stir in water, egg, and oil. Beat at low speed of electric mixer for ½ minute, scraping sides of bowl. Beat 3 minutes at high speed. By hand, stir in enough of the remaining flour to make a moderately stiff dough. Turn out onto floured surface and knead about 5 minutes or till smooth. Place in a greased bowl, turning once. Cover; let rise till double (about 1 hour). Divide dough; place in two greased 9x9x2-inch baking pans *or* three 8x1½-inch round baking pans (sprinkle bottoms of pans with cornmeal, if desired). With well-oiled hands, pat dough out to fit pan, making a ½-inch rim around edges. Cover; let rise 30 minutes.

In skillet cook sausage and chopped onion till meat is brown; drain. Stir in tomato sauce, oregano, and dash *pepper*. Simmer, covered, 10 minutes.

When dough has risen, spread with a thin layer of the meat mixture. Arrange onion rings and mushrooms atop; sprinkle with mozzarella cheese. Spoon remaining meat mixture over. Bake in 425° oven for 25 minutes. Arrange tomato slices and green pepper rings on pizzas; sprinkle with parmesan cheese and basil. Bake 5 to 10 minutes more. Serves 6.

Sausage Nibbles

9 canned water chestnuts
1½ cups packaged biscuit mix
½ pound bulk Italian sausage

1 cup shredded sharp
  cheddar cheese
  (4 ounces)

Quarter water chestnuts; set aside. In bowl combine biscuit mix, *uncooked* sausage, and cheese; mix with hands till completely blended. Shape some of the mixture around a piece of water chestnut to form a 1¼-inch meatball. Place on baking sheet. Bake in 400° oven about 15 minutes. Makes 36.

Microwave cooking directions: Prepare meatballs as above. Arrange about half at a time in 12x7½x2-inch nonmetal baking dish. Cover with waxed paper or clear plastic wrap; cook in countertop microwave oven for 2 minutes. Rearrange; cover and micro-cook about 2 minutes or till done.

French Lima Stew

8 cups water
1 pound dry lima beans
1 pound bulk pork sausage
1 cup cubed fully cooked ham
½ cup chopped onion

1 10¾-ounce can condensed
  golden mushroom soup
2 tablespoons catsup
¼ teaspoon garlic powder
1 bay leaf

In 4-quart Dutch oven bring water and beans to boiling. Reduce heat; simmer 2 minutes. Cover; let stand 1 hour. (Or, soak beans in water overnight.) *Do not drain.* Simmer, covered, 1¼ to 1½ hours. Drain; reserve 1½ cups liquid. In skillet cook sausage, ham, and onion till meat is browned; drain fat. Add meat mixture to beans. Stir in reserved liquid and remaining ingredients. Cover; simmer 20 minutes. Remove bay leaf. Serves 6 to 8.

Chili-Spaghetti Dinner

½ pound bulk pork sausage
¼ cup chopped onion
¼ cup chopped carrot
1¼ cups tomato juice
1 8-ounce can red kidney
  beans, drained

½ teaspoon salt
½ teaspoon chili powder
  Dash pepper
½ cup broken uncooked
  spaghetti

In saucepan cook sausage, onion, and carrot till meat is browned. Drain off fat. Stir in tomato juice, kidney beans, salt, chili powder, and pepper. Place uncooked spaghetti in a 1-quart casserole; add meat mixture. Bake in 375° oven for 55 to 60 minutes or till spaghetti is tender, stirring twice. Serves 2 or 3.

Lentils Coriander

1 pound Italian
  sausage links,
  cut in 1-inch pieces
2 large onions, thinly sliced
2 teaspoons ground
  coriander
1½ teaspoons salt

½ teaspoon ground ginger
7 cups water
2 cups dry lentils
1 tablespoon lemon juice
  Dairy sour cream
8 lemon slices

In Dutch oven brown sausage; stir in onions. Cover and cook till onion is tender but not brown. Drain off excess fat. Stir in coriander, salt, and ginger. Stir in water and lentils. Bring mixture to boiling. Reduce heat; cover and simmer for 50 minutes. Stir in lemon juice. Serve in soup bowls; top with a dollop of sour cream and a lemon slice. Makes 8 servings.

Tamale-Franks

1 15-ounce can tamales
1 pound frankfurters (8 to 10), cut up
1 11¼-ounce can condensed chili beef soup
1 8-ounce can tomato sauce
½ cup shredded cheddar cheese (2 ounces)
Corn chips

Drain tamales, reserving sauce. Remove paper from tamales and cut each tamale in thirds. In 1½-quart casserole combine the reserved tamale sauce, frankfurters, soup, and tomato sauce. Top with tamales. Cover and bake in 350° oven for 35 minutes. Top with cheese and bake, uncovered, 10 minutes more. Serve with corn chips. Makes 6 servings.

Golden-Sauced Franks

1 15¼-ounce can pineapple chunks
2 17-ounce cans sweet potatoes, cut up
1½ pounds frankfurters (12 to 15), cut in 1-inch pieces
⅓ cup packed brown sugar
2 tablespoons cornstarch
½ teaspoon finely shredded orange peel
½ cup orange juice
¼ cup water
2 tablespoons vinegar
2 tablespoons chili sauce

Drain pineapple, reserving syrup. In 3-quart casserole combine pineapple, sweet potatoes, and franks. In small saucepan combine brown sugar and cornstarch. Stir in reserved pineapple syrup, orange peel, orange juice, water, vinegar, and chili sauce. Cook and stir over medium heat till thickened and bubbly. Pour over mixture in casserole. Cover and bake in 350° oven for 25 to 30 minutes or till heated through. Makes 8 servings.

Microwave cooking directions: Drain pineapple, reserving syrup. In 3-quart nonmetal casserole combine pineapple, sweet potatoes, and franks. In a 2-cup glass measure combine the brown sugar and cornstarch. Stir in the reserved pineapple syrup, orange peel, orange juice, water, vinegar, and chili sauce. Cook, uncovered, in countertop microwave oven about 3 minutes or till thickened and bubbly; stir after each minute. Pour sauce over mixture in casserole. Micro-cook, covered, for 12 minutes, stirring every 3 minutes.

Corn and Sausage Scallop

1 cup milk
2 eggs
1 tablespoon all-purpose flour
1 16-ounce can cream-style corn
1 3-ounce can chopped mushrooms, drained
3 cups bite-size shredded corn cereal, crushed (1½ cups crushed)
1 8-ounce package brown-and-serve sausage links

In mixing bowl combine milk, eggs, and flour; beat till smooth. Stir in cream-style corn, mushrooms, and *1 cup* of the crushed corn cereal. Turn into an 8x1½-inch round baking dish. Arrange sausages atop in spoke design. Sprinkle with remaining ½ cup crushed corn cereal. Bake in 350° oven for 40 to 45 minutes or till knife inserted just off-center comes out clean. Makes 4 or 5 servings.

Frank-Potato Chowder

2 cups chopped potatoes
1 10-ounce package frozen
   mixed vegetables
¼ cup chopped onion
1 tablespoon snipped
   parsley
2 teaspoons instant chicken
   bouillon granules

½ teaspoon salt
   Dash pepper
5 or 6 frankfurters,
   thinly sliced
4 cups milk
¼ cup all-purpose flour
   Paprika

In saucepan combine potatoes, frozen vegetables, onion, parsley, bouillon granules, salt, pepper, and 1 cup *water;* bring to boiling. Cover; simmer about 15 minutes or till vegetables are tender. Add frankfurters. Blend ½ *cup* of the milk into the flour; stir into vegetables. Add the remaining milk. Cook and stir till thickened and bubbly; cook and stir 2 minutes more. Sprinkle each serving with paprika. Makes 6 to 8 servings.

Choucroute Garni

When selecting the link sausages for Choucroute Garni, *you may use 1 pound of any one particular sausage, or a combination of sausages to make 1 pound. Bratwurst, bockwurst, and thuringer links are also available precooked. These precooked types may be heated in boiling water as directed for the knackwurst and franks.*

1 medium onion, sliced
1 tablespoon bacon
   drippings *or* lard
3 fresh pork hocks (1½
   pounds) *or* 2 pounds pork
   spareribs, cut in 3-rib
   portions
1 2-pound smoked pork
   shoulder roll *or* 3 or
   4 smoked pork loin
   chops, cut ¾ inch thick
   (1½ pounds)
3 16-ounce cans sauerkraut,
   rinsed and drained
2 cooking apples, peeled,
   cored, and cut in wedges

2 tablespoons brown sugar
4 whole cloves
3 juniper berries, crushed
   (optional)
2 small cloves garlic, minced
1 bay leaf
⅛ teaspoon freshly ground
   black pepper
1½ cups rhine wine
1 pound sausage links
   (use desired combi-
   nation of fresh bratwurst,
   bockwurst, or thuringer
   or knackwurst *or*
   frankfurters)
   Boiled potatoes

In 4½- or 5-quart Dutch oven cook onion in bacon drippings or lard about 5 minutes or till tender; remove from heat. Add pork hocks or spareribs. Cut pork shoulder roll crosswise in ¾-inch slices; add shoulder slices or loin chops to Dutch oven. In large bowl stir together the sauerkraut, apples, brown sugar, cloves, juniper berries, garlic, bay leaf, and pepper. Spoon over meats. Pour wine over all. Cover and bake in 375° oven about 2½ hours or till meats are tender.

Meanwhile, prepare desired combination of sausages. For bratwurst, bockwurst, and thuringer, place in unheated skillet with 2 to 3 tablespoons *water;* cover and cook over low heat 5 to 8 minutes. Uncover and continue cooking 5 to 8 minutes more or till water has evaporated and sausages are cooked through. For knackwurst and frankfurters, add to boiling water in saucepan; cover and simmer 5 to 10 minutes or till heated through.

Mound sauerkraut mixture on deep, wide serving platter or in large bowl. Arrange meats and sausages around and atop sauerkraut. Add boiled potatoes to platter or pass separately. Makes 6 servings.

Translated "sauerkraut with all the trimmings," Choucroute Garni *is a hearty country dish. Choose from four pork cuts and five types of link sausages for the "trimmings."*

Polish Sausage Stew

1 27-ounce can sauerkraut, drained
1 10¾-ounce can condensed cream of celery soup
1 soup can water (1¼ cups)
⅓ cup packed brown sugar

1½ pounds Polish sausage, cut in 2-inch pieces
4 medium potatoes, peeled and cubed
1 cup chopped onion
1 cup shredded monterey jack cheese (4 ounces)

In Dutch oven combine sauerkraut, soup, water, and sugar. Stir in sausage, potatoes, and onion. Cover and simmer about 45 minutes or till potatoes are tender. Spoon off fat. Stir in cheese. Spoon into serving bowls. Pass additional shredded cheese to sprinkle atop, if desired. Makes 6 to 8 servings.

Crockery cooker directions: In electric slow crockery cooker combine all ingredients omitting water and reserving cheese. Cover and cook on low-heat setting for 8 hours. (*Or,* cook on high-heat setting for 4 hours.) Spoon off excess fat. Stir in cheese and serve as above.

Hot Smoky Potato Salad

4 slices bacon
5 fully cooked smoked sausage links, sliced
½ cup chopped onion
1 10¾-ounce can condensed cream of celery soup
¼ cup water

2 tablespoons sweet pickle relish
2 tablespoons vinegar
¼ teaspoon salt
1 16-ounce package frozen French-fried potatoes, halved crosswise

In skillet cook bacon till crisp. Drain, reserving 2 tablespoons drippings; set bacon aside. Cook sausage and onion in drippings about 5 minutes or till meat is browned and onion is tender. Stir in soup, water, pickle relish, vinegar, and salt. Bring to boiling; add potatoes and cook, covered, for 10 minutes, stirring once or twice. To serve, crumble the reserved bacon over top of potato salad. Makes 4 to 6 servings.

Sausage Supper Salad

4 cups torn lettuce
8 ounces assorted dry and semi-dry sausages (salami, cervelat, pepperoni, mortadella)
½ of a 15-ounce can garbanzo beans, drained (1 cup)
1 cup sliced celery
½ cup chopped onion

2 hard-cooked eggs, cut in wedges
½ cup mayonnaise *or* salad dressing
2 tablespoons milk
1½ teaspoons prepared horseradish
½ teaspoon dry mustard

Place lettuce in a large bowl. Cut meats in thin slices, then in bite-size pieces. Arrange meats, beans, celery, onion, and egg wedges atop lettuce. Blend together mayonnaise or salad dressing, milk, horseradish, and mustard; dollop in center of salad. To serve, carefully toss mayonnaise mixture with vegetables and meat. Makes 4 to 6 servings.

It's easy to create your own favorite version of Sausage Supper Salad. For a selection of sausages to try, check the dry and semi-dry listings on pages 123 to 125.

Corn Con Carne Salad

Salami is a general name for a large variety of dry and semi-dry sausages. See page 125 for suggested types to try in these recipes.

6 cups torn lettuce
1 15½-ounce can chili-style beans in chili gravy, chilled
1 12-ounce can whole kernel corn with sweet peppers, chilled and drained
4 ounces sliced salami, cut in 2-inch strips (1 cup)

½ cup chopped celery
2 tablespoons finely chopped onion
¼ cup mayonnaise *or* salad dressing
½ teaspoon worcestershire sauce
¼ teaspoon salt
¼ teaspoon chili powder

In large salad bowl combine lettuce, chili-style beans, corn, salami, celery, and onion; stir lightly. In small bowl blend together mayonnaise, worcestershire, salt, and chili powder. Add mayonnaise mixture to vegetables and meat in salad bowl; toss well to coat. Makes 8 servings.

Salami-Bean Casserole

1 16-ounce can pork and beans in tomato sauce
⅓ cup catsup
2 tablespoons brown sugar

2 cups frozen hash brown potatoes with onion and peppers
4 ounces sliced salami

Combine pork and beans, catsup, and brown sugar; stir in hash brown potatoes. Turn into a 1-quart casserole. Bake, covered, in 375° oven for 20 minutes; stir. Roll salami slices into logs; arrange atop casserole, pressing into bean mixture slightly. Bake, covered, 10 to 15 minutes more or till potatoes are done. Makes 4 servings.

Microwave cooking directions: Combine pork and beans, catsup, and brown sugar; stir in potatoes. Turn into a 1-quart nonmetal casserole. Cover with waxed paper or clear plastic wrap. Cook in countertop microwave oven for 5 minutes; stir. Roll salami slices into logs; arrange atop casserole, pressing into bean mixture slightly. Micro-cook, covered, about 5 minutes more or till potatoes are done.

A Soup for All Seasons

10 cups water
1 pound dry lentils
8 ounces pepperoni, thinly sliced and halved
1 large onion, chopped
1 6-ounce can tomato paste
2½ teaspoons salt
½ teaspoon dried oregano, crushed

¼ teaspoon ground sage
¼ teaspoon cayenne
4 tomatoes, cut up
2 medium carrots, sliced
2 stalks celery, sliced
3 cups water
1½ teaspoons salt
1½ cups bulgur wheat

In Dutch oven combine 10 cups water, lentils, pepperoni, onion, tomato paste, 2½ teaspoons salt, oregano, sage, and cayenne. Bring to boiling. Reduce heat; cover and simmer 30 minutes, stirring occasionally. Add tomatoes, carrots, and celery; cover and simmer 40 minutes more.

Meanwhile, in saucepan bring 3 cups water and 1½ teaspoons salt to boiling; stir in bulgur wheat. Reduce heat; cover and simmer 25 minutes. Mound the cooked bulgur wheat in soup bowls; spoon the lentil mixture over. Makes 10 to 12 servings.

Variety meats include the organs and other nonfleshy parts of a meat animal used for food. They're usually removed before the meat is divided into wholesale cuts; retail stores must order them specially. All are very perishable and so are best cooked the same day purchased. Liver, heart, and kidneys are ready to cook after the meat is trimmed and any membranes or veins have been removed. Tongue, tripe, chitterlings, and usually sweetbreads and brains are simmered in water before completing cooking. Since variety meats are boneless, you can plan on 4 servings per pound when served as the meat course, or 6 servings per pound when served in creamed dishes with eggs or cheese.

Liver

Best known and most popular of the variety meats. Most of the liver sold is beef or baby beef (calf) liver. Pork, veal, and lamb livers are less common. Livers differ slightly in taste, with beef and pork livers generally more flavorful than baby beef, veal, or lamb livers. Prepare for cooking by removing any tough outer membrane (usually, the retailer has already removed this membrane for

you). Also, cut out any veins or hard portions that are present. Then cut into thin slices. Beef liver is usually

panfried, allowing only 2 to 3 minutes per side so as not to overcook. Pork liver is always cooked well-done and often braised to keep the meat moist. Lamb and veal livers are tender enough for broiling. Brush the surface with bacon drippings or melted butter to keep the meat from drying out.

Kidneys

Organ meats taken from the loin sections of beef, pork, lamb, and veal. Kidneys range in flavor from delicate lamb, through veal and pork, to beef, which has the most pronounced taste.

Prepare for cooking by removing any membranes and white hard portions from the center of kidneys. Cook beef kidneys in liquid about 2 hours, or braise.

Braise pork kidneys to assure thorough cooking. Lamb and veal kidneys are tender enough for broiling. Because of their small size, lamb kidneys are usually served whole.

Sweetbreads

The thymus glands from the neck or throat of young animals, usually beef. Although not widely available, some sweetbreads also come from the pancreas. Sweetbreads have a delicate flavor, and are often the most expensive of the variety meats. Cook

by simmering in a covered pan of salted water about 20 minutes or till tender. Add vinegar or lemon juice to the cooking water to keep sweetbreads white and firm. Remove the thin membrane coverings.

Sweetbreads may then be broiled, sliced and panfried, or served in creamed mixtures.

Tripe

Actually the stomach lining from beef. Honeycomb is the preferred type. It has the lacy construction of a honeycomb and is more delicate than the plain variety. Plain tripe is smooth and somewhat rubbery

in texture. Tripe is available fresh, canned, and pickled. Cook fresh tripe as a whole piece or cut into strips or serving-size pieces.

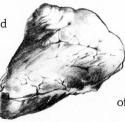

Simmer, covered, in salted water till tripe has a clear, jellylike appearance. Then fry; broil, basting with butter; or use in a prepared dish.

Brains

Have a delicate flavor and soft consistency. Before cooking, cover brains with cold water. Add a small amount of vinegar or lemon

juice to the water to keep the meat firm and white.
Soak for 30 minutes; drain.
Remove the loose fatty membrane. Simmer brains in enough salted water to cover for 20 to 30 minutes.

May then be broiled, panfried, or cooked with another food. Cooked brains are often cut up and scrambled with eggs or served in a white sauce.

Heart

Beef heart is the largest and most commonly sold. It is usually cut or split. The meat is firm, resembling typical muscle meat. Prepare for cooking by cutting out

any hard portions such as arteries, and trimming off any fat. Leave whole or slice. The heart is a hard-working muscle. Consequently, it is one of the less tender cuts of

meat. This means that it requires slow, moist-heat cooking to give a tender product. Heart may be braised or simmered, covered, in a large amount of liquid until tender. Or stuff the heart and bake, covered, with added liquid.

Tongue

Most tongue sold is beef, which may be fresh, pickled, or smoked. The flavor and texture of fresh beef tongue are similar to a fine-grained beef roast. Pork and lamb tongues are used in blood and tongue sausage. Tongue is not a tender meat and needs long, slow cooking in liquid to make it tender. Cook fresh tongue by simmering, covered, in enough salted water to cover until

tender. Seasonings may be added to the cooking water. Allow a cooking time of about 1 hour per pound of meat. Cut away any gristle. Slit the skin lengthwise and peel off. Thinly slice meat and serve hot or cold. If planning to serve cold, cool tongue in cooking liquid in the refrigerator to retain juiciness.

Chitterlings

The small intestines of a pig. They're used in some regional dishes, especially in the South. Also called chitlins. Available cleaned, frozen, and ready to cook, or canned and

ready to eat. If using fresh chitterlings, trim away any fat. Simmer in water for 2 to 3 hours or until tender.

Seasonings may be added to the cooking water. Cooked chitterlings may then be panfried or deep-fat fried for serving.

Tongue with Raisin and Onion Sauce

1 4-pound fresh beef tongue	¼ cup chopped celery
2 sprigs parsley	2 tablespoons butter *or*
4 stalks celery with leaves,	margarine
cut up	½ cup dry white wine
1 carrot, cut up	1 tablespoon instant beef
1 onion, cut up	bouillon granules
3 whole allspice	1 bay leaf
1 bay leaf	Dash pepper
1 clove garlic	2 cups pearl onions
½ teaspoon dried thyme,	(8 ounces)
crushed	½ cup raisins
¼ cup shredded carrot	2 tablespoons cornstarch

Place tongue in Dutch oven. Cover with 3 quarts salted *water*. Add parsley, the cut-up celery, carrot, and onion, the allspice, the first bay leaf, garlic, and thyme. Simmer, covered, about 3½ hours or till meat is tender. Remove tongue from pan. Strain broth; set aside 1 cup of the broth. Return tongue and remaining broth to pan; keep hot over low heat. Cook the shredded carrot and chopped celery in butter or margarine for 5 minutes. Stir in the 1 cup reserved broth, the wine, bouillon granules, the remaining bay leaf, and pepper. Add pearl onions and raisins. Bring to boiling. Reduce heat and simmer, covered, 15 minutes or till onions are tender.

Blend 2 tablespoons cold *water* into cornstarch. Add to onion mixture; cook and stir till thickened and bubbly. Cook 1 to 2 minutes longer. Remove bay leaf. Remove tongue from broth. Cut off gristle from large end of tongue. Slit skin on tongue; peel off. Thinly slice meat crosswise. Arrange on platter; spoon some sauce over. Garnish with additional parsley, if desired. Pass remaining sauce. Makes 12 servings.

Tongue and Lima Skillet

Variety meats are good buys not only because they're low in cost (you'll discover they're boneless and practically waste-free), but also because they're especially high in protein and iron.

1 2- to 4-pound fresh beef	1 teaspoon instant beef
tongue	bouillon granules
2 tablespoons chopped	½ teaspoon worcestershire
onion	sauce
1 tablespoon butter *or*	¼ teaspoon dried thyme,
margarine	crushed
1⅓ cups water	⅓ cup catsup
1 10-ounce package frozen	1 tablespoon cornstarch
baby lima beans	

Place tongue in large saucepan; cover with salted water. Simmer, covered, till meat is tender (allowing about 1 hour per pound). Drain tongue; cool. Cut off gristle from large end of tongue. Slit skin on tongue; peel off. Thinly slice crosswise, slicing enough meat for 4 servings. Refrigerate remaining meat for sandwiches or other casseroles.

In medium skillet cook onion in butter or margarine till tender but not brown. Stir in water, limas, bouillon granules, worcestershire, and thyme. Cover and cook according to lima package directions. Blend catsup into cornstarch. Stir into *undrained* lima mixture. Cook and stir till thickened and bubbly. Stir in tongue; heat through. Makes 4 servings.

Robust Tongue and Lima Skillet *is a hearty main dish that will please the family while also stretching the budget and providing good nutrition.*

You can relax when you serve Devilish Liver Fondue. *Just invite your friends over, set up the fondue pot, and let everyone be their own cook.*

Devilish Liver Fondue

For more information on preparing meat fondues, see page 24.

2 tablespoons cooking oil
1 tablespoon dijon-style mustard
1 tablespoon lemon juice
1 tablespoon catsup
1½ teaspoons worcestershire sauce
¼ teaspoon onion powder

⅛ teaspoon cayenne
1 pound beef liver, cut in 1½x½-inch strips
½ cup fine dry bread crumbs
Cooking oil
1 teaspoon salt
Hot-style catsup
Bacon Butter

Combine the 2 tablespoons cooking oil, the mustard, lemon juice, the 1 tablespoon catsup, the worcestershire, onion powder, and cayenne; mix well. Add liver; stir to coat. Refrigerate 3 to 4 hours, turning meat occasionally. Remove liver from mustard mixture; roll in bread crumbs.

Pour cooking oil into metal fondue cooker to no more than half capacity or to depth of 2 inches. Heat over range to 375°. Add the salt. Transfer cooker to fondue burner. Spear liver with fondue fork. Fry in hot oil about 1 minute or till browned. Transfer to dinner fork before eating. Serve with hot-style catsup or Bacon Butter. Makes 4 or 5 servings.

Bacon Butter: Cream ½ cup *butter* till light. Blend in 1 teaspoon prepared *mustard* and 4 slices *bacon,* crisp-cooked, drained, and crumbled.

Liver and Sausage Supper

½ pound pork sausage links,
cut into 1-inch pieces
½ pound beef *or* pork liver,
cut into strips
1 small onion, sliced

1 1-ounce envelope brown
gravy mix
1 8-ounce can mixed
vegetables, drained
Hot cooked rice

In 10-inch skillet cook sausage over medium heat for 8 to 10 minutes or till browned; drain off all but 1 tablespoon drippings. Push sausage pieces to one side. Add liver and onion; cook over medium-high heat about 4 minutes or just till liver is cooked. Sprinkle gravy mix over all; stir to blend. Add 1½ cups *water*. Cook and stir till mixture is thickened and bubbly; stir in vegetables and heat through. Serve meat-vegetable mixture over hot cooked rice. Makes 4 servings.

Sweet-and-Sour Beef Liver

½ cup finely chopped onion
¼ cup butter *or* margarine
2 tablespoons cooking oil
1½ pounds beef liver, cut
into strips
All-purpose flour

¼ cup dry white wine
2 tablespoons wine vinegar
¼ teaspoon salt
Brown Sauce
1 cup dairy sour cream

In skillet cook onion in butter or margarine till tender but not brown. Remove mixture and set aside. Heat cooking oil in the same skillet. Coat liver lightly with flour and cook quickly in hot oil about 5 minutes or till browned. Remove liver and set aside. Return onion mixture to skillet; add wine, vinegar, and salt. Cook till mixture is reduced by half. Stir Brown Sauce into sour cream; add to onion-wine mixture. Stir in liver; heat through. Season to taste with salt and pepper. Serve with hot cooked noodles or mashed potatoes, if desired. Makes 4 servings.

Brown Sauce: In saucepan melt 2 tablespoons *butter or margarine;* stir in 2 tablespoons all-purpose *flour.* Cook over low heat, stirring constantly, till flour is browned. Add one 10½-ounce can condensed *beef broth.* Bring to boiling and cook for 3 to 5 minutes.

Liver Dijon

1 pound beef liver
¼ cup all-purpose flour
2 tablespoons butter *or*
margarine
1 tablespoon cooking oil
1 clove garlic, minced
3 tablespoons dijon-style
mustard

3 tablespoons finely snipped
parsley
2 tablespoons finely
chopped green onion
2¼ cups soft bread crumbs
(3 slices)
¼ cup butter *or* margarine,
melted

Sprinkle liver with a little salt and pepper; coat with flour. In large skillet heat together the 2 tablespoons butter and the oil. Add liver; brown quickly, about 1 minute on each side. Remove from skillet, reserving drippings; set liver aside. In small bowl blend garlic, mustard, parsley, and green onion. Gradually add drippings from skillet. Spread both sides of liver slices with mustard mixture; coat with bread crumbs.

Place liver on unheated rack in broiler pan. Drizzle with half the melted butter. Broil 2 inches from heat for 3 minutes. Turn liver; drizzle with remaining butter. Broil 2 minutes more. Arrange on platter. Serves 4.

Sweetbreads Elegante

1 pound sweetbreads
1 tablespoon vinegar
1 tablespoon all-purpose
  flour
3 tablespoons butter
¼ cup dry vermouth
2 tablespoons snipped parsley

1 tablespoon sesame seed,
  toasted
½ teaspoon instant chicken
  bouillon granules
½ teaspoon dried tarragon,
  crushed
Hot cooked rice

In saucepan combine sweetbreads, vinegar, 4 cups *water*, and ½ teaspoon *salt*. Bring to boiling; reduce heat and simmer, covered, 20 minutes or till tender. Drain; remove white membranes and cut sweetbreads into bite-size pieces. Coat with flour. In skillet brown sweetbreads in butter. Add vermouth, parsley, sesame seed, bouillon, tarragon, ½ cup *water*, ¼ teaspoon *salt*, and dash *pepper*. Cook and stir till bubbly. Reduce heat; cover and simmer for 8 to 10 minutes. Serve over rice. Makes 4 servings.

Sweetbreads Divan-Style

1 pound sweetbreads
1 tablespoon vinegar
1 pound fresh broccoli
3 tablespoons butter
3 tablespoons all-purpose
  flour
⅛ teaspoon white pepper
2¼ cups milk

½ cup shredded process
  Swiss cheese (2 ounces)
¼ cup fine dry bread crumbs
¼ cup grated parmesan
  cheese
2 tablespoons snipped
  parsley
2 tablespoons butter, melted

In saucepan combine sweetbreads, vinegar, 4 cups *water*, and ½ teaspoon *salt*. Bring to boiling; reduce heat and simmer, covered, 20 minutes or till tender. Drain; remove white membranes and slice sweetbreads.

Cut broccoli stalks lengthwise into uniform spears, following branching lines. In covered pan cook broccoli in boiling salted water 12 to 15 minutes or till tender. Drain. In saucepan melt the 3 tablespoons butter; blend in flour, white pepper, and ½ teaspoon *salt*. Add milk all at once. Cook and stir till thickened and bubbly. Stir in Swiss cheese.

Arrange broccoli in bottom of 10x6x2-inch baking dish; top with sweetbreads. Cover with cheese sauce. Combine fine dry bread crumbs, parmesan cheese, parsley, and the melted butter. Sprinkle over sauce. Bake in 350° oven for 30 to 35 minutes. Makes 4 servings.

Kidneys in Wine Sauce

1 pound beef *or* lamb kidneys
1 10½-ounce can condensed
  beef broth
½ cup chopped onion
1 small clove garlic, minced
¼ teaspoon salt

½ cup chopped carrot
½ cup chopped celery
2 tablespoons dry red wine
3 tablespoons all-purpose
  flour
Chow mein noodles

Remove membranes and hard portions from kidneys; cut meat crosswise into ½-inch slices. Set aside ¼ *cup* of the beef broth. In saucepan combine kidneys, remaining beef broth, onion, garlic, and salt. Cover and simmer for 1½ hours. Add carrot and celery; simmer, covered, 25 minutes more or till kidneys are tender. Blend wine and reserved beef broth into flour; add to kidney mixture. Cook and stir till thickened and bubbly. Season to taste with salt and pepper. Serve over chow mein noodles. Makes 4 servings.

Savory Heart and Stuffing Casserole *offers affordable beef eating at its best. The colorful stuffing is a deftly-seasoned corn bread and bread cube combination.*

Savory Heart and Stuffing Casserole

1 2-pound beef heart
1 13¾-ounce can chicken broth
1 bay leaf
1 cup chopped celery
¼ cup chopped onion
3 tablespoons butter *or* margarine
4 cups crumbled corn bread

2 cups dry bread cubes
1 10-ounce package frozen mixed vegetables, cooked and drained
1 teaspoon ground sage
½ teaspoon salt
1 10¾-ounce can condensed golden mushroom soup

Remove hard portions and fat from heart. In Dutch oven combine heart, broth, and bay leaf. Cover; simmer about 2½ hours or till tender. Cook celery and onion in butter till tender. For stuffing combine corn bread, bread cubes, mixed vegetables, sage, salt, and celery mixture. Drain and slice heart; reserve 1 cup liquid. Toss liquid with stuffing. Turn into 12x7½x2-inch baking dish; top with heart. Combine soup and ¼ cup *water*; spoon over heart. Cover; bake in 350° oven for 45 minutes. Serves 8.

Heart and Vegetable Platter

½ cup chopped onion
½ cup chopped green pepper
1 fresh red chili pepper, seeded and chopped
2 cloves garlic, minced
1 teaspoon ground sage
2 tablespoons butter
1 medium sweet potato, peeled

1 medium turnip, peeled
¼ cup soy sauce
½ teaspoon instant beef bouillon granules
1 2-pound beef heart
2 tablespoons all-purpose flour
2 tablespoons vinegar
Hot cooked rice

In Dutch oven cook onion, peppers, garlic, and sage in butter till tender. Chop potato and turnip; add to pan. Stir in soy, bouillon, and ½ cup *water*. Bring to simmering. Remove hard portions and fat from heart. Add meat to broth mixture; cover and simmer about 1½ hours. Remove meat; slice thinly. Keep warm. Blend ¼ cup cold *water* into flour; stir into broth mixture. Cook and stir till bubbly. Stir in vinegar. Season with some salt and pepper. Spoon rice onto platter; top with broth and meat. Makes 8 servings.

Western Baked Beef Heart

1 2-pound beef heart
  Garlic salt
½ of an 8-ounce package brown-and-serve sausage links, cut up

½ cup chopped onion
¼ cup chopped green pepper
½ cup long grain rice
1 10¾-ounce can condensed tomato soup

Remove hard portions and fat from heart. Close slit with metal skewers; lace with string, forming a pocket. Sprinkle pocket with a little garlic salt; set aside. In saucepan cook sausage, onion, and green pepper till vegetables are tender. Drain well. Stir in uncooked rice, ½ *cup* of the soup, ½ cup *water*, ½ teaspoon *salt*, and ⅛ teaspoon *pepper*. Cover; simmer 10 minutes. Stuff heart with some of the rice mixture; place in 2-quart casserole. Spoon remaining rice mixture around heart. Spoon remaining soup over heart. Cover; bake in 325° oven for 1½ hours. Spoon cooking liquid over heart. Cover; bake 1 to 1½ hours more or till tender. Makes 8 servings.

Philadelphia Pepper Pot Soup

2 pounds beef tripe
1 1½-pound veal knuckle
3 medium carrots, sliced
1 large onion, sliced
½ cup sliced celery
2 tablespoons snipped parsley
4 whole cloves
2 bay leaves
1 teaspoon dried marjoram, crushed

1 teaspoon dried summer savory, crushed
1 teaspoon dried basil, crushed
½ teaspoon dried thyme, crushed
½ teaspoon whole black pepper
⅛ to ¼ teaspoon cayenne
2 medium potatoes, peeled and cubed

In Dutch oven cover tripe with salted water. Simmer, covered, 3 to 4 hours or till tripe looks like jelly, drain. Cut into ½-inch pieces; chill. Combine veal, carrots, onion, celery, parsley, remaining seasonings, and 1 teaspoon *salt*. Add 6 cups *water*. Simmer, covered, about 2 hours or till veal comes off bone. Strain; return meat to broth. Reserve 4 cups; chill. Skim fat, then heat broth; add tripe and potatoes. Simmer 15 minutes. Serves 6.

Game and other wild meats once were man's
primary source of meat. Today, however, hunting is usually
a sport rather than a necessity, and so these
meats comprise only a small proportion of our meat supply.
However, venison cuts and domestic
rabbit can still be found in specialty meat shops.
Proper handling is extremely important to
preserve the distinctive flavor and to prevent spoilage of
any wild meat. Unless you are returning home
immediately, eviscerate the animal in the field and hang
it so air can circulate through the body
cavity to thoroughly cool the meat. Cut up and refrigerate
or freeze the meat as soon as possible.
When cooking these meats, follow the same general guidelines
as for other meats—use dry heat for
young meat or tender cuts, and moist heat for older meat or
tough cuts. If you cannot determine the age
of the animal, use moist heat cooking methods.

Venison

The meat of any antlered animal is called venison, of which deer meat is the most common type. To cut up a whole deer into steaks, roasts, stew meat, etc., use the beef diagram on page 6 as a guide. Trim the fat well because it quickly becomes rancid. Then wrap the cuts in moisture-vaporproof freezer wrap. Store the meat at 0° F. for up to 9 months. In addition to the following recipes, you can substitute venison in recipes calling for comparable beef cuts. But you'll probably find that venison meat is a little drier than beef.

Rabbit

Rabbit, often compared in flavor to chicken, can be used in your favorite chicken recipes. Every hunter has a favorite way of preparing rabbit, but soaking the rabbit in vinegar, wine, or salt water is frequently recommended.

The approximate age of rabbits can be determined from their weight —young rabbits usually weigh less than 4 pounds.

When skinning and cleaning a rabbit, carefully examine the liver. If you find white spots on the liver, the animal may have tularemia. Discard the rabbit and wash hands and work area with disinfectant.

Squirrel

Gray squirrels are the most common type and usually weigh about 1 pound. Young squirrel is one of the more tender wild meats. Like rabbit, squirrel resembles chicken in flavor and can be used in a variety of chicken recipes.

Opossum

Although popular as a food primarily in southern states, opossums roam most areas of the country. This meat resembles pork in flavor. Remove the glands under the front legs and at the small of the back and trim off excess fat when cleaning the animal. Pot-roast or braise opossum, or fry after parboiling.

Marinated Venison Chops

4 venison chops *or* steaks
    cut ¾ inch thick (about
    1 pound)
¼ cup wine vinegar
¼ cup cooking oil
¼ cup catsup
1 tablespoon worcester-
    shire sauce
1 teaspoon salt
½ teaspoon dry mustard
⅛ teaspoon pepper
1 clove garlic, minced

Place venison in plastic bag; set in shallow dish. For marinade combine vinegar, oil, catsup, worcestershire, salt, mustard, pepper, and garlic. Pour over meat in bag; close bag. Chill several hours. Turn occasionally. Drain venison; reserve marinade. Place chops on unheated rack in broiler pan. Broil 3 inches from heat till desired doneness; turn once and baste occasionally with marinade (allow about 12 minutes total time for medium-rare; 14 minutes for medium; and 16 minutes for well-done). Serves 4.

Stuffed Venison Steaks

For more ways to cook and serve venison, try your favorite beef marinades and sauces.

2 pounds venison steak, cut
    ¾ inch thick
1½ cups milk
6 slices bacon
⅓ cup sliced green onion
¼ cup all-purpose flour

Cut venison into 6 pieces. Place in plastic bag; set in shallow pan. Pour milk over meat in bag; close. Refrigerate overnight, turning meat several times. Drain meat; pat dry with paper toweling. Discard milk. Cook bacon till crisp. Drain; reserve 2 tablespoons drippings. Crumble bacon; set aside.

With a sharp knife, carefully cut a pocket in one side of each piece of meat. Mix bacon and green onion; stuff mixture into pockets in meat. Brown steaks on both sides in reserved bacon drippings. Season with some salt and pepper. Add ½ cup *water*. Cover and simmer over low heat for 45 to 60 minutes or till venison is tender. Remove meat to platter.

Measure pan juices; add enough water to make 1½ cups. Blend ½ cup cold *water* slowly into flour. Stir into pan juices. Cook and stir till thickened and bubbly. Season to taste with salt and pepper. Makes 6 servings.

Savory Chicken and Rabbit Pie

1 1½- to 2-pound rabbit
½ cup finely chopped celery
¼ cup finely chopped onion
¼ cup snipped parsley
3 tablespoons butter
3 tablespoons all-purpose
    flour
1 teaspoon salt
½ teaspoon ground savory
¼ teaspoon ground nutmeg
¼ teaspoon pepper
¼ teaspoon dried thyme,
    crushed
⅛ teaspoon ground cloves
1½ cups chicken broth
2 cups diced cooked chicken
1 package piecrust mix
    (for 2-crust pie)

Simmer rabbit in large amount boiling salted water about 1 hour or till tender. Drain; set aside to cool. Remove meat from bones; chop. In saucepan cook celery, onion, and parsley in butter till tender. Stir together flour, salt, savory, nutmeg, pepper, thyme, and cloves. Stir into celery mixture; stir in chicken broth. Cook and stir till thickened and bubbly. Add rabbit and chicken. Prepare pastry mix according to package directions. Roll out half of pastry; fit into 9-inch pie plate. Spoon in meat mixture. Roll out remaining pastry for top crust; adjust and seal. Cut slits for escape of steam. Bake in 375° oven about 40 minutes or till done. Cover edges with foil if needed to prevent over browning. Serves 6.

Rabbit in Wine-Mustard Sauce

1 1½- to 2-pound rabbit,
    cut up
¼ cup all-purpose flour
⅛ teaspoon ground nutmeg
2 slices bacon
8 to 12 whole boiling onions
½ cup dry white wine
¼ cup water
1 bay leaf, crumbled

1 teaspoon instant chicken
    bouillon granules
¼ teaspoon dried thyme,
    crushed
½ cup light cream
2 egg yolks
1 tablespoon prepared
    mustard
2 tablespoons snipped
    parsley

Coat rabbit pieces with mixture of flour, nutmeg, and dash *pepper*. In 10-inch skillet cook bacon; drain, reserving drippings in pan. Crumble bacon; set aside. Brown rabbit in reserved drippings about 5 minutes per side. Add onions, wine, water, bay leaf, bouillon, thyme, and crumbled bacon. Cover and simmer about 1 hour or till rabbit is tender. Remove rabbit, onions, and bacon to platter; keep warm. Strain pan juices. Return ½ cup juices to skillet. Beat cream with egg yolks, mustard, ¼ teaspoon *salt,* and dash *pepper;* slowly stir into pan juices. Cook and stir till thickened; *do not boil.* Serve over rabbit; sprinkle with parsley. Makes 2 or 3 servings.

Rabbit Brunswick Stew

1 2-pound rabbit, cut up
1½ teaspoons salt
⅛ teaspoon pepper
2 medium onions, sliced
2 slices bacon, cut up
½ teaspoon dried rosemary,
    crushed
½ teaspoon dried basil,
    crushed

2 medium potatoes
1 16-ounce can tomatoes,
    cut up
1 8¾-ounce can whole
    kernel corn, drained
1 8½-ounce can lima beans,
    drained
2 tablespoons all-purpose
    flour

Sprinkle rabbit with the salt and pepper. Place rabbit pieces in a large kettle or Dutch oven; add 2 cups *water.* Stir in onions, bacon, rosemary, and basil. Bring to boiling. Cover and reduce heat; simmer for 45 minutes.

Peel and cube potatoes; add to kettle. Stir in *undrained* tomatoes, the corn, and limas. Cover; simmer 30 minutes longer or till meat is done and potatoes are tender. Blend ¼ cup *cold water* into flour; stir into hot stew. Cook and stir until thickened and bubbly. Makes 5 or 6 servings.

'Possum Supper

Opossum is often said to have a pork-like flavor.

1 1½- to 2-pound opossum
2 medium sweet potatoes

Butter, melted
Cayenne

Wash opossum; trim off excess fat. Season cavity with salt and pepper; close with skewers. Tie legs together. Scrub sweet potatoes; do not peel. Place opossum and potatoes in shallow roasting pan. Add ½ cup *water.* Brush meat and potatoes with ¼ *cup* melted butter. Sprinkle with cayenne and some salt. Bake, covered, in 350° oven about 1¼ hours or till meat and potatoes are tender; baste occasionally with melted butter. Uncover; bake 15 to 20 minutes more or till brown, basting often with butter. Serves 2.

Celebrate the end of the hunt with a meal to make both the hunter and the cook proud. Rabbit in Wine-Mustard Sauce *features a creamy-rich sauce spooned over rabbit pieces.*

Rabbit Fricassee

Young tender rabbits have a taste similar to chicken and can be substituted in chicken recipes.

¼ cup all-purpose flour
½ teaspoon salt
⅛ teaspoon pepper
1 2- to 2½-pound rabbit, cut up
1 tablespoon butter
1 cup water
2 parsley sprigs
¼ teaspoon dried marjoram, crushed
¼ teaspoon dried oregano, crushed
⅛ teaspoon ground allspice
⅛ teaspoon ground cloves
1 teaspoon lemon juice
2 tablespoons cold water
1 tablespoon all-purpose flour
Hot cooked rice

In paper or plastic bag combine the ¼ cup flour, salt, and pepper. Add rabbit pieces; shake to coat. In a skillet brown rabbit slowly in butter. Reduce heat; add the 1 cup water, parsley, marjoram, oregano, allspice, and cloves. Cook, covered, about 1 hour or till tender. Remove rabbit; keep warm. Discard parsley. Skim fat from pan juices; measure juices. Add the lemon juice and enough water to make 1 cup liquid; return to skillet. Blend the 2 tablespoons cold water into the 1 tablespoon flour; stir into cooking liquid. Cook and stir till bubbly; cook 2 minutes more. Season to taste with salt and pepper. Serve gravy over rice. Makes 4 servings.

Hasenpfeffer

Translated from the German, this dish is literally "hare in pepper." It is a highly seasoned, hearty stew.

1 1- to 2-pound rabbit, cut up
2 cups dry red wine
1 cup water
1 medium onion, sliced
¼ cup vinegar
2 tablespoons sugar
2 teaspoons salt
1 teaspoon mixed pickling spice
¼ teaspoon pepper
2 tablespoons all-purpose flour
2 tablespoons cooking oil
4 gingersnaps, coarsely crushed (¼ cup crumbs)

Place rabbit pieces in plastic bag; set in shallow dish. For marinade combine wine, water, onion, vinegar, sugar, salt, mixed pickling spice, and pepper. Pour over rabbit in bag; close. Refrigerate for 2 days. Remove rabbit from marinade; pat dry with paper toweling. Reserve marinade.

In a paper or plastic bag shake rabbit pieces in flour to coat. Brown rabbit pieces in hot oil. Drain off excess oil. Gradually stir in 1 cup reserved marinade. Cover and simmer 45 to 60 minutes or till tender (add more marinade if necessary). Remove rabbit. Skim off fat from pan juices; measure and add enough water to equal 1 cup. Stir in gingersnaps. Cook and stir till thickened and bubbly. Serve with rabbit. Makes 2 to 3 servings.

Squirrel in Cider Sauce

2 1- to 2-pound squirrels, halved
2 tablespoons butter *or* margarine
1 cup apple cider *or* juice
¼ cup chopped onion
1 teaspoon honey
1 bay leaf
1 tablespoon cold water
2 teaspoons cornstarch

Sprinkle squirrel halves with some salt and pepper. In medium skillet brown squirrels in butter. Add cider, onion, honey, and bay leaf. Simmer, covered, about 1 hour or till tender. Remove meat to heated platter. Remove bay leaf. Blend cold water into cornstarch. Stir into pan juices. Cook and stir till thickened and bubbly. Pass with meat. Serves 4.

Hearty Brunch Ring

2 cups finely chopped fully
  cooked ham, cooked
  beef, *or* cooked pork
1 cup shredded cheddar *or*
  Swiss cheese (4 ounces)
3 slightly beaten eggs
1 4-ounce can mushroom
  stems and pieces, drained
2 tablespoons snipped parsley

¼ teaspoon salt
1 tablespoon butter *or*
  margarine
3 tablespoons sesame seed
1 package (8) refrigerated
  crescent rolls
1 2-ounce jar sliced
  pimiento, drained
1 tablespoon milk

Combine meat and cheese; set aside. Stir together eggs, mushrooms, parsley, and salt. Cook egg mixture in butter till almost set, stirring frequently; remove from heat and set aside. Grease a 5½-cup ring mold; sprinkle sides and bottom of mold with *2 tablespoons* of the sesame seed. Separate crescent roll dough into 4 rectangles, pressing perforations to seal. Using three of the pieces, roll *each* to an 8x5-inch rectangle. Carefully fit dough lengthwise into prepared ring mold, overlapping slightly and sealing ends to completely line bottom and sides of mold.

Spoon meat mixture evenly into lined mold; arrange pimiento atop. Spoon cooked egg mixture over all. Cut remaining piece of dough in half crosswise; cut each half diagonally into quarters, forming 8 triangles. Arrange around top. Brush with milk; sprinkle with remaining 1 tablespoon sesame seed. Bake in 375° oven for 25 to 30 minutes. Invert onto wire rack; invert again. Let stand 5 to 10 minutes before slicing. Makes 6 servings.

Beef Pie with Caper Sauce

¼ cup chopped onion
1 tablespoon butter *or*
  margarine
3 tablespoons all-purpose
  flour
1 teaspoon instant beef
  bouillon granules
¼ teaspoon ground nutmeg
⅛ teaspoon pepper

1 cup water
1 tablespoon anchovy paste
1 tablespoon chopped capers
2 cups finely chopped cooked
  beef
1 package piecrust mix
  (for 2-crust pie)
Caper Sauce

Cook onion in butter or margarine till tender but not brown; blend in flour, bouillon granules, nutmeg, and pepper. Stir in water. Cook over medium heat, stirring constantly, till thickened and bubbly. Stir in anchovy paste and capers. Add beef; mix well.

Prepare pastry according to package directions. On floured surface roll out half the pastry; fit into a 9-inch pie plate. Spoon in the hot meat mixture. Roll out remaining pastry. Adjust top crust; seal edges. Cut slits in top crust for escape of steam. Bake in 350° oven for 50 to 60 minutes (cover the edge of pastry with foil, if necessary, to prevent overbrowning). Let stand about 15 minutes for easier slicing. Serve with Caper Sauce. Serves 6.

Caper Sauce: In saucepan melt 2 tablespoons *butter or margarine.* Blend in 2 tablespoons all-purpose *flour*, 1 teaspoon instant *chicken bouillon granules*, and ½ teaspoon *worcestershire sauce.* Stir in 1 cup *water.* Cook and stir till bubbly. Stir in 1 tablespoon *capers.* Makes 1 cup.

Hearty Brunch Ring *makes for interesting dining. Nestled under a flaky blanket of pastry are mushroom scrambled eggs atop a layer of meat and cheese.*

Ham and Cabbage Rolls

Ham and Cabbage Rolls puts the leftovers from a baked ham to good use.

⅓ cup long grain rice
1 teaspoon instant chicken bouillon granules
2 beaten eggs
¼ cup finely chopped onion
¼ cup finely chopped green pepper
¼ teaspoon salt
¼ teaspoon dried thyme, crushed
¼ teaspoon dried savory, crushed
3 cups ground fully cooked ham
12 large cabbage leaves
1 teaspoon instant chicken bouillon granules
1 cup dairy sour cream
2 tablespoons all-purpose flour

In saucepan bring rice, 1 teaspoon bouillon granules, and 1 cup *water* to boiling. Reduce heat; cover and simmer about 20 minutes or till rice is done. Combine cooked rice, eggs, onion, green pepper, salt, thyme, savory, and dash *pepper*. Add ham; mix well. Cut about 2 inches of heavy center vein out of each cabbage leaf. Immerse leaves in boiling water about 3 minutes or just till limp; drain. Place about ¼ cup meat mixture in center of each leaf; fold in sides. Fold ends so they overlap atop meat mixture.

Place, seam side down, in 10-inch skillet. Dissolve 1 teaspoon bouillon granules in 1 cup hot *water*; pour over cabbage rolls. Simmer, covered, about 25 minutes. Remove to warm platter; keep warm. Combine sour cream and flour; stir into pan juices. Cook and stir till bubbly. Spoon over cabbage rolls. Top with snipped chives, if desired. Makes 6 servings.

Stuffed Acorn Squash

2 small acorn squash, halved lengthwise and seeds removed
¼ cup chopped celery
2 tablespoons chopped onion
2 tablespoons chopped green pepper
¼ cup butter *or* margarine
1 cup finely chopped fully cooked ham
1½ cups soft bread crumbs
½ teaspoon salt
2 tablespoons butter *or* margarine, melted

Place squash, cut side down, in shallow baking pan. Bake in 350° oven for 45 to 50 minutes or till done. Meanwhile, cook celery, onion, and green pepper in the ¼ cup butter just till tender. Scoop out squash pulp, being careful not to break shells. Mash squash; fold in cooked vegetables, ham, *half* of the crumbs, and salt. Return squash mixture to shells. Toss remaining crumbs with the 2 tablespoons melted butter; sprinkle around edge of squash. Bake about 10 minutes more or till heated through. Serves 4.

Armenian Pilaf

¾ cup fine noodles
2 tablespoons cooking oil
2 cups chopped cooked lamb *or* beef
¾ cup long grain rice
½ cup raisins
1 tablespoon instant beef bouillon granules
½ teaspoon dried mint, crushed
¼ cup toasted slivered almonds

In skillet brown *uncooked* noodles in hot oil till golden. Stir in meat, *uncooked* rice, raisins, bouillon granules, mint, 3 cups *water,* and 1 teaspoon *salt.* Bring to boiling; turn into 2-quart casserole. Bake, covered, in 325° oven 30 to 40 minutes or till liquid is absorbed; stir once after 20 minutes. Sprinkle with almonds. Makes 6 servings.

Chinese Fried Rice with Pork

2 beaten eggs
2 tablespoons cooking oil
¼ cup sliced green onion
1 clove garlic, minced
4 cups cooked rice (1⅓ cups uncooked)
½ cup coarsely shredded cooked pork
3 tablespoons soy sauce
¼ teaspoon crushed red pepper
Soy sauce

In 12-inch skillet cook eggs in *1 tablespoon* of the oil, without stirring, till set. Invert skillet over a baking sheet to remove cooked eggs; cut into short, narrow strips. In the same skillet cook green onion and garlic in the remaining oil till onion is tender. Stir in cooked rice, shredded cooked pork, the 3 tablespoons soy sauce, red pepper, and egg strips. Heat through. If desired, sprinkle with additional sliced green onion. Pass soy sauce. Makes 6 to 8 servings.

Delicatessen Casserole

8 slices rye bread
¼ cup butter *or* margarine, softened
¼ cup grated parmesan cheese
1½ cups thinly sliced cooked beef
8 ounces sliced salami (1½ cups)
2 beaten eggs
1 16-ounce carton cream-style cottage cheese
1 cup shredded mozzarella cheese (4 ounces)
½ cup grated parmesan cheese
½ cup sliced dill pickle
½ cup milk

Spread one side of each bread slice with butter or margarine; sprinkle with the ¼ cup parmesan cheese. Cut into ½-inch cubes. Cut beef and salami in bite-size strips. In bowl combine eggs, cottage cheese, mozzarella cheese, the ½ cup parmesan cheese, dill pickle, milk, and meat. Spread *half* of the bread cubes in a 12x7½x2-inch baking dish. Spread with cottage cheese mixture. Top with the remaining bread cubes. Bake in 375° oven 45 to 50 minutes or till heated through. Makes 8 servings.

Puffy Beef Casserole

2 tablespoons butter *or* margarine
2 tablespoons all-purpose flour
1 teaspoon prepared mustard
½ teaspoon salt
½ teaspoon prepared horseradish
1 cup milk
1 cup shredded sharp American cheese (4 ounces)
2 cups chopped cooked beef
1 16-ounce can cut green beans, drained
3 egg whites
Dash salt
3 egg yolks

In saucepan melt butter or margarine. Blend in flour, mustard, ½ teaspoon salt, and horseradish. Add milk all at once; cook and stir till thickened and bubbly. Stir in ½ *cup* of the cheese; stir in beef and beans. Turn into a 1½-quart casserole. In large mixing bowl beat egg whites and dash salt till stiff peaks form. In small mixing bowl beat egg yolks till thick and lemon-colored; stir in the remaining ½ cup cheese. Fold yolk mixture into whites; spread atop hot beef mixture. Bake in 375° oven for 30 to 35 minutes or till golden. Makes 6 servings.

Potato-Topped Goulash

2 cups cubed cooked beef, lamb, *or* pork
1 medium rutabaga, peeled and chopped (2 cups)
3 large carrots, chopped
1 large onion, sliced
1½ cups water
½ cup apple juice
1 tablespoon snipped parsley
1 teaspoon salt

¼ teaspoon dried marjoram, crushed
¼ teaspoon dried thyme, crushed
½ cup cold water
¼ cup all-purpose flour
1 teaspoon kitchen bouquet
4 or 5 servings hot mashed potatoes

In large saucepan combine meat, rutabaga, carrots, and onion. Stir in the 1½ cups water, apple juice, parsley, salt, marjoram, and thyme. Cover and simmer about 30 minutes or till vegetables are tender. Blend the ½ cup cold water into flour; stir into meat mixture. Cook, stirring constantly, till thickened and bubbly. Stir in kitchen bouquet. Transfer to serving dish; spoon mashed potatoes around edge. Sprinkle with additional snipped parsley, if desired. Makes 4 or 5 servings.

Pork and Pea Pods

2 medium onions, cut in thin wedges
2 tablespoons butter
¾ cup water
2 tablespoons soy sauce
2 tablespoons dry sherry
2 teaspoons instant beef bouillon granules

1 teaspoon sugar
⅛ teaspoon ground ginger
2 cups cubed cooked pork
¼ cup cold water
4 teaspoons cornstarch
1 6-ounce package frozen pea pods, partially thawed

In 2-quart saucepan cook onions in butter till tender but not brown. Add ¾ cup water, soy sauce, dry sherry, beef bouillon granules, sugar, and ginger. Stir in pork. Cover and simmer for 10 minutes. Blend ¼ cup cold water into cornstarch; stir into meat mixture. Cook, stirring constantly, till thickened and bubbly. Stir in pea pods; cover and simmer for 3 minutes. Transfer to serving dish. Makes 4 servings.

Ham Stew

Pour this hot stew into wide-mouth vacuum bottles for your children's lunch-box lunches (you can omit the hot pepper sauce if you like).

1 16-ounce can tomatoes, cut up
1 16-ounce can mixed vegetables
1 cup cubed fully cooked ham
¼ cup water
1 tablespoon snipped parsley

½ teaspoon dried thyme, crushed
½ teaspoon instant chicken bouillon granules
Dash pepper
Dash bottled hot pepper sauce

In saucepan combine *undrained* tomatoes and mixed vegetables, the ham, water, parsley, thyme, chicken bouillon granules, pepper, and hot pepper sauce. Bring to boiling; reduce heat. Cover and simmer about 10 minutes, stirring occasionally. Makes 4 servings.

Start with cubes of cooked meat to create Potato-Topped Goulash *and* Pork and Pea Pods. *Both main dishes are geared for hearty family eating.*

Brussels Sprouts and Ham

1 10-ounce package frozen
  brussels sprouts
¼ cup chopped onion
4 tablespoons butter *or*
  margarine
2 tablespoons all-purpose
  flour
¼ teaspoon dried marjoram,
  crushed

Dash dried rosemary,
  crushed
2¼ cups milk
½ cup shredded American
  cheese (2 ounces)
2 cups cubed fully cooked
  ham
1½ cups herb-seasoned
  stuffing mix

Cook brussels sprouts according to package directions. Drain; halve sprouts. Cook onion in *3 tablespoons* of the butter or margarine till tender but not brown. Blend in flour, marjoram, and rosemary. Add milk all at once. Cook and stir till thickened and bubbly. Stir in shredded cheese. Stir in ham, *1 cup* of the stuffing mix, and brussels sprouts. Turn into 1½-quart casserole. Melt the remaining 1 tablespoon butter or margarine; toss with the remaining ½ cup stuffing mix. Sprinkle around edge of casserole. Bake, covered, in 350° oven for 25 to 30 minutes. Makes 4 to 6 servings.

Manicotti

8 manicotti shells
1 10-ounce package frozen
  chopped spinach
3 tablespoons butter *or*
  margarine
3 tablespoons all-purpose
  flour
½ teaspoon salt
⅛ teaspoon cayenne
1 cup milk
2 slightly beaten eggs
¼ cup grated parmesan
  cheese
2 tablespoons milk
½ teaspoon garlic salt

½ teaspoon dried oregano,
  crushed
Dash pepper
1½ cups chopped cooked
  beef *or* pork
1 medium onion, chopped
1 tablespoon cooking oil
1 8-ounce can tomato sauce
1 teaspoon dried basil,
  crushed
½ teaspoon sugar
½ teaspoon salt
Dash pepper
2 tablespoons grated
  parmesan cheese

Cook manicotti in boiling salted water 15 to 20 minutes or till just tender. Drain and rinse in cold water; set aside. Cook spinach according to package directions. Drain and press out excess moisture; set aside.

For sauce, in small saucepan melt butter or margarine; blend in flour, ½ teaspoon salt, and cayenne. Add 1 cup milk all at once; cook and stir till thickened and bubbly. Spread about ½ cup of the sauce over bottom of 12x7½x2-inch baking dish; reserve remaining sauce.

In bowl combine eggs, the ¼ cup parmesan, 2 tablespoons milk, garlic salt, oregano, and dash pepper; mix well. Stir in cooked spinach and meat. Spoon about ⅓ cup meat mixture into each manicotti shell; place atop sauce in baking dish.

In skillet cook onion in hot oil till tender but not brown; drain. Stir in tomato sauce, basil, sugar, ½ teaspoon salt, and dash pepper. Pour over manicotti in pan; top with reserved sauce and remaining 2 tablespoons cheese. Bake, covered, in 350° oven for 40 to 45 minutes. Let stand 10 minutes. Makes 6 to 8 servings.

Hamwiches

¼ cup mayonnaise *or* salad
   dressing
1 teaspoon bottled steak sauce
½ teaspoon minced dried
   onion
6 slices Swiss cheese
6 slices fully cooked
   ham
1 large dill pickle
6 club rolls, split

Combine mayonnaise or salad dressing, steak sauce, and onion. Place a cheese slice atop each ham slice; spread with mayonnaise mixture. Cut pickle in 6 strips; place a strip across end of each cheese slice. Roll up; place in split rolls. Place on baking sheet. Bake in 400° oven for 8 to 10 minutes. Makes 6 servings.

Breakfast Wheels

2 English muffins, split and
   toasted
Butter *or* margarine
Currant jelly
4 slices fully cooked ham
1 apple, peeled, cored, and
   thinly sliced
4 slices Swiss cheese

Spread muffin halves with butter or margarine and currant jelly. Place a ham slice, 2 or 3 apple slices, and a cheese slice atop each. Place on baking sheet. Broil 4 inches from heat for 3 to 4 minutes or till cheese is melted and lightly browned. Makes 4 sandwiches.

Microwave cooking directions: Spread muffin halves with butter and jelly; set aside. Place ham slices in a 10x6x2-inch nonmetal baking dish; top each with 2 or 3 apple slices. Cook, covered with waxed paper or clear plastic wrap, in countertop microwave oven 1 to 1½ minutes or till hot. Uncover; top each with a cheese slice. Micro-cook about 1 minute or till cheese melts. Place atop muffins.

Beer-Sauced Sandwiches

1 medium onion, chopped
1 medium green pepper,
   chopped
2 tablespoons butter *or*
   margarine
⅔ cup beer
⅓ cup bottled barbecue sauce
2 cups cooked beef, pork, *or*
   lamb cut in thin strips
2 tablespoons cold water
1 tablespoon cornstarch
6 individual French rolls *or*
   8 frankfurter buns, split

In skillet cook onion and green pepper in butter or margarine till tender. Blend in beer and barbecue sauce. Stir in meat; heat through. Blend cold water into cornstarch; stir into meat mixture. Cook and stir till thickened and bubbly. Spoon into rolls. Makes 6 to 8 sandwiches.

Meat-Cabbage Sandwich Filling

⅓ cup mayonnaise *or* salad
   dressing
¼ cup chili sauce
2 teaspoons prepared
   mustard
½ teaspoon salt
¼ teaspoon pepper
3 cups chopped cabbage
2 cups chopped cooked lamb
   or beef

In bowl blend together mayonnaise or salad dressing, chili sauce, mustard, salt, and pepper. Stir in chopped cabbage and meat; mix well. Chill to blend flavors, if desired. Spread mixture on your favorite bread or rolls for sandwiches. Makes 8 sandwiches (about 2½ cups filling).

Honeydew Fruit Salad

1 honeydew melon
1 cup cubed cooked pork
1 orange, peeled and
  sectioned
1 large nectarine, chopped
½ cup seedless green grapes,
  halved

½ cup fresh dark sweet
  cherries, halved and
  pitted
¼ cup chopped celery
½ cup peach yogurt
¼ cup mayonnaise *or* salad
  dressing

Chill all ingredients thoroughly. Cut melon into quarters; remove seeds. Separate melon from shell; cut into pieces, leaving pieces in shell. Combine pork, orange sections, nectarine, green grapes, cherries, and celery. Toss to mix. Spoon the fruit mixture onto melon quarters. Blend peach yogurt and mayonnaise; spoon over fruit mixture on melon. Makes 4 servings.

Meaty Pasta-Filled Tomatoes

½ cup tiny shell macaroni
4 firm ripe tomatoes
1 cup cooked beef *or* lamb
  cut in thin strips
¼ cup bias-sliced celery
¼ cup chopped green pepper
¼ cup chopped onion
⅓ cup mayonnaise

⅓ cup shredded Swiss *or*
  cheddar cheese
1 tablespoon prepared
  mustard
½ teaspoon poppy seed
  (optional)
Lettuce

Cook macaroni according to package directions. Rinse in cold water; drain. Turn tomatoes stem end down. Make 5 or 6 wedges by cutting down to, *but not through,* base. Scoop out some of the center pulp; set aside. Sprinkle tomatoes with a little salt; invert on paper towel-lined plate and chill. Combine meat, celery, green pepper, onion, tomato pulp, and drained macaroni. Combine mayonnaise, cheese, mustard, poppy seed, ¼ teaspoon *salt,* and dash *pepper.* Add to meat mixture, tossing to coat. Cover and refrigerate at least 1 hour. To serve, place each tomato, cut side up, on a lettuce-lined plate. Fill with meat mixture. Garnish with sliced pitted ripe olives, if desired. Makes 4 servings.

Curried Meat in Avocados

1 egg
1 cup mayonnaise *or* salad
  dressing
⅓ cup grated parmesan cheese
1 single-serving envelope
  instant onion soup mix
1 teaspoon curry powder

⅛ teaspoon garlic powder
2 cups chopped fully cooked
  ham *or* cooked pork
1 cup cooked rice
3 medium to large avocados
Lemon juice
Lettuce

In small mixer bowl combine egg, mayonnaise, cheese, soup mix, curry powder, and garlic powder. Beat at medium speed of electric mixer for 20 to 30 seconds or till smooth and creamy. Stir in meat and rice. Cover; chill.

To serve, cut avocados in half lengthwise; carefully remove pits. Brush cut surfaces with lemon juice. Place each half on lettuce-lined salad plate. Mound about ½ cup meat mixture atop each. Sprinkle with chopped salted peanuts and chopped tomato, if desired. Makes 6 servings.

Refreshingly light yet filling, Honeydew Fruit Salad, Meaty Pasta-Filled Tomatoes, *and* Curried Meat in Avocados *make the most of any cooked meat you have on hand.*

Orange-Pork Salad

3 tablespoons frozen orange
  juice concentrate,
  thawed
3 tablespoons salad oil
1 tablespoon sugar
1 tablespoon vinegar
⅛ teaspoon dry mustard
  Dash salt
  Few drops bottled hot
    pepper sauce
¼ cup mayonnaise *or* salad
    dressing

2 cups cubed cooked pork
1 cup bias-sliced celery
½ cup sliced pitted ripe
  olives
  Leaf lettuce
1 medium avocado, peeled
  and sliced
1 medium orange, peeled and
  sectioned
¼ cup toasted slivered
  almonds

Stir together orange juice concentrate, oil, sugar, vinegar, dry mustard, salt, and pepper sauce. Fold in mayonnaise. Add pork, celery, and olives; toss lightly. Cover and chill. To serve, arrange lettuce, avocado slices, and orange sections on individual plates. Mound pork mixture in center. Sprinkle with almonds. Makes 3 or 4 servings.

Royal Reuben Salad

8 cups torn leaf lettuce
1 cup cooked corned beef cut
  in thin strips
1 8-ounce can sauerkraut,
  rinsed, drained, and
  chilled

1 cup cubed Swiss
  cheese (4 ounces)
1 cup Rye Croutons
¾ cup thousand island
  salad dressing
½ teaspoon caraway seed

Place lettuce in large salad bowl. Arrange corned beef, sauerkraut, cheese, and 1 cup Rye Croutons atop lettuce. Combine salad dressing and caraway seed; pour over salad and toss. Makes 6 servings.

Rye Croutons: Brush both sides of 5 slices *rye bread* with 3 tablespoons softened *butter or margarine;* cut in ½-inch cubes. Place on baking sheet. Bake in 300° oven for 20 to 25 minutes or till croutons are dry and crisp. Store croutons in a plastic bag. Makes 2 cups.

Spinach-Egg Toss

½ cup mayonnaise *or* salad
  dressing
½ cup dairy sour cream
¼ cup milk
2 teaspoons prepared
  mustard
½ teaspoon curry powder
3 eggs
2 tablespoons snipped
  parsley

2 tablespoons milk
⅛ teaspoon salt
  Dash pepper
1 tablespoon butter *or*
  margarine
4 cups torn fresh spinach
2 cups torn leaf lettuce
1 cup fully cooked ham cut
  in thin strips

For dressing combine mayonnaise or salad dressing, sour cream, ¼ cup milk, mustard, and curry powder. Cover and chill at least 1 hour.

Beat together eggs, parsley, 2 tablespoons milk, salt, and pepper. In 10-inch skillet melt butter or margarine. Pour in egg mixture; cook over low heat, without stirring, till set. Invert skillet over a baking sheet to remove cooked eggs; cut in ½-inch strips. In salad bowl combine spinach, lettuce, ham, and egg strips. Spoon dressing over salad; toss. Makes 4 servings.

Molded Ham and Potato Salad

1 envelope unflavored gelatin
¼ cup cold water
1 10¾-ounce can condensed cream of potato soup
½ cup milk
½ cup dairy sour cream
1 teaspoon lemon juice
1 teaspoon prepared mustard
1 cup finely chopped fully cooked ham
½ cup chopped celery
2 tablespoons chopped pimiento
2 tablespoons sliced green onion
¼ teaspoon dried dillweed
Lettuce

Soften unflavored gelatin in cold water. In saucepan combine soup, milk, and softened gelatin. Stir over low heat till gelatin is dissolved. Remove from heat; stir in sour cream, lemon juice, and mustard. Chill gelatin mixture till partially set. Fold in ham, celery, pimiento, green onion, and dillweed. Turn into a 9x5x3-inch loaf pan. Chill 4 to 5 hours or overnight. Unmold onto lettuce-lined platter. Garnish with hard-cooked egg slices and parsley, if desired. Makes 4 servings.

Pineapple-Beef Salad

⅓ cup white wine vinegar
⅓ cup salad oil
2 tablespoons chopped green onion
2 tablespoons snipped parsley
1 teaspoon dry mustard
¼ teaspoon salt
¼ teaspoon dried tarragon, crushed
2 cups cooked beef, cut in julienne strips
3 cups torn mixed salad greens
1 15¼-ounce can pineapple chunks, drained
3 tomatoes, cut in wedges
1 green pepper, cut in strips

For marinade, in screw-top jar combine vinegar, oil, onion, parsley, mustard, salt, and tarragon. In bowl sprinkle beef with a little salt and pepper; pour marinade over. Cover and marinate for several hours in refrigerator. To serve, drain beef, reserving marinade. Place greens in large salad bowl. Top with beef strips, pineapple, tomatoes, and green pepper; pour marinade over all. Toss lightly. Makes 4 servings.

Tangy Stuffed Pepper Salad

If you like, precook the raw peppers until crisp-tender. Remove the tops from green peppers, halve lengthwise, and remove the seeds as directed. Then immerse in boiling salted water for 2 minutes and invert to drain. Cover and chill.

2 cups shredded cabbage
1 cup chopped fully cooked ham *or* cooked beef
½ cup coarsely shredded carrot
¼ cup sliced radish
¼ cup chopped unpeeled cucumber
1 8-ounce carton plain yogurt
2 teaspoons sugar
1 teaspoon lemon juice
½ teaspoon celery seed
¼ teaspoon garlic salt
¼ teaspoon onion salt
Dash freshly ground black pepper
2 large green peppers

In bowl combine shredded cabbage, meat, carrot, radish, and cucumber. Combine yogurt, sugar, lemon juice, celery seed, garlic salt, onion salt, and pepper; mix well. Pour over vegetable mixture, tossing to coat. Cover and chill at least 1 hour.

Remove tops from green peppers. Cut peppers in half lengthwise and remove seeds. Spoon vegetable mixture into pepper cups. If desired, garnish with more sliced radish or chopped hard-cooked egg. Serves 4.

MEAT GUIDE

The following eight pages present an assortment of information that will help you understand meat terminology and make the best meat buys. In addition to specific buying guides and preparation tips, you'll find a dictionary of meat terms, carving instructions, recipes for beef stock and pan gravy, and a guide to recommended storage times.

Meat Terms

Aging An expensive process used on high quality beef. Wholesale or retail cuts are hung to dry in a temperature-controlled, low-humidity cooler for 2 to 6 weeks. During this time, enzymes in the meat break down some of the tendons and fibers, thus making the meat more tender. At the same time, evaporation of meat liquids causes the meat to become firmer and to shrink. This shrinkage means less meat per pound, and so increases the cost.

Au jus Served in natural meat juices from roasting.

Bake To cook covered or uncovered in an oven or oven-type appliance.

Baste To moisten foods during cooking with pan drippings or a special sauce to add flavor and to help prevent the food from drying out.

Boil To cook in liquid at boiling temperature (212°F. at sea level) where bubbles rise to the surface and break. In a full rolling boil, bubbles form rapidly throughout the mixture.

Braise To cook slowly with a small amount of liquid in a tightly covered pan on range top or in oven.

Bread To coat with bread crumbs before cooking.

Broil To cook by direct heat, usually in broiler.

Butterfly To split almost entirely and spread apart, making flat piece.

Dice To cut food in small cubes of uniform size.

Dredge To sprinkle or coat with flour or other fine substance.

Filet A strip of lean meat.

Frenching Trimming a small amount of meat from end of a bone.

Fry To cook in hot fat. **Panfrying** is to cook in a small amount of shortening or other fat. **Deep-fat frying** is to cook immersed in large amount of cooking oil or other fat.

Garnish To trim with small pieces of colorful foods such as green pepper, pimiento, or lemon.

Julienne Match-like strips of vegetables, fruits, or meats.

Larding Adding fat to meat before it is cooked. Specifically used in French cooking, it refers to inserting narrow strips of fat into a piece of meat—a roast, for example—at equal intervals.

London broil A thin steak that is broiled and then carved in very thin diagonal slices. A flank steak is the cut most commonly used.

Marbling The interior fat in meat that is recognizable as flecks of white interspersed in the red meat fibers.

Marinate To add flavor to food by allowing it to stand in a liquid.

Mince To chop food into extremely small pieces.

Panbroil To cook uncovered on a hot surface, such as a skillet, removing fat as it accumulates.

Pounding A tenderizing method in which a wooden or metal mallet is used to strike heavy repeated blows on the surface of meat.

Roast To cook uncovered without water added, usually in an oven.

Roux A mixture of flour and fat that is cooked, sometimes till the flour browns, and used to thicken soups and sauces.

Sauté To brown or cook in a small amount of hot fat.

Score To cut narrow grooves or slits into the outer surface of food, making a diamond pattern.

Sear To brown the surface of meat very quickly by cooking over intense heat. Recent tests have questioned the old theory that this helps to seal in meat juices.

Simmer To cook food in liquid over low heat at a temperature below boiling (185° to 210°F.) where bubbles form at a slow rate and burst before reaching the surface.

Stew To simmer slowly in a small amount of liquid.

Type of Meat	Servings Per Pound
Boneless meat (ground, stew, or variety meats)	4 or 5
Cuts with little bone (beef round or ham center cuts, lamb or veal cutlets)	3 or 4
Cuts with medium amount of bone (whole or end cuts of beef round, bone-in ham; loin, rump, rib, or chuck roasts; steaks, chops)	2 or 3
Cuts with much bone (shank, spareribs, short ribs)	1 or 2

In addition to price per serving, also consider the following things. Do you plan to serve only one meal from a particular cut? (Leftovers can become planned-overs with a little forethought.) What kinds and amounts of food are you serving with the meat? Do the people you plan to serve have light or hearty appetites? (Age makes a difference; so does activity level.) Do you have adequate refrigerator or freezer storage? How much time do you have for preparation? (A roast will take longer than ground beef.)

How Much to Buy

Price per pound is what you see, but price per serving is what you want to consider. A boneless piece of meat that is well trimmed of fat may be priced higher per pound but actually cost less per serving because there's more edible meat. This guide to servings per pound will help you comparison-shop.

Beef is sold by the hanging or gross weight. You pay for the entire weight of the carcass before cutting, including bones and fat. As a general rule, a beef carcass will give 25% ground beef or stew meat, 25% steaks, 25% roasts, and 25% waste.

If you are buying a quarter, you'll note that the hindquarter will be more costly per pound than either a forequarter or half, but it contains the loin and round where many tender steaks and roasts are located. The majority of the cheaper forequarter is made up of less tender cuts. Sometimes you can save more by watching the supermarket specials for pot roasts and ground beef than by purchasing a forequarter.

If your freezer space is limited or if your family doesn't want all the cuts that are part of a half or quarter, ask about buying a wholesale cut. Check the identification charts on pages 6 to 9 for information on retail cuts found in each wholesale cut.

Buying Beef in Quantity

Before you buy a beef half or quarter, consider these questions. Will your family eat all the cuts? Do you know how to prepare all the cuts? Can your budget stand the cash outlay required to buy a quarter or half? Do you have enough freezer space?

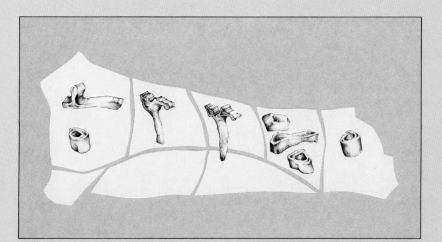

Bone Shapes

Use the identifying bone from each area to predict the degree of tenderness. The center loin is the most tender area. Cuts become less tender closer to each end. The blade bone and round arm and leg bones indicate a need for moist-heat cooking.

Understanding Meat Labels

As the label at right shows, the meat cut name can be broken into the following three parts: 1) the kind of meat—beef, veal, pork, lamb; 2) the wholesale (or primal) cut—chuck or shoulder, rib, loin, or round or leg; and 3) the retail cut—blade roast, loin chop, etc. Learn to read the label so you'll be sure to get the exact cut you want. (If your local market hasn't adopted URMIS guidelines, encourage them to do so.)

MEAT DEPARTMENT		
WEIGHT Lb. Net	PAY	PRICE Per Lb.
0.00	$0.00	0.00

BEEF CHUCK
BLADE STEAK

(kind of meat)   (wholesale cut)
BEEF   **CHUCK**
(standard name for specific cut packaged)
BLADE STEAK

The saying "A rose by any other name . . ." well applies to cuts of meat—a delmonico steak is a fillet steak is a beauty steak is a beef rib eye steak. And undoubtedly, like everyone else, you find all these names for the same cut very confusing.

That's why, a few years ago, the meat industry established voluntary guidelines (called Uniform Retail Meat Identity Standards, or URMIS) in an effort to standardize meat cut names throughout the country. Since these guidelines are followed in this book, if your local supermarket has also adopted them, it's easy to identify meat cuts just by looking at the label.

Inspection vs. Grading

Although inspection and grading both refer to ways of measuring meat quality, they are entirely different procedures. Meat inspection, which assures that the meat is fit for human consumption, is required by law. Grading, however, is voluntary since it deals with palatability and yield.

Every packinghouse and processing plant in the United States must meet strict requirements for the sanitation and wholesomeness of its meats. These are checked by government officials who then give carcasses a round inspection stamp.

Many beef, veal, and lamb packers also choose to have their product graded according to federal standards. These packers pay to have government employees examine each carcass and evaluate the visible characteristics that relate to tenderness, juiciness, and flavor. Only meat graded U.S. Prime, Choice, Good, or Standard is sold in retail stores, with U.S. Choice the grade most commonly available. This grading is indicated by a shield-shaped stamp on the carcass. (Pork is not graded.)

Ground Beef

What are you getting when you buy hamburger, ground beef, ground chuck, ground round, or ground sirloin? There's no one answer. Unless your store grinds under federal inspection, buys ground meat from a processor who is federally inspected, or is regulated by specific state or local laws, there is no hard and fast percentage of lean to fat for each type.

A store that uses labels with percentages of lean may be working under URMIS guidelines (see Understanding Meat Labels above). These are:

1. All ground beef should contain at least 70 percent lean. The label should read "ground beef," and state the lean-to-fat ratio as "not less than X% lean."

2. Ground beef should contain beef only and no other meat trimmings.

3. Unless labeled otherwise, ground beef should contain only skeletal meat (no variety meats).

4. A descriptive name should be used if meat is from a specific cut, i.e., ground beef chuck.

What Does Cooking Do?

Properly done, cooking improves the flavor, tenderness, and palatability of meat. To understand how it does this, we need to know a little about the composition of meat. Meat is actually skeletal muscle which is interspersed with fat and connective tissue. A large muscle, such as the eye of the round, is made up of many bundles of muscles, giving the meat a grain. These bundles are held together by connective tissue which in turn is made up of the protein collagen which is softened by cooking and the protein elastin which is not tenderized by cooking. There are two primary methods of cooking meat—dry heat cooking and moist heat cooking.

Dry heat cooking (roasting, broiling, panbroiling, and frying): Only tender cuts of meat can satisfactorily be prepared by these methods since no moisture is added to help tenderization. Heat solidifies the protein in meat, and that's why an overdone steak may taste tough. The longer it cooks, the more solid the protein becomes, making the meat harder to chew. Overcooking or cooking at too high a temperature also increases the evaporation and loss of drippings so the meat is drier and less juicy.

Moist heat cooking (stewing, simmering, and braising): Less tender cuts of meat are usually prepared by these methods. The added moisture and long, slow cooking time help to tenderize the meat by breaking down the connective tissues so they become more gelatinous and easier to eat.

Tenderness of Meat

Tenderness depends both on the type of animal and its maturity. Lamb and pork come from younger animals so they are more naturally tender than beef. And individual cuts vary in tenderness depending on where they come from on the carcass. As a general rule, cuts from the loin area (the part of the animal that gets the least exercise) are the most tender. Tenderness tends to decrease for cuts taken farther from this area.

As you look at the meat identity charts, you'll notice that the majority of meat cuts come from the less tender areas of the animal. These cuts are usually a good buy, but how can you make them more tender?

Using moist heat cooking is the easiest way (see What Does Cooking Do? above). In addition to cooking, pounding with a meat mallet and using powdered instant meat tenderizers also help increase tenderness.

Probably the most effective home tenderizing method is to pound the meat surface with a meat mallet. This physical action breaks down some of the meat fibers. When choosing a meat mallet, make sure it's fairly heavy but comfortable to hold and swing.

Powdered instant meat tenderizers are available both seasoned and unseasoned. The main ingredient in most of them is a plant-produced enzyme that acts chemically to break down the meat protein. Be sure to follow the directions suggested for using each one.

Meat Thermometers

Timings given in recipes and roasting charts are always approximations. No two ovens cook exactly the same way, and no two roasts are shaped exactly alike or have the same amount of bone or fat. Because of these variations, a meat thermometer is your best guide to judging doneness.

To get the most accurate reading, make sure the tip of the thermometer isn't resting on bone, fat, gristle, or the bottom of the pan. Oftentimes, especially with a large roast, it's a good idea to check the temperature more than once. When the thermometer indicates the desired degree of doneness, push it into the meat a little farther. If the temperature drops, leave the roast in longer and check again.

Meat thermometers are instruments, usually needle-shaped, with a tube of mercury in the center. Prices vary depending on how well the mercury is protected.

Perfect Pan Gravy

Add special flavor to meats with browned flour gravy. In small skillet cook 1 cup all-purpose flour over medium-high heat, stirring constantly, 10 to 15 minutes or till it turns light brown. Store in covered container.

Browning flour reduces its thickening power by nearly one-half, so adjust amounts accordingly when substituting it for regular flour in gravy making.

When you're cooking a large roast in a roasting pan, it's easy to make use of those flavorful drippings by making the gravy in the pan. First, remove the meat to a warm platter and cover with foil to keep warm. Leaving the crusty bits in the pan, pour the fat and meat juices into a large liquid measuring cup. Continue as directed below, thickening either by blending with drippings or by combining with liquid.

BLEND WITH DRIPPINGS

For 2 cups gravy: Skim fat from pan juices, reserving 3 to 4 tablespoons. Return the reserved fat to the roasting pan. Blend in ¼ cup all-purpose *flour*. Place over medium heat and stir till bubbly. Add 2 cups *liquid* (pan juices plus water, milk, or broth) all at once. Cook and stir till thickened and bubbly. Season to taste with salt and pepper.

COMBINE WITH LIQUID

For 2 cups gravy: Skim fat from pan juices. Add enough water to the pan juices to measure 1½ cups. Return juices to roasting pan. Put ½ cup cold *water* in screw-top jar; add 2 tablespoons *cornstarch* (or ¼ cup all-purpose *flour*). Shake well. Stir into juices. Cook, stirring constantly, till mixture is thickened and bubbly. Season to taste with salt and pepper.

Basic Beef Stock

After making the broth, don't toss out the meat and bones. Use the cooked beef in soups or stews. When bones are cool, remove the meat from bones. Store meat in covered container in refrigerator or wrap in moisture-vaporproof freezer wrap; seal, label, and freeze. Makes 2 cups.

4 pounds meaty beef bones
3 medium onions, quartered
1½ cups celery leaves
6 sprigs parsley
4 or 5 whole peppercorns
2 or 3 bay leaves
1 or 2 cloves garlic, halved
1 tablespoon salt
2 teaspoons dried thyme, crushed, *or* 1 tablespoon dried basil, crushed
10 cups water
   Use any 2 or 3 of the following vegetable trimmings

(approximate amounts):
1½ cups potato peelings
1½ cups carrot peelings
1½ cups turnip tops *or* peelings
1½ cups parsnip tops *or* peelings (wax removed)
4 or 5 outer leaves of cabbage
¾ cup sliced green onion
¾ cup sliced leek tops
1 eggshell, crushed
1 egg white
¼ cup water

In large kettle or Dutch oven combine beef bones, quartered onions, celery leaves, parsley, peppercorns, bay leaves, garlic, salt, and thyme or basil. Add 10 cups water and 2 or 3 of the vegetable trimmings, using only approximate measures for trimmings. Bring mixture to boiling. Cover and simmer for 2½ to 3 hours.

Using slotted spoon, remove meat and bones (use as directed in note, left). Strain stock, discarding vegetables and herbs. To clarify stock, combine eggshell, egg white, and ¼ cup water. Stir into hot stock; bring to boiling. Remove from heat; let stand 5 minutes.

Strain stock through a double thickness of cheesecloth. Skim off excess fat or chill and lift off the fat. Pour stock into pint or quart jars or containers; cover and chill. (Store stock in refrigerator up to 2 weeks or in freezer up to 6 months.) Use stock in any recipe that calls for broth, or serve alone. Makes 7 to 8 cups.

Storage

Keep meat at its best by protecting against spoilage with proper care and storage. Bring meat home and place in the refrigerator or freezer as soon as possible.

Fresh meat purchased pre-cut and wrapped in clear flexible packaging may be refrigerated as purchased. If it is to be frozen, remove the clear packaging material and tightly wrap the meat in moisture-vaporproof freezer paper. (See Wrapping Meat for the Freezer, below.)

Occasionally check the temperature of your refrigerator meat keeper. It should be between 36° and 40°F. Upright or chest freezers and refrigerator-freezers should maintain 0°F. or lower.

Maximum Meat Storage Times

Safeguard your meat against spoilage with proper handling and storage. Preventing potentially dangerous bacterial growth on meat is mostly a matter of avoiding exposure to warm temperatures and improper wrapping. Always purchase meat that's sealed tightly and feels cold.

Keep the working areas clean by scrubbing cutting boards and utensils with hot soapy water before and after each use. Diluted bleach also helps clean up wooden cutting boards. This is very important because bacteria can be transmitted from an unwashed cutting board to the meat.

MEAT	REFRIGERATOR (36° to 40°F.)	FREEZER (0° or lower)
BEEF		
Roasts	2 to 4 days	6 to 12 months
Steaks	2 to 4 days	6 to 12 months
Ground Beef, Stew Meat	1 to 2 days	3 to 4 months
PORK		
Roasts (fresh)	2 to 4 days	3 to 6 months
Chops, Spareribs (fresh)	2 to 4 days	3 to 6 months
Ground Pork	1 to 2 days	1 to 3 months
Hams, Picnics (whole)	7 days	2 months
Bacon	5 to 7 days	1 month
VEAL		
Roasts	2 to 4 days	6 to 9 months
Chops	2 to 4 days	6 to 9 months
LAMB		
Roasts	2 to 4 days	6 to 9 months
Chops	2 to 4 days	6 to 9 months
Ground lamb	1 to 2 days	3 to 4 months
VARIETY MEATS	1 to 2 days	3 to 4 months
COOKED MEATS	4 to 5 days	2 to 3 months

Wrapping Meat for the Freezer

Properly wrapped meat helps assure against dehydration (freezer burn). Use wrapping 1½ times as long as needed to go around meat. Place meat in the center. The coated side of wrapping paper should be next to the meat. Bring sides of wrapping together at the top. Fold edges down in a series of locked folds. Press the wrapping securely against the meat. Crease the ends of wrapping into points. Press wrapping to remove pockets of air. Bring both ends of the wrapping together at the top. Secure ends with freezer tape. Label package with the contents and the date.

Meat Carving

Carving meat can be baffling, especially when it comes to slicing all types of meat cuts. To carve meat successfully, keep the knife's cutting edge very sharp. For best results, sharpen knives with a hand-held sharpening steel or stone before each use. With steel or stone in one hand, hold knife in the other hand at a 20° angle to the sharpener. Draw the blade edge over the sharpener, using a motion that goes across and down at the same time. Turn blade over, reverse directions, and sharpen other side, an equal number of times.

To keep knives clean, wipe them with a wet cloth after each use, then dry. And, to keep knives in good condition, proper storage is essential. Keep knives separated, either in a holder or in a rack, to prevent them from becoming blunted.

Beef Rib Roast

Carving the rib roast is easier if the chine bone (part of backbone) is removed and the rib bones are cut short by the meatman. Place rib roast on warm platter with largest end down. This forms a solid base for carving. Insert carving fork between top two ribs. Starting on fat side of the piece of meat, slice across the meat to rib bone. Use tip of knife to cut along rib bone to loosen each slice, if whole rib is not served. Keep as close to rib bones as possible, making the largest serving of meat.

Beef Flank Steak

Place the flank steak on a wooden cutting board, holding the meat steady on the board with the carving fork. With the narrow end of the steak to carver's right, begin slicing. With the knife blade at an angle parallel to board, cut the meat in very thin slices all at the same angle. Carving this way cuts with the grain of the flank steak.

Crown Roast

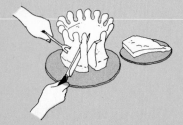

Crown roast should have all of the center stuffing removed before carving. Using fork to steady, start carving where ribs are tied. Cut between ribs. Remove to plate.

Beef brisket is sliced at an angle across the grain, ⅛ to ¼ inch thick. Carve from two sides since the grain goes in several directions.

Beef Brisket

Leg of Lamb

With shank on carver's right, cut 2 or 3 slices from thin side parallel to leg bone; turn leg to rest on this base.

Steady with carving fork. Beginning at shank end, cut ¼-inch slices down to leg bone. Continue cutting till bone pointing upward is reached. With fork

still in place, start at shank end and cut along leg bone to release slices. Tip roast on side to carve the remaining meat.

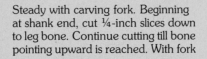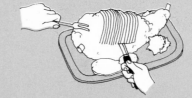
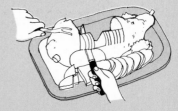

Beef Porterhouse Steak

Place steak on cutting board. Hold steak steady with a carving fork. Using the tip of knife, start at the top of the T-shaped bone and cut down and around to the bottom of bone. Start at the top of the bone on the other side and cut around to the bottom. Lift out the bone and discard. Slice across the full width of

the steak, cutting through both the top loin and the tenderloin muscles.

Trim off any fat and discard. For thick steaks, diagonal slicing rather than crosswise slicing is recommended.

Shank Half of Ham

With shank at the carver's left, turn ham so that the thick cushion side is up. Steady ham with carving fork. Using sharp knife, cut along the top

of the leg and the shank bones and under fork to lift off the boneless cushion. Remove the cushion and place it on a cutting board. Cut perpendicular slices, as shown. Cut around the leg bone with the tip of

the knife to remove any meat from this bone. Turn meat so that the broadest side is down. Cut perpendicular slices in same manner as the boneless cushion piece.

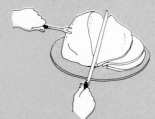

Beef Chuck Blade Pot Roast

Place pot roast on cutting board. Steady meat with carving fork. Trim away any excess fat. Cut between the

muscles and around the bones to remove one solid section of roast at a time. Turn section just removed so meat fibers are parallel to board. This

makes it possible to carve across the grain of meat. Cut the slices about ¼ inch thick.

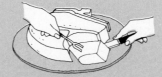
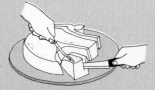

Index

A-B

Appetizers
  Cumberland-Style Bacon Rolls ... 72
  Sausage Nibbles 128
Apple Stuffing, Pork Steaks with 50
Apricot-Ham Patties 98
Apricot Stuffing, Pork Crown
  Roast with 46
Armenian Pilaf 154
Asparagus-Sauced Pork Tenderloin 48
Aspic, Veal in 15
Autumn Chowder 28
Bacon
  Bacon Butter 140
  Bacon-Leek Pie 74
  Cumberland-Style Bacon Rolls ... 72
  Dilled Veal Special 95
  Hearty Brunch Casserole 71
  Hot Potato Salad 72
  Lamb and Sausage Terrine 104
  Lamb Patties with Dill Sauce 96
  Lemon-Pepper Sandwich Loaf ... 74
  Mushroom-Bacon Scramble 71
  Spaghetti with Canadian Bacon .. 71
Barbecue Apple-Beef Pie 119
Barbecue-Glazed Ham and Pineapple 64
Basic Beef and Broth 38
Bean Pot, Steak and 28
Beef (see also *Corned Beef*)
  Armenian Pilaf 154
  Beef-Barley Stew 35
  Beef Borscht Stew 37
  Beef Fondue 24
  Beef Pie with Caper Sauce 153
  Beer-Sauced Sandwiches 159
  Burgundy Beef Casserole 40
  Chinese Beef Casserole 39
  Cranberry Beef Stew 37
  Delicatessen Casserole 155
  Devilish Liver Fondue 140
  Easy Beef-Vegetable Soup 35
  Fruited Beef with Bulgur 39
  Heart and Vegetable Platter 144
  Hearty Brunch Ring 153
  Kidneys in Wine Sauce 142
  Leek and Beef Stew 37
  Liver and Sausage Supper 141
  Liver Dijon 141
  Manicotti 158
  Meat-Cabbage Sandwich Filling .. 159
  Meaty Pasta-Filled Tomatoes 161
  Oxtail-Vegetable Soup 33
  Philadelphia Pepper Pot Soup 144
  Pineapple-Beef Salad 163
  Potato-Topped Goulash 156

Beef *(continued)*
  Puffy Beef Casserole 155
  Rio Grande Stew 39
  Savory Heart and Stuffing
    Casserole 143
  Sweet-and-Sour Beef Liver 141
  Sweetbreads Divan-Style 142
  Sweetbreads Elegante 142
  Tangy Stuffed Pepper Salad 163
  Texas Chili Pie 40
  Tongue and Lima Skillet 138
  Tongue with Raisin and Onion
    Sauce 138
  Western Baked Beef Heart 144
Beef, Ground
  Barbecue Apple-Beef Pie 119
  Beef Crepes Florentine 109
  Beef-Stuffed Tomatoes 115
  Burgers Florentine 100
  Colossal Cornburger 102
  Confetti Hamburger Salad 117
  Creole Beef Pie 119
  Dilly Burgers 100
  Double-Decker Burgers 96
  Eggplant Roll-Ups 114
  Elegant Meat Loaf Wellington 103
  Fiesta Meatballs in Almond
    Sauce 95
  Grilling Chart 99
  Ground Beef Curry with Custard
    Topping 111
  Hearty Beef Turnovers 116
  Hearty Mexican Casserole 110
  Italian Meat Loaf 103
  Meat Loaf Potato Splits 107
  Meat Loaf Supreme 102
  Mexican Beef in Corn Bread 108
  Mexican Meat Loaf 102
  Moussaka 111
  Multipurpose Meatballs 92
  Olive-Burger Pizza 120
  Oriental Meatball Salad 92
  Pinwheel Burgers 100
  Pita Burgers 101
  Saucy Meatball Platter 94
  Serves-a-Dozen Lasagna 120
  Sour Cream-Onion Burgers 99
  Spaghetti Pie 118
  Spanish Rice Skillet 112
  Stuffed Peppers Sicilian 115
  Sweet-Sour Beef 'n Cabbage 112
  Swiss-Style Meatballs 94
  Taco Burgers 99
  Taco Casserole 112
  Tamale Pie 119
  Up-North Gumbo 94
  Vegetable Burger Cups 114
Beef, Ribs
  Deviled Beef Bones 33
  Short Ribs and Limas 33
  Wined Short Ribs 33

Beef, Roasts
  Beef Roast with Vegetable
    Stuffing 16
  Beef Wellington 12
  Burgundy Beef Roast 17
  Chateaubriand with Bearnaise
    Sauce 10
  Chinatown Chuck Roast 17
  Horseradish- and Barley-Stuffed
    Rib Roast 10
  Macaroni-Stuffed Brisket 18
  Roasting Chart 13
  Roast with Barbecue Gravy 17
  Saucy Beef Sandwiches 16
  Sauerbraten-Style Roast 12
  Standing Rib Roast with
    Yorkshire Pudding 10
Beef, Steaks
  Autumn Chowder 28
  Beef Jerky 28
  Beef Rolls and Kraut 30
  Broiling Chart 23
  Deviled Blade Steak Broil 22
  Grilling Chart 23
  London Broil 24
  Mock Gyros 82
  Moussaka Sandwiches 32
  Mushroom-Stuffed Steaks 21
  Saucy Steak and Vegetable Platter 25
  Seafood-Steak Roll-Ups 21
  Spanish-Style Round Steak 30
  Spinach Beef Roll 29
  Steak and Bean Pot 28
  Steak and Oyster Pie 32
  Steak au Poivre 22
  Steak with Chicken Livers 24
  Stir-Fried Beef 30
  Summer Swiss Steak 32
  Tahiti Beef and Lobster Kabobs .. 22
  T-Bone Steaks with Sauteed
    Vegetables 21
  Two-Dinner Round Steak 29
Beer-Sauced Sandwiches 159
Brats Sausage 126
Breaded Pork Tenderloin 48
Breakfast Wheels 159
Brown Sauce 141
Brussels Sprouts and Ham 158
Brussels Sprouts Saute, Roast Pork
  with 49
Burgers Florentine 100
Burgundy Beef Casserole 40
Burgundy Beef Roast 17

C-F

Caper Sauce 153
Casseroles
  Armenian Pilaf 154
  Bacon-Leek Pie 74

Casseroles *(continued)*
Barbecue Apple-Beef Pie 119
Beef Pie with Caper Sauce 153
Brussels Sprouts and Ham 158
Burgundy Beef Casserole 40
Chili-Spaghetti Dinner 128
Chinese Beef Casserole 39
Choucroute Garni 131
Corn and Sausage Scallop 129
Creole Beef Pie 119
Delicatessen Casserole 155
Fruited Beef with Bulgur 39
German Pork and Sauerkraut 60
Golden-Sauced Franks 129
Ground Beef Curry with Custard
Topping 111
Ham and Egg Pie 67
Hearty Brunch Casserole 71
Hearty Mexican Casserole 110
Lamb Stuffing Bake 83
Manicotti 158
Moussaka 111
Oven-Baked Pork Stew 62
Pork-Noodle Casserole 110
Puffy Beef Casserole 155
Salami-Bean Casserole 134
Savory Chicken and Rabbit Pie . . 147
Savory Heart and Stuffing
Casserole 143
Serves-a-Dozen Lasagna 120
Spaghetti Pie 118
Steak and Bean Pot 28
Steak and Oyster Pie 32
Sweetbreads Divan-Style 142
Taco Casserole 112
Tamale-Franks 129
Tamale Pie 119
Texas Chili Pie 40
Chateaubriand with Bearnaise Sauce 10
Chicken and Rabbit Pie, Savory . . . 147
Chicken Livers, Steak with 24
Chili Barbecued Pork Chops 51
Chili-Spaghetti Dinner 128
Chili, Zesty Pork 61
Chinatown Chuck Roast 17
Chinese Beef Casserole 39
Chinese Curried Lamb 87
Chinese Fried Rice with Pork 155
Chop Suey, Pork 54
Choucroute Garni 130
Chuck Wagon Bean Soup 70
Chutney Chops with Pineapple 51
Chutney Lamb Loaf 104
Colossal Cornburger 102
Confetti Hamburger Salad 117
Corn and Sausage Scallop 129
Corn Con Carne Salad 134
Corned Beef
Corned Beef Platter 18
Corned Beef with Wine Sauce . . . 18
Royal Reuben Salad 162

Country-Style Ham 65
Country-Style Sausage 126
Cranberry Beef Stew 37
Cranberry-Lemon Glaze 81
Creole Beef Pie 119
Crepes Florentine, Beef 109
Crockery Cooking
Autumn Chowder 28
Curry-Sauced Ham 67
Italian Soup 117
Polish Sausage Stew 132
Short Ribs and Limas 33
Croutons, Rye 162
Crown Roast of Lamb with Rice
Stuffing 78
Cucumber Sauce 104
Cumberland-Style Bacon Rolls 72
Curried Cranberry Glaze 67
Curried Lamb Madras 88
Curried Meat in Avocados 161
Curry-Sauced Ham 67
Delicatessen Casserole 155
Deviled Beef Bones 33
Deviled Blade Steak Broil 22
Devilish Liver Fondue 140
Dilled Veal Special 95
Dilly Burgers 100
Divan-Style, Sweetbreads 142
Double-Decker Burgers 96
Dumplings 65
Easy Beef-Vegetable Soup 35
Egg-Lemon Sauce 115
Egg Pie, Ham and 67
Eggplant Roll-Ups 114
Elegant Meat Loaf Wellington 103
Fiesta Meatballs in Almond Sauce . . 95
Five Spice Powder 58
Fondue, Beef 24
Fondue, Devilish Liver 140
Frankfurters
Choucroute Garni 130
Frank-Potato Chowder 131
Golden-Sauced Franks 129
Tamale-Franks 129
Frank-Potato Chowder 130
French Lima Stew 128
Fresh Mint Sauce 81
Fried Apples 74
Fried Rice with Pork, Chinese 155
Fruited Beef with Bulgur 39
Fruit-Glazed Ham Slice 69
Fruit-Stuffed Pork Rib Roast 46

G-K

German Cheese Schnitzel 26
German Ham and Dumplings 65
German Pork and Sauerkraut 60
Glazed Ham-Bran Balls 95
Glazes *(see Sauces and Glazes)*

Golden-Sauced Franks 129
Grape Leaves, Lamb-Stuffed 115
Green Goddess Sauce 24
Gremolada 34
Grilled Rice-Stuffed Pork Chops 51
Ground Beef Curry with Custard
Topping 111
Ham
Barbecue-Glazed Ham and
Pineapple 64
Breakfast Wheels 159
Brussels Sprouts and Ham 158
Chuck Wagon Bean Soup 70
Country-Style Ham 65
Curried Meat in Avocados 161
Curry-Sauced Ham 67
Fruit-Glazed Ham Slice 69
German Ham and Dumplings 65
Ham and Egg Pie 67
Ham Caribbean 69
Ham Stew 156
Hamwiches 159
Hearty Brunch Ring 153
Hot and Hearty Ham Soup 70
Lamb and Sausage Terrine 104
Layered Ham Florentine 69
Molded Ham and Potato Salad . . . 163
Planked Ham 64
Roasting Chart 66
Scandinavian Jul Ham 65
Spinach-Egg Toss 162
Stuffed Acorn Squash 154
Tangy Stuffed Pepper Salad 163
Tenderloin Pinwheels 48
Veal Cordon Bleu 26
Ham, Ground
Apricot-Ham Patties 98
Glazed Ham-Bran Balls 95
Ham and Cabbage Rolls 154
Ham Omelet Roll 109
Ham-Yam Loaf 106
Individual Ham Souffles 110
Mini Apple-Ham Loaves 106
Mustard-Glazed Ham Loaf 106
Picnic Ham Packages 116
Pinwheel Ham 116
Harvest Pot Roast 45
Hasenpfeffer 150
Heart
Heart and Vegetable Platter 144
Savory Heart and Stuffing
Casserole 143
Western Baked Beef Heart 144
Hearty Beef Turnovers 116
Hearty Brunch Casserole 71
Hearty Brunch Ring 153
Hearty Mexican Casserole 110
Herbed Center-Cut Leg of Lamb . . . 83
Herbed Lamb Kabobs 87
Homemade Taco Sauce 112
Honeydew Fruit Salad 161

Horseradish- and Barley-Stuffed
   Rib Roast 10
Horseradish Sauce 24
Hot and Hearty Ham Soup 70
Hot Potato Salad 72
Hot Smoky Potato Salad 132
Individual Ham Souffles 110
Italian Lamb Shoulder Chops 85
Italian Meat Loaf 103
Italian Soup 117
Jicama and Pork 55
Kidneys in Wine Sauce 142

L-O

Lamb
   Armenian Pilaf 154
   Beer-Sauced Sandwiches 159
   Chinese Curried Lamb 86
   Curried Lamb Madras 88
   Herbed Lamb Kabobs 87
   Kidneys in Wine Sauce 142
   Lamb and Sausage Terrine 104
   Lamb Shanks in Pineapple-Dill
      Sauce 90
   Lamb Shanks Paprikash 88
   Lamb Shish Kabobs 86
   Meat-Cabbage Sandwich Filling . . 159
   Meaty Pasta-Filled Tomatoes 161
   Moroccan-Style Lamb 90
   Plum-Sauced Lamb Kabobs with
      Peaches 87
   Potato-Topped Goulash 156
   Scotch Broth 88
   Spicy Lamb Stew 90
Lamb, Chops
   Broiling Chart 86
   Italian Lamb Shoulder Chops 85
   Lamb Loin Chops with Walnut
      Glaze 85
   Lamb Stuffing Bake 83
   Lemony Lamb Shoulder Chops . . 85
   Parmesan Lamb Chops 83
Lamb, Ground
   Chutney Lamb Loaf 104
   Eggplant Roll-Ups 114
   Lamb Patties with Dill Sauce 96
   Lamb-Stuffed Grape Leaves 115
   Moussaka 111
   Pita Burgers 101
   Savory Lamb Burgers 98
Lamb, Roasts
   Crown Roast of Lamb with Rice
      Stuffing 78
   Herbed Center-Cut Leg of Lamb . 83
   Lamb Shoulder Roast with Curry
      Sauce 80
   Mock Gyros 82
   Orange-Sauced Lamb Roll 78
   Roasting Chart 81

Lamb, Roasts *(continued)*
   Rolled Lamb Shoulder with
      Vegetables 80
   Seasoned Leg of Lamb 82
Layered Ham Florentine 69
Leek and Beef Stew 37
Lemon-Pepper Butter 74
Lemon-Pepper Sandwich Loaf 74
Lemony Lamb Shoulder Chops 85
Lentils Coriander 128
Liver
   Devilish Liver Fondue 140
   Liver and Sausage Supper 141
   Liver Dijon 141
   Sweet-and-Sour Beef Liver 141
Lobster Kabobs, Tahiti Beef and 22
London Broil 24
Macaroni-Stuffed Brisket 18
Make Your Own Sausage 126
Manicotti 158
Marinated Venison Chops 147
Meatballs
   Dilled Veal Special 95
   Fiesta Meatballs in Almond Sauce 95
   Glazed Ham-Bran Balls 95
   Multipurpose Meatballs 92
   Oriental Meatball Salad 92
   Saucy Meatball Platter 94
   Swiss-Style Meatballs 94
   Up-North Gumbo 94
Meat-Cabbage Sandwich Filling 159
Meat Loaves
   Chutney Lamb Loaf 104
   Elegant Meat Loaf Wellington 103
   Ham-Yam Loaf 106
   Italian Meat Loaf 103
   Meat Loaf Potato Splits 107
   Meat Loaf Supreme 102
   Mexican Meat Loaf 102
   Mini Apple-Ham Loaves 106
   Mustard-Glazed Ham Loaf 106
   Pork Loaf with Olives 104
   Raisin-Veal Loaf 107
Meaty Pasta-Filled Tomatoes 160
Mexican Beef in Corn Bread 108
Mexican Meat Loaf 102
Microwave Recipes
   Barbecue-Glazed Ham and
      Pineapple 64
   Breakfast Wheels 159
   Golden-Sauced Franks 129
   Meat Loaf Potato Splits 107
   Mexican Meat Loaf 102
   Multipurpose Meatballs 92
   Plantation Spareribs 58
   Pork in Sweet-Sour Sauce 55
   Salami-Bean Casserole 134
   Sausage Nibbles 128
   Vegetable Burger Cups 114
Mini Apple-Ham Loaves 106
Mock Gyros 82

Molded Ham and Potato Salad 163
Moroccan-Style Lamb 90
Moussaka 111
Moussaka Sandwiches 32
Multipurpose Meatballs 92
Mushroom-Bacon Scramble 71
Mushroom-Stuffed Steaks 21
Mustard-Glazed Country Ribs 56
Mustard-Glazed Ham Loaf 106
Mustard Sauce 106
Olive-Burger Pizza 120
Olive Sauce 24
Omelet Roll, Ham 109
Onion Burgers, Sour Cream 99
Orange-Glazed Smoked Shoulder . . 65
Orange-Pork Salad 162
Orange-Sauced Lamb Roll 78
Orange-Sauced Pork Roast 45
Oriental Meatball Salad 92
Oriental Spareribs 58
Osso Bucco 34
Oven-Baked Pork Stew 62
Oxtail-Vegetable Soup 33

P-R

Parmesan Lamb Chops 83
Pea Pods, Pork and 156
Philadelphia Pepper Pot Soup 144
Picnic Ham Packages 116
Pie, Barbecue Apple-Beef 119
Pie, Creole Beef 119
Pie, Tamale 119
Pilaf, Armenian 154
Pineapple-Beef Salad 163
Pineapple-Chutney Glaze 81
Pinwheel Burgers 100
Pinwheel Ham 116
Pita Burgers 101
Pizza, Olive-Burger 120
Pizza Supreme, Sicilian 127
Planked Ham 64
Plantation Spareribs 58
Plum-Sauced Lamb Kabobs with
   Peaches 87
Polish Sausage Stew 132
Pork (see also *Bacon, Ham*)
   Beer-Sauced Sandwiches 159
   Chinese Fried Rice with Pork 155
   Choucroute Garni 131
   Chuck Wagon Bean Soup 70
   Curried Meat in Avocados 161
   German Pork and Sauerkraut 60
   Hearty Brunch Ring 153
   Honeydew Fruit Salad 161
   Hot and Hearty Ham Soup 70
   Jicama and Pork 55
   Liver and Sausage Supper 141
   Manicotti 158
   Orange-Glazed Smoked Shoulder 65

Pork (continued)
Orange-Pork Salad 162
Oven-Baked Pork Stew 62
Pork and Brew 60
Pork and Cabbage Soup 60
Pork and Fruit Kabobs 54
Pork and Pea Pods 156
Pork and Vegetable Stew 61
Pork Chop Suey 54
Pork in Sweet-Sour Sauce 55
Pork Steaks with Apple Stuffing . . 50
Pork Stroganoff For a Crowd 62
Potato-Topped Goulash 156
Side Pork Fry 74
Skewered Pork and Vegetable
Bundles 52
South American Pork Soup 61
Special Hungarian Goulash 35
Spicy Hopping John 70
Stir-Fried Pork and Rice 54
Zesty Pork Chili 61
Pork, Chops
Chili Barbecued Pork Chops 51
Chutney Chops with Pineapple . . 51
Grilled Rice-Stuffed Pork Chops . . 51
Pork Chops with Anise-Corn
Stuffing 52
Skillet Pork Chops and Hot Slaw 50
Smoky Pork Skillet 50
Pork, Ground
Apricot-Ham Patties 98
Fiesta Meatballs in Almond Sauce 95
Glazed Ham-Bran Balls 95
Ham-Yam Loaf 106
Italian Soup 117
Meat Loaf Supreme 102
Mini Apple-Ham Loaves 106
Mustard-Glazed Ham Loaf 106
Pork Loaf with Olives 104
Pork-Noodle Casserole 110
Spicy Apple-Pork Patties 96
Swiss-Style Meatballs 94
Pork, Ribs
Mustard-Glazed Country Ribs 56
Oriental Spareribs 58
Plantation Spareribs 58
Portuguese Marinated Ribs 59
Smoked Pineapple Pork Ribs 59
Spanish Spareribs 59
Spiced Orange-Apricot Ribs 56
Pork, Roasts
Asparagus-Sauced Pork
Tenderloin 48
Breaded Pork Tenderloin 48
Fruit-Stuffed Pork Rib Roast 46
Harvest Pot Roast 45
Orange-Sauced Pork Roast 45
Pork Crown Roast with Apricot
Stuffing 46
Pork Loin with Curry-Horseradish
Sauce 45

Pork, Roasts (continued)
Roasting Chart 49
Roasting Chart (Smoked) 66
Roast Pork with Brussels Sprouts
Saute 49
Tenderloin Pinwheels 48
Portuguese Marinated Ribs 59
'Possum Supper 148
Potato Chowder, Frank- 131
Potato-Topped Goulash 156
Puffy Beef Casserole 155
Quantity Recipes (10 or more
servings)
Beef Wellington 12
Eggplant Roll-Ups 114
Horseradish- and Barley-Stuffed
Rib Roast 10
Macaroni-Stuffed Brisket 18
Mock Gyros 82
Orange-Sauced Lamb Roll 78
Planked Ham 64
Pork Crown Roast with Apricot
Stuffing 46
Pork Loin with Curry-Horseradish
Sauce 45
Pork Stroganoff For a Crowd 62
Saucy Beef Sandwiches 16
Sauerbraten-Style Roast 12
Scandinavian Jul Ham 65
Serves-a-Dozen Lasagna 120
Swiss-Style Meatballs 94
Texas Chili Pie 40
Veal a la Royale 15
Quick Raisin Sauce 67
Rabbit
Hasenpfeffer 150
Rabbit Brunswick Stew 148
Rabbit Fricassee 150
Rabbit in Wine-Mustard Sauce . . . 148
Savory Chicken and Rabbit Pie . . 147
Raisin-Veal Loaf 107
Rice Stuffing, Crown Roast of
Lamb with 78
Rio Grande Stew 39
Roast Pork with Brussels Sprouts
Saute 49
Roast with Barbecue Gravy 17
Rolled Lamb Shoulder with
Vegetables 80
Round Steak Stroganoff 29
Royal Reuben Salad 162
Rye Croutons 162

S

Salads
Confetti Hamburger Salad 117
Corn Con Carne Salad 134
Curried Meat in Avocados 161
Honeydew Fruit Salad 161

Salads (continued)
Hot Potato Salad 72
Hot Smoky Potato Salad 132
Meaty Pasta-Filled Tomatoes 161
Molded Ham and Potato Salad . . . 163
Orange-Pork Salad 162
Oriental Meatball Salad 92
Pineapple-Beef Salad 163
Royal Reuben Salad 162
Sausage Supper Salad 132
Spinach-Egg Toss 162
Tangy Stuffed Pepper Salad 163
Salami-Bean Casserole 134
Sandwiches
Beer-Sauced Sandwiches 159
Breakfast Wheels 159
Dilly Burgers 100
Double-Decker Burgers 96
Hamwiches 159
Hearty Beef Turnovers 116
Lemon-Pepper Sandwich Loaf . . . 74
Meat-Cabbage Sandwich Filling . . 159
Mock Gyros 82
Moussaka Sandwiches 32
Picnic Ham Packages 116
Pinwheel Burgers 100
Pita Burgers 101
Saucy Beef Sandwiches 16
Savory Lamb Burgers 98
Sour Cream-Onion Burgers 99
Taco Burgers 99
Sauces and Glazes
Bacon Butter 140
Brown Sauce 141
Caper Sauce 153
Cranberry-Lemon Glaze 81
Cucumber Sauce 104
Curried Cranberry Glaze 67
Egg-Lemon Sauce 115
Fresh Mint Sauce 81
Green Goddess Sauce 24
Homemade Taco Sauce 112
Horseradish Sauce 24
Mustard Sauce 106
Olive Sauce 24
Pineapple-Chutney Glaze 81
Quick Raisin Sauce 67
Spicy Strawberry Glaze 66
Sweet and Pungent Sauce 58
Sweet-Sour Sauce, Pork in 55
Tangy Tomato Sauce 109
Wine-Olive Sauce 103
Saucy Beef Sandwiches 16
Saucy Meatball Platter 94
Saucy Steak and Vegetable Platter . . 25
Saucy Swiss Steak 29
Sauerbraten-Style Roast 12
Sauerkraut, German Pork and 60
Sausages (see also Frankfurters)
Beef Rolls and Kraut 30
Chili-Spaghetti Dinner 128

Sausages (continued)
- Choucroute Garni 131
- Corn and Sausage Scallop 129
- Corn Con Carne Salad 134
- Delicatessen Casserole 155
- French Lima Stew 128
- Hot Smoky Potato Salad 132
- Lamb and Sausage Terrine 104
- Lentils Coriander 128
- Liver and Sausage Supper 141
- Make Your Own Sausage 126
- Polish Sausage Stew 132
- Salami-Bean Casserole 134
- Sausage Nibbles 128
- Sausage Supper Salad 132
- Sicilian Pizza Supreme 127
- Soup for All Seasons, A 134
- Veal a la Royale 15
- Savory Chicken and Rabbit Pie . . . 147
- Savory Heart and Stuffing
  Casserole 143
- Savory Lamb Burgers 98
- Scandinavian Jul Ham 65
- Scotch Broth 88
- Seafood-Steak Roll-Ups 21
- Seasoned Leg of Lamb 82
- Sensational Veal Stew 34
- Serves-a-Dozen Lasagna 120
- Short Ribs and Limas 33
- Sicilian Pizza Supreme 127
- Side Pork Fry 74
- Skewered Pork and Vegetable
  Bundles 52
- Skillet Pork Chops and Hot Slaw . . . 50
- Smoked Pineapple Pork Ribs 59
- Smoky Pork Skillet 50
- Souffles, Individual Ham 110
- Soups
  - Autumn Chowder 28
  - Chuck Wagon Bean Soup 70
  - Easy Beef-Vegetable Soup 35
  - Frank-Potato Chowder 131
  - Hot and Hearty Ham Soup 70
  - Italian Soup 117
  - Lentils Coriander 128
  - Oxtail Vegetable Soup 33
  - Philadelphia Pepper Pot Soup . . . 144
  - Pork and Cabbage Soup 60
  - Scotch Broth 88
  - Soup for All Seasons, A 134
  - South American Pork Soup 61
  - Up-North Gumbo 94
- Sour Cream-Onion Burgers 99
- South American Pork Soup 61
- Spaghetti Pie 118
- Spaghetti with Canadian Bacon . . . 71
- Spanish Rice Skillet 112
- Spanish Spareribs 59
- Spanish-Style Round Steak 30
- Special Hungarian Goulash 35
- Spiced Orange-Apricot Ribs 56

- Spicy Apple-Pork Patties 96
- Spicy Hopping John 70
- Spicy Italian Sausage 126
- Spicy Lamb Stew 90
- Spicy Strawberry Glaze 66
- Spinach Beef Roll 29
- Spinach-Egg Toss 162
- Squirrel in Cider Sauce 150
- Standing Rib Roast with Yorkshire
  Pudding 10
- Steak and Bean Pot 28
- Steak and Oyster Pie 32
- Steak au Poivre 22
- Steak with Chicken Livers 24
- Stews
  - Beef-Barley Stew 35
  - Beef Borscht Stew 37
  - Cranberry Beef Stew 37
  - French Lima Stew 128
  - Ham Stew 156
  - Leek and Beef Stew 37
  - Oven-Baked Pork Stew 62
  - Polish Sausage Stew 132
  - Pork and Vegetable Stew 61
  - Potato-Topped Goulash 156
  - Rabbit Brunswick Stew 148
  - Rio Grande Stew 39
  - Sensational Veal Stew 34
  - Special Hungarian Goulash 35
  - Spicy Lamb Stew 90
- Stir-Fried Beef 30
- Stir-Fried Pork and Rice 54
- Stroganoff For a Crowd, Pork 62
- Stroganoff, Round Steak 29
- Stuffed Acorn Squash 154
- Stuffed Peppers Sicilian 115
- Stuffed Venison Steaks 147
- Summer Swiss Steak 32
- Sweet and Pungent Sauce 58
- Sweet-and-Sour Beef Liver 141
- Sweetbreads Divan-Style 142
- Sweetbreads Elegante 142
- Sweet-Sour Beef 'n Cabbage 112
- Swiss Steak, Saucy 29
- Swiss Steak, Summer 32
- Swiss-Style Meatballs 94

T-Z

- Taco Burgers 99
- Taco Casserole 112
- Tahiti Beef and Lobster Kabobs . . . 22
- Tamale-Franks 129
- Tamale Pie 119
- Tangy Stuffed Pepper Salad 163
- Tangy Tomato Sauce 109
- T-Bone Steaks with Sauteed
  Vegetables 21
- Tenderloin Pinwheels 48
- Texas Chili Pie 40

- Tomato-Cucumber Relish 96
- Tomatoes, Beef-Stuffed 115
- Tongue and Lima Skillet 138
- Tongue with Raisin and Onion
  Sauce 138
- Two-Dinner Round Steak 29
- Up-North Gumbo 94
- Veal
  - German Cheese Schnitzel 26
  - Osso Bucco 34
  - Roasting Chart 13
  - Sensational Veal Stew 34
  - Special Hungarian Goulash 35
  - Veal a la Royale 15
  - Veal Cordon Bleu 26
  - Veal in Aspic 15
  - Veal Scallopini with Wine 26
- Veal, Ground
  - Dilled Veal Special 95
  - Raisin-Veal Loaf 107
  - Stuffed Peppers Sicilian 115
  - Swiss-Style Meatballs 94
  - Veal Patties 98
- Vegetable Burger Cups 114
- Venison Chops, Marinated 147
- Venison Steaks, Stuffed 147
- Western Baked Beef Heart 144
- Wined Short Ribs 33
- Wine-Olive Sauce 103
- Yorkshire Pudding, Standing Rib
  Roast with 10
- Zesty Pork Chili 61

Tips
- Cooking Bacon 72
- Grilling Pork 56
- Ground Beef Labels 107
- Microwave Cooking 55
- Shaping Ground Meat Patties 98
- Shaping Meatballs 92
- Stretch a Leg of Lamb Into
  Three Meals 87
- Use Your Broiler 52

Meat Guide
- Basic Beef Stock 168
- Bone Shapes 165
- Buying Beef in Quantity 165
- Carving 170-171
- Ground Beef 166
- How Much to Buy 165
- Inspection vs. Grading 166
- Maximum Meat Storage Times . . . 169
- Meat Terms 164
- Perfect Pan Gravy 168
- Storage 169
- Tenderness of Meat 167
- Understanding Meat Labels 166
- What Does Cooking Do? 167
- Why Use a Meat Thermometer? . . 167
- Wrapping Meat for the Freezer . . . 169